HIGH
OCTANE
TRADING

Other Books by Steve Wirrick

High Octane Investing
High Octane Options

HIGH OCTANE TRADING

**Simple, time-tested,
bread and butter strategies
to help you make serious money
trading stocks and options!**

Steve Wirrick

Planet Cash, Inc.
Seattle

This book is for educational purposes only. The information provided has been obtained from sources deemed reliable, but is not guaranteed as to accuracy or completeness. The author and publisher specifically disclaim any liability resulting from the use or application of the contents of this book.

It should not be assumed the ideas, strategies, and information presented in this book will be profitable or that they will not result in losses. Past performance does not guarantee future results.

Under no circumstances does the information in this book represent a recommendation to buy or sell stocks and/or options, or to provide investment advice. Consult a licensed professional broker regarding your personal investments.

The examples in this book do not include commissions and other costs. All stock and option transactions have important tax considerations so please consult your tax advisor.

Options involve risk and are not suitable for every investor. Prior to buying or selling an option, you must receive and read Characteristics and Risks of Standardized Options. Copies of this document are available from your broker or the Chicago Board Options Exchange, 400 S. LaSalle Street, Chicago, IL 60605.

Published by Planet Cash, Inc.
POB 1711
Issaquah, WA 98027
support@planetcash.com

ISBN 0-9727071-0-7

Printed in the United States of America

To my Mom and Dad

Acknowledgements

It's often been said that in order to reach the stars you need to stand on the shoulders of giants! To say the least, I've had many "giants" in my life who have allowed me to stand on their shoulders, enabling me to attain breathtaking heights I only dreamed of.

A special and heartfelt thanks goes to my incredible Mom and Dad who provide a never-ending supply of love and encouragement. They instilled in me a strong work ethic and provided a healthy environment of rewarding and challenging experiences. It goes without saying that I wouldn't have accomplished a fraction of what I've been able to without their love, support, and sacrifice.

I also owe a debt of gratitude to my remarkable sister and her husband, Jenni and Chris Cirillo, and to my indispensable brothers, Mike and Jon Wirrick, for helping me behind the scenes (in every way, shape, and form) with Planet Cash, Inc. and MyTradingDiary.com. They are truly my unsung heroes!

I'm indebted to Kirt Barrett for his humor, clever insights, and endless supply of creativity. His editorial and literary input, sprinkled throughout the book, is priceless. Frankly, if it weren't for him it would have never been completed, let alone published.

I'm eternally grateful to Monique Redford for her deft editorial prowess and keen sense of style. She not only helped make this a better book, but she is also an incredible blessing in my life.

I want to express my deep gratitude to Elijah Cardon, a great friend and mentor. He taught me the magic of enthusiasm and the power of thinking big!

I can't say enough about Ken Machen and Tracy Childers. Their technical expertise, ingenuity, and countless hours of hard work keep my various websites up and running, including: planet-cash.com, killertradingsecrets.com, and mytradingdiary.com. They are true team players in every sense of the word.

An extra special thanks goes to Robert Machen, who was the genius behind my wildly popular software programs, Option Explorer and Option Explorer Pro. He endured many a sleepless night (literally!) making it happen. Thank you!

I'm thankful to John Childers, who taught me how to be a more effective and productive communicator and teacher. He opened my eyes to the importance of not only what to say, but how to say it.

I'm grateful to Wade Cook for introducing me to the wonderful world of options and teaching me how to treat my investments like a business.

Brent Magarrell has worked with me from day one putting together all my home study materials and special reports. His help, hard work, and creative input have been priceless.

Many thanks to Candee Casazza, Megan Johnson and Mike Spencer, who did an outstanding job designing the cover and for-matting the book. Hats off to you!

Ricardo Rabago has been an invaluable resource, helping me cre-ate and market the ebook version of High Octane Trading. He is also the technical wizard behind getrichswingtrading.com and highoctaneinvesting.com. You're the best!

I also want to thank my wonderful sisters and their husbands, Kim and Troy Romero, Julie and Mike Jorgensen, Jodi and Doug Finch, for all their love, support, and help along the way.

One of the most enjoyable and rewarding roles I've been blessed with is that of being an Uncle to 14 amazing nieces and nephews: Brittany, Taylor, Zack, Lexi, Halli, Sydney, Teagan, Callie, Josh, Malorie, Anna, Grace, Olivia, and Benjamin. Thanks for all the wonderful memories and making me laugh!

And finally, a big thank you goes to the many students and read-ers of my books and homestudy materials. Without you, none of this would be possible!

Table of Contents

Preface

"Train up a child in the way he should go: and when he is old, he will not depart from it."
– Proverbs 22:6)

"As the twig is bent, so the tree's inclined." (Alexander Pope, *Moral Essays*, vol. 2 of *The Works of Alexander Pope, Esq.*, "Epistle I: To Sir Richard Temple, Lord Cobham" [1776], 119; line 150)

As I lecture and teach both stateside and internationally, I'm often asked how and when I began my investment career. Frequently, my knee-jerk reaction is 1994. However, upon a little introspection I recognize it started earlier than that – *much* earlier.

The seeds of my entrepreneurial career began being sown when I was but five years of age. Little did I know at that time, but I harnessed two of the most important principles related to running a successful business – big profits and a never-ending demand for the product or service.

You see, I noticed that when I sprayed water onto the fence surrounding our house that it looked brand new! I said to myself, "WOW, won't Mom and Dad be pleased. In fact, I bet they'd pay me to 'paint' the entire fence." Heck, the water was free and the fence appeared to go on forever. Talk about a no-brainer!

So there I was, with my bucket of water and paintbrush, merrily painting the fence (as much as I could reach), winning the amusing pleasure of my parents and earning a few nickels for myself in the process. So not only did my parents support my desire to work, they also taught me the rewards of ingenuity, creativity and recognizing "hidden" opportunities around me.

In retrospect that was really the genesis of my career as an entrepreneur and investor. But more importantly, the lessons I learned in my youth laid the foundation for what would become an integral part of my success later in life.

Let me explain…

Like many kids, during hot, summer days I'd set up a lemonade stand. Here I learned the importance of seasonality and striking while the iron was hot. In other words, I learned how to capture a brief, explosive trend – critical to succeeding on Wall Street.

I was fascinated by magic growing up – and I still am! So much so that I took lessons. I loved putting on magic shows, baffling family and friends alike with various tricks and illusions. However, to do so effectively required countless hours of practice and study. Similarly, becoming a better trader also requires practice and study. I've spent countless hours over the years looking at charts and studying the market. And frankly, it sometimes reminds me of magic – entertaining and totally baffling!

For many years I had a paper route. In fact, it turned into a family affair as everyone ultimately got into the act. I'm sure my brothers and sisters still rue the day when I, as a third grader, talked my parents into letting me have a paper route of my own.

That was the beginning of a 15-year "love" affair with *The Seattle Times*. I learned the principle of delivering the paper on time regardless of how tired I was or how bad the weather was. This required commitment and discipline, two traits critical to trading successfully.

As a family we had a goal of buying a pop-up trailer but they cost a lot of money. So my Mom and Dad, never missing an opportunity to teach us the value of work, encouraged us to think of creative ways to earn the money. But how? As I soon discovered, the opportunity was right under my nose.

You see, as I delivered newspapers, I began to notice that many people would stack their old ones in the garage. Soon it dawned on me that those stacks of old newspaper were a veritable gold mine. To say the least, there was plenty of money to be made recycling old newspaper.

So every Saturday, I, along my younger brothers or sisters, would take our wagons around the neighborhood collecting these stacks of old newspaper. I also promised our neighbors that if they'd continue to collect the newspaper I'd be sure to come by every few weeks and pick them up. It worked like a charm! Pretty soon we were collecting so much newspaper that my Dad had to drive us around in the stationwagon! As you might imagine, it wasn't too long before we were able to buy the pop-up trailer.

We created a systematic routine whereby we knew what to do and when to do it. Therein lies the beauty of having a plan, system, or way of making money. The key is repetition and duplication – creating a cookie cutter approach to making money. And so it is with trading. By creating a game plan you'll know exactly when to buy and sell. It doesn't get any simpler than that!

All those experiences helped mold me into the person I am today, enabling me to draw upon those skills in my present-day endeavors – writing, speaking, teaching and investing.

However, there is one more invaluable and priceless lesson I learned (although I didn't realize until many years later) that my Mom taught me in elementary school that is the foundation for lasting trading success – or any other endeavor you may choose.

My Mom had a passionate love for the great artists of the world – both musically and artistically. She loved it so much that she volunteered at my elementary school as the "Art Lady". Once a month she would come into our classroom and teach us about a world-famous artist. One of her favorite artists was Claude Monet.

Around the year 1890 a French writer, Guy de Maupassant, had many opportunities to watch Claude Monet paint. He described exactly how the artist captured his impressions of life. "Actually, he was no longer a painter," he wrote, "but a hunter." You see, by this time in his painting career Monet had become such a master of the art of Impressionism that he would paint five or six canvases at the same time, experimenting with different brushstrokes, in order to perfectly capture his subjects.

And how perfect his brushstrokes were! For today his masterpieces are recognized around the world as priceless works of art. But the real lesson to be gleaned from Monet, the master artist, is that there is an eternal principle that goes to the very core of his paintings. Monet's paintings are masterpieces because...

He developed, applied, and mastered a painting technique according to a disciplined apprenticeship program.

Monet (at the tender age of fifteen) "realized what painting could be." You see, he was exposed, tutored, and mentored for two years by another master painter named Eugene Boudin. And from that apprenticeship he subsequently spent eight additional years studying and painting in Paris with associates of Boudin. Monet developed his artistic talents via an apprenticeship program (tailored for his chosen discipline), which provided him with the knowledge, skill, experience, expertise and freedom to express his ideas artistically. Needless to say, Monet's impressionistic views, as expressed on canvas, have become timeless treasures.

As in Monet's painting technique, trading also requires an apprenticeship program. (Any program or person that claims otherwise is not a true master of options trading techniques.) Let's face it, forgoing an opportunity to learn, experience and apply trading techniques under a master's watchful eye will directly equate to disastrous results for any new trader. Remember, an apprentice is a person who learns a skill or trade by working under the guidance and tutelage of a skilled master. Milestones of knowledge, skill, experience and expertise must be obtained by anyone expecting to trade options effectively.

So it is with Monet in mind that I present to you, *High Octane Trading* – an invitation to become an apprentice of the important skills, techniques and strategies that I will share with you throughout this book. This information will not only help you survive but thrive in good times or bad!

In a way this book brings me full circle, returning me to my roots. By tapping into the same lessons I learned as a child: developing a game plan, commitment, discipline, persistence, recognizing an explosive opportunity, and acting upon it, I hope, in some small way, this book will mentor you to greater success and more profitable results.

Moreover, by learning from the mistakes I've made along the way, you can shorten your own learning curve, thereby helping you achieve success quicker and more efficiently.

As you read each chapter you'll be further prepared to go on to the next level of understanding until you've attained a master-like touch in trading stocks and/or options. So here's your chance to participate in a one-of-a-kind apprenticeship program. You won't believe how simple and easy it is to become a better trader!

Introduction

"The only thing more expensive than education is ignorance."
– Benjamin Franklin

We all have ambitions. However, for most of us the size and scope of our aspirations shrink. Why? Because the longer we toil in unproductive endeavors, squander our time in off-hand wasteful ways, refuse to learn from past experiences and fail to seize upon rich educational opportunities we risk remaining ignorant. And…

Ignorance is a Dream Killer!

You see, in order to have everything you want (socially, intellectually, temporally and spiritually) you need to keep your dreams alive. Avoiding "dream evaporation" involves creating a life full of passion to cultivate, pursue and realize your dreams.

The purpose of this book is to breath life back into your temporal aspirations by showing you a specific path, that if followed, will allow you to experience the excitement of seeing your financial dreams come true!

CHAPTER 1

Time is Your
Most Precious Asset

Only you really know why you are reading this book. It may be partly due to the fact that you're looking for a change in your financial well-being. I assure you, the doubt and worry you may feel from time to time, I have felt. Like a lot of individuals, I have also sought for and made changes. Rest assured, you are not alone in your quest!

If one of the reasons behind your desire to pursue other sources of income (a reason stated by most everyone) is that you are not satisfied with your current lifestyle or financial situation then this book is for you. However, if you are currently satisfied with your finances, then this book is still for you. In fact, I would be so bold as to say that it is much easier to squander and lose a fortune in the stock market than it is to acquire one. Just ask those who watched their networth literally vaporize before their eyes during the horrific stock market meltdown in 2000-01. By understanding the principles and strategies presented in this book you'll be able to build, protect, and hold onto the money that you have worked so hard to obtain. All that stands between you and your dreams is *time*.

Some of the questions you need to ask yourself (before you read any further) are: 1) Am I progressing financially the way I wish? 2) Am I at a point in my life where I can support (without going any further into debt) the lifestyle that I would like to enjoy? 3) Do I have the financial resources available to me that would allow me to enhance my current lifestyle?

These three questions can truly only be answered with some soul-searching. There is no doubt in my mind that if you answered in the negative to any of these questions, then this book will provide you with a myriad of bread and butter techniques, insights, and strategies to dispel your financial concerns.

> The wonderful thing about time, particularly if you view it as a precious commodity, is that everyone has been allocated the same amount of it. Time is equal for all of us.

The wonderful thing about time, particularly if you view it as a precious commodity, is that everyone has been allocated the same amount of it. Time is equal for all of us. The number of minutes in your day that can be used in pursuit of your dreams is identical to anyone else's. So are your hours, days, weeks, or months.

If you are going to properly use your allotted time and leverage it in order to obtain your financial goals and dreams, it is nice to know that no one has any specific advantage or disadvantage over anyone else.

The playing field is level. We all start pursuing our financial aspirations on equal footing. I cannot emphasize this enough! Psychologically, this is quite comforting, since

> How you make use of your time is the deciding factor in how productive and rewarding your life is.

you know that you have every opportunity to achieve your financial goals, no matter what they are.

So what is the importance of time as a commodity? It is only important in its relevance to how you use it. Do you take advantage of your time? Do you put it to good use? Did you take some time today to better yourself? Have you made any financial decisions today that will help yourself and your family in the future?

There are hundreds of questions that you could ask yourself regarding your finances. The enlightening thing is that all of these questions have a relationship with time. How you make use of your time is the deciding factor in how productive and rewarding your life is.

You probably won't become a "zillionaire" overnight, but if you take action today, you will be sowing something that you will be able to reap in the future. This is not a new or hard concept to grasp. You ultimately reap what you sow, something you undoubtedly understand. So start taking steps today to better prepare and improve yourself for tomorrow!

Please take out a pen and sheet of paper. Let's take a simple test to see if you are prepared to pursue your financial dreams by trading stocks and/or options. But first, do you remember how we stated the premise of this book? Do you recall the quote by Benjamin Franklin in the Introduction? He stated,

"The only thing more expensive than education is ignorance."

Benjamin Franklin held a belief that man was bound by duty to take advantage of his time. He said that man had a stewardship for his time and that he was to be held accountable for what he did or accomplished with it. He knew that anyone could prosper greatly if they would but learn from life's experiences. Life would bear the sweetest fruit if new educational challenges, which are invariably in front of all of us, were readily embraced.

The "Franklin scale" was a tool and a methodical exercise that Benjamin Franklin invented as a measuring device that weighted the pluses (+) and minuses (-) of every decision he could or would possibly want to make. Since Franklin's day, this approach has been used by millions of people to determine if they can or should attempt to do a specific activity. (The decision can involve anything and is not merely confined to the pursuit of financial endeavors.)

> The only thing more expensive than education is ignorance.

Take your paper and draw a line down the center of it. Draw a second, horizontal line about one inch down from the top of the paper from edge to edge. On the left side of the paper, above the horizontal line, draw a plus (+) sign. On the right side of the paper, above the horizontal line, place a negative (-) sign. Under the plus sign, list every positive experience or result that may occur from trading stocks and/or options. It can be anything. Let your imagination fly. Don't hold back. This is truly an opportunity to dream! Then, in the opposite column, list those items that you perceive to be a negative.

On the positive side you will be listing, more likely than not, temporal or physical items. For example, your monetary gains may well be used to remodel a bathroom or kitchen. Perhaps on a grander level you will be able to add an addition to your home. Who knows, maybe you will be able to afford a new home! How about a new car or boat in your driveway or garage?

Maybe a new car or home are not things you need or are interested in right now. Maybe you're interested in just having enough extra money to sign the kids up for piano or dance lessons.

Maybe your interests revolve around traveling. Make a long list of all the places you would like to go or have dreamed of visiting. Maybe traveling in the United States or Canada doesn't excite you. Does the idea of international travel intrigue you? Would you like to travel to Paris, Rome, Hong Kong, or the French Riviera? If so, write it down. Remember, the world is your playground!

Make an extensive list of all the things that you've always wanted to do in your life. Have you ever wanted to play golf at Pebble Beach? Well write it down. Have you ever been on an African safari? Have you ever taken your family on a cruise during the winter? Have you sat down in the Louvre and copied a work of a master painter? Have you walked the Great Wall of China, kayaked the beautiful waters of New Zealand, studied the rare birds of the Amazon, or toured the canals of Venice by gondola? The sky's the limit - dream big!

After you have made your list, you will begin to realize just what money can do for you, your family, and others around you. Money gives you freedom! It gives you the opportunity to choose from a multitude of wonderful choices. It gives you financial independence!

Benjamin Franklin was a big dreamer. He constantly used the Franklin scale as a tool to take the first steps in mapping out his aspirations and goals. He realized early on that in order to make his dreams come true he would have to reach a certain level of financial independence.

Historically, it has been pointed out that Benjamin Franklin was quite an entrepreneur. And he was an entrepreneur because of his financial independence. He was able to pursue his joys because he had the means to do so. His businesses, which were many, were positioned to allow him to go after his personal interests and aspirations with vigor.

It has also been noted that Benjamin Franklin didn't have a purely financial interest in everything that he did. Not all of his dreams were financially oriented. Some of his more charitable endeavors were accomplished because he had the capital that afforded him more choices and greater interests than others of his era.

When you take a look at your own Franklin scale everything won't be monetarily driven. For example, there will be things that will be oriented around your charitable interests. There will be charities that you'll want to donate your time or money to. Maybe the same will be true for a church or religious faith that you share a kinship with. Wanting to help your children with their educational interests (paying for tuition, books, and room and board) is a huge act of charity and goodness.

Your personal financial independence will provide huge benefits to society. Your money and time will help many others. Your community will become a better place and benefit with your help. Remember, your desires and ultimately the degree to which you can help yourself, others, and society depends upon your ability to become financially independent.

Are you an individual who works at a nine-to-five job? Do you regret having to get up to go to work? Must you ask permission from a supervisor in order to get vacation time? Have you hit a ceiling in regard to potential future earnings? Does your paycheck always look the same? Are you worried about retirement? Will you be able to make ends meet? Are you going to have enough from Social Security and retirement benefits to live on when you choose to retire? Are you depressed about your financial future?

If you answered yes to any of these questions, then your choices, your freedom, and ultimately your financial independence is being hampered.

There are many statistics out there that bring to light issues addressing exactly what the American lifestyle is like. It is estimated that about 90% of Americans engage in the "nine-to-five" rat race. And for many, it is truly a rat race. An interesting statistic put out by the American Medical Association states that antidepressants are among the fastest-selling drugs. Wow! You can really see that many people perceive there is no real freedom, no real choices, and no true independence.

The bottom line is that your own Franklin scale will show you how bound to your current lifestyle you really are. But on the other hand, your list will also show you how liberated you could really be if you had more money. I promise you that the plus side of your Franklin scale will far outweigh the negative. The negative side will probably list just one thing — the loss of money. Period. (As you'll soon learn, the key to your success is keeping those losses small.)

However, the underlying reason for losing too much money is rooted in fear, greed, and a lack of knowledge. If these things are holding you back, your dreams will disappear and evaporate. Life doesn't have to be full of fear, doubt, and worries, because the proper knowledge can be easily acquired to allay all of these.

If you don't like the way your life is going, take the time and change it. Learn from the past and take advantage of your future. Realize the power of a second, a minute, an hour, a day, a week, and a year to change your life for the better. Make a decision today, right now, to treat time as a precious commodity. Commit to making the most of your time, never wasting it again.

It's true that America is a land where everyone can sow and cultivate the seeds of their dreams. In fact, the American Dream has sprouted, developed and flourished for millions of people. The secret is finding the perfect opportunity.

Key Points to Remember

➤ All that stands between you and your dreams is time.

➤ How you make use of your time is the deciding factor in how productive and rewarding your life will be.

➤ The "Franklin scale" was a tool and a methodical exercise that Benjamin Franklin invented as a measuring device that weighted the pluses (+) and minuses (-) of every decision he could or would possibly want to make.

➤ Under the plus sign, list every positive experience or result that may occur from trading stocks and/or options. This is truly an opportunity to dream!

➤ In the opposite column, list those items that you perceive to be a negative.

➤ Make a decision today, right now, to treat time as a precious commodity.

CHAPTER 2

Three Lost Secrets to Financial Freedom

"Every man is rich or poor according to the degree in which he can afford to enjoy the necessaries, conveniences, and amusements of human life."
Adam Smith, *The Wealth of Nations,* 1776

As a youth, I was friends with a kid who lived in a large, beautiful, and obviously very expensive house. In addition to a beautiful home he always had the newest and best toys to play with. His family was the first in our school to have a large-screen television set, and as I recall, everyone had a permanent invitation to go over to his house to watch "Monday Night Football." They were generous people, always willing to go out of their way for someone else.

In high school, this same friend was the first to wear a nice watch. He always wore the trendiest fashion clothes and of course, he was always going out with the best-looking girl in school. In our junior and senior years, he drove the coolest and most expensive car (and that even included those that the school faculty drove).

Soon, I became curious and bold enough to ask my friend what his dad did for a living. (I assumed he was a president of some large, high-profile corporation.) "Oh, he owns his own business," was his reply.

It was at that moment I realized that true lasting fortunes are founded in the basic premise that it might be better to work for yourself rather than for someone else.

> J. Paul Getty firmly believed that in order to succeed in the business world you had to work for yourself.

J. Paul Getty firmly believed that in order to succeed in the business world you had to work for yourself. I believe he was right. There are a lot of benefits that can be derived from running and operating your own business. Undoubtedly, you have already listed some on your Franklin scale. But the big question that you are faced with is: What business should you go into? Are you still wondering if you should pursue the business of trading stocks and/or options?

Go ahead and make another Franklin scale. List all the positives and negatives to any particular business that you'd like to start. But before you start writing, let me suggest some of the reasons why you shouldn't go into any business other than trading stocks or options.

Remember, a high percentage of new companies fail. Why? The costs of running the business are too high. Even established companies that have been around for 25, 50, and even 100 years are constantly fighting employee and production cost overruns. Fortunately, as a trader you won't have to face many of the problems that plague other businesses.

In fact, when I was trying to decide if I was going to get into the options business, I drafted my own Franklin scale. I'm sure your scale will have many of these same items listed below. You won't:

Need more than $5,000 to get started (and you can open an account for much less than that).

Need a bank loan.

Have any employees.

Have to go to any lame office holiday parties.

Have to worry about employees calling in sick with tired, worn-out excuses.

Need an attorney.

Need full-time accountants or bookkeepers.

Have to worry about payroll.

Have an inventory to keep track of.

Have to worry about the quality or control of merchandise.

Have customers to deal with.

Have to worry about customer relations.

Have to worry about customer complaints. (Heck, if you don't want to be nice one day at work you don't have to be.)

Have to rent or lease office space.

Have to worry about insurance.

Waste countless hours commuting to and from work.

Have to go to bed early because you have to get up early to go to work.

Need to spend eight hours a day running your business.

Need an advertising budget.

Have to purchase an endless supply of office products.

Get the picture? The list of benefits could go on forever, and I'm only listing the subtle nuisances and big problems that you'll avoid.

At this point, a few of you still may not yet be entirely sold on the prospect of trading options, even though you'd actually be starting up your own business. But when you think about it, no one is going to look out for your or your family's future unless you do. As the saying goes, "If it is to be, it's up to me!"

Many attendees at my workshops come to learn how to achieve the "American Dream." They have a strong desire to change their financial situation, taking it upon themselves to learn how. Many believe investing in the stock market is the answer. Perhaps you feel the same way.

> The three Rs are: Revenue, write-offs, and retirement.

To stimulate their thinking, I like to ask the following questions: "Why do you want to invest in the first place? What did you come to learn about? What are you hoping to gain from the information I will share with you today?" Invariably, the responses revolve around the three Rs, also know as *the three lost secrets to financial freedom:* Revenue, write-offs, and retirement.

Let me explain…

The number one reason why people want to invest (it doesn't matter whether it's in the stock market, real estate, a business, or a franchise) is to make more money. They need more revenue. Obviously, that comes as no surprise. In fact, how many times do you find yourself with more month than money?

Plus, as people live longer, more and more families and individuals will need a bigger nest egg to retire on.

Finally, you are probably getting sick and tired of working for somebody else. You want to get paid what you are really worth and you want to call your own shots. Having your own business provides such opportunities.

Generate More Revenue

The secret lies in working smarter, not harder. You need to develop a cookie-cutter approach to making money – a system that will not only generate additional streams of revenue for you and your family, but will run on autopilot as well.

Many a great entrepreneur has a rags-to-riches story to tell. Often, through hard work and perseverance, these individuals rise from impoverished beginnings and climb the ladder of success, attaining great wealth in the process. Such is the case of Tom Monaghan, founder of Domino's Pizza.

He parlayed his ownership of three pizzerias into a world-famous pizza chain with more than 5,000 stores worldwide. Not only did he love to work, but he was able to create a system whereby he easily duplicated his approach to making fresh pizzas.

He conceived of two innovations that many of us take for granted today. According to Daniel Gross' *Greatest Business Stories of All Time,* he devised "the square, multi-sized corrugated box (strong and easily stackable) and the 'hot box,' or insulated pouch, to keep the pizza hot during delivery. He is also credited with designing the conveyor oven, pizza trays, and a vertical cutter." All these things helped streamline the pizza-making process, generating more revenue for his business in the process.

He helped pioneer the concept of free home delivery. In fact, his promise of hot pizza in 30 minutes or less became the signature hallmark of the Domino's franchise.

Every step of the way, Monaghan was constantly looking for different ideas and techniques that would produce pizza more efficiently without lessening the quality. In short, he developed a cookie-cutter approach to making pizza and became a billionaire in the process.

You see, the money is made from the system. The bottom-line key to wealth is repetition and duplication. You find something that works and you do it over and over again. Regardless of the Domino's Pizza you visit or order from, the process by which pizza is made is the same. The secret to obtaining true financial freedom is creating a money-making system that will run with or without you.

That's why running and operating your own business is really the only way to pursue the American Dream. Further, it helps protect you and your family from two "American Dream Killers," taxes and inflation.

Cut Your Taxes

The first "American Dream Killer," hindering your ability to get rich, is taxes. Most likely, you pay too much! Legally avoiding taxes should become an integral part of your financial affairs. In fact, Judge Learned Hand gave you permission to do so when he said, "Anyone may so arrange his affairs that his taxes shall be as low as possible. ...There is not even a patriotic duty to increase one's taxes."

> The bottom-line key to wealth is repetition and duplication. You find something that works and you do it over and over again.

Sadly, most people work almost six months out of the year for Uncle Sam before they see a dime (affectionately known as, *Tax Freedom Day*). Let's face it, you can't achieve financial independence if you continue to share 40% to 60% of what you make with someone else.

In fact, it doesn't take long before you realize that the harder you work the less you keep. It saps initiative and deflates your aspirations. In the *1996 Report of the National Commission on Economic Growth and Tax* they point out, "Why dream bigger, when little dreams are less expensive? ...In the famous 1819 United States Supreme Court case, *McCulloch v. Maryland*, Chief Justice John Marshall wrote: 'The power to tax involves the power to destroy.'"

The report also points out that *The New York Times*, in a 1909 editorial opposing the very first income tax, predicted: "When men get in the habit of helping themselves to the property of others, they cannot easily be cured of it."

Thus, it should come as no surprise that the current Tax Code, with accompanying regulations, has grown to more than 7,000,000 words! Moreover, you have more than 400 tax forms to choose from. That's why the lobbying industry, which employs more than 67,000 people, is the largest private sector employer in Washington, D.C. The only reason many of these lobbyists exist is to protect or add special tax breaks to the Tax Code. No wonder it's so onerous and complex!

You need to learn how to reduce your taxes so you have more money to spend on your family, home, business interests, hobbies, and favorite charities. Either you can write out a check to the "I-R-S" or you can write it out to "Y-O-U," – it's your choice. There's absolutely no reason why you should pay more than your fair share.

If you take a look at the history of the United States, you'll quickly discover that the country was founded on tax protest. Just consider a few of the more famous events that illustrated the lengths to which people would go to fight the oppression of unfair and burdensome taxes.

> Either you can write out a check to the "I-R-S" or you can write it out to "Y-O-U," – it's your choice.

To begin with, one of the most effective political dramas ever staged was the Boston Tea Party. It was a protest of British tax policies on tea imported to the American Colonies.

John Adams said of the event, "There is a dignity, a majesty, a sublimity, in this last effort of the patriots that I greatly admire."

His cousin, Samuel Adams, stated, "Fellow countrymen, we cannot afford to give a single inch! If we retreat now, everything we have done becomes useless..."

In essence, the citizens of Boston would not permit the unloading of three British ships that arrived in their port, but the royal governor of Massachusetts would not let the tea ships return to England until the duty had been paid. The situation was at an impasse.

As a result, on the evening of December 16, 1773, a group of 60 Colonists, disguised as Mohawk Indians, boarded the ships at Griffin's Wharf. With the aid of the ships' crew, they tossed 342 chests of tea into Boston Bay, boycotting the English Parliament's tax on tea. "Taxation without representation!" was their cry as they destroyed the tea. The news of the destruction of the tea raised the spirit of resistance in the Colonies.

After this incident, the English Parliament began passing more legislation to raise money, which only further enraged the colonists. This was but a prelude to April 1775, when British and Colonial forces met on the battlefield, ready to wage war. Mystery surrounds that fateful day, as nobody knows who fired the first shot. But the "shot heard around the world" triggered the fighting and as they say, the rest is history.

After the American Revolution, taxes also led to an uprising in Massachusetts, commonly referred to as "Shay's Rebellion." Daniel Shays, a former captain in the American Revolutionary army, headed the group of mostly poor farmers who were fed up with excessive land taxation, high legal costs, and economic depression.

Among other things, they demanded a radical reduction in taxes. This, as well as many other protests during this period, helped push the nation's leaders to form and ratify the fledgling Constitution of the United States.

While I'm not advocating that you go out and lead a rebellion or stage a tax protest, I *am* suggesting that you become proactive when it comes to cutting your taxes. Believe it or not, there are some simple, legal, and ethical things you can do to reduce your tax burden. In short, you need more write-offs! Many come as a perk to running and operating your own business. As a result, I firmly believe that you need to start some type of small business.

For example, are there more tax deductions available to a small business than an individual? Of course there are. You see, there are things that you currently spend money on as an individual that you can't write off; yet when purchased for business purposes, you can write off. What are some of those things? Cars, gas, insurance, computers, postage, office supplies, meals, and entertainment, to name only a few.

> I firmly believe that you need to start some type of small business.

In fact, that's why I love the seminar business. Instead of taking vacations, I take business trips! If you happen to run into the beach, pool, or Mickey Mouse on your way to a business seminar, so be it. Such is life when running and operating your own business. (Make sure you consult your tax advisor before doing any of the above, though.)

Simply put, do more in the name of business. Most likely than not, you're overpaying your taxes because you don't take advantage of all the deductions legally available to you.

Develop a Financially Secure Retirement

The final "R" that my seminar attendees want to learn more about is how to develop a financially secure retirement. Most Americans are forced to retire on much less than they need because they didn't adequately plan for their future.

In fact, numerous studies and surveys point out that many individuals are clueless when it comes to the financial facts of life. Supporting this claim is a study by the Securities and Exchange Commission (SEC) that showed 49% of adults flunked a basic economic literacy test.

Since retirement isn't a priority for most people, it should come as no surprise that 51% of Americans don't even have a retirement plan. Even more alarming is a study by the Employee Benefit Research Institute (EBRI) that found 55% have never even *tried* to calculate what they'll need for retirement!

In addition, the SEC discovered that, "two out of three households in America – an estimated 65 million households – will probably fail to realize one or more of their major life goals because they've failed to develop a comprehensive financial plan."

Think about it. Will you be able to retire on Social Security (or, I should say, Social "Insecurity") alone? While many believe it won't be their major source of retirement income, the statistics dictate otherwise. Sadly, the EBRI found that more than 66% of retirees rely almost totally on Social Security, mainly because they didn't know they needed to save (which is what the statistics I cited support). As a result, many spend their golden years just trying to make ends meet.

Perhaps you're lucky enough to have a pension plan. Many aren't. According to the Department of Labor, less than half of American workers are covered by a pension plan. Even if you *do* enjoy the benefit of having a pension plan, will it be enough to secure your future? Have you considered what will happen to your pension check if the company you retired from goes broke or out of business? Your pension checks will dry up! You'll be left high and dry!

My telling you about those statistics isn't meant to scare or intimidate you, but to help you realize that you need to get back in control of your retirement *now!* A simple solution is getting more educated about financial matters, which is exactly what you're doing by reading this book. Congratulations!

More important, by learning how to sow various "money trees" you can develop multiple streams of revenue so you won't need to rely solely on Social Security or a company pension plan for financial support. You can become financially independent on your own.

Inflation, the Second "American Dream Killer"
Finally, the second "American Dream Killer" you need to guard against is inflation. Have you ever considered the ravaging effects of inflation and what it may do to the purchasing power of your future nest egg?

Inflation is the monster that eats away at your future a small bite at a time. I wouldn't worry so much about your $1,000 to $5,000 trading account (that's small pickings). To be frank, you should be more concerned about how your retirement, Social Security, pension, and any other possible savings/investments are going to hold up under the severe pressure of inflation.

Let's take a look at some of the financial tools that allegedly will help you fight inflation and, more important, help provide for an enjoyable retirement.

Stocks

Do you own stocks? If you do, do you receive dividends on a quarterly, semi-annually, or annualized basis? Do you know what your yield is from those dividends? Pretty low, isn't it? Dividends are at their lowest level ever! The dividend yield on the Standard & Poor's 500 (S&P 500) Index is less than 1.5%. If you're looking to get rich at 1.5% a year, is it going to happen? No. It's like treading water – you're working hard but going nowhere. In fact, if you mix in a little inflation, are you going forward or backward? You may actually be losing ground!

Bonds, CDs, and Savings Accounts

Do you think a savings account will protect you against inflation? No way! Why? Bonds, CDs (certificates of deposit, or as I like to call them, "certificates of depreciation") and savings accounts are based upon a fixed-rate-of-return. With interest rates so low, your rate of return is in the low single digits and it may not even keep up with the cost of living. If the cost of living is around 3% annually and you are only earning 2.5% interest annually, then you're not even keeping your head above water. Such poor rates of return will eventually drown you.

Life Insurance

Many individuals have life insurance benefits that they believe will aid their families upon their deaths. There are some things you should be aware of. First of all, the IRS will undoubtedly be first in line to get their "fair" share. Once you do get your hands on what's left over, statistics show that recipients of these cash lump-sum payments tend to spend the money foolishly before they allow themselves time to invest it. Post-grief spending can be costly and detrimental to your future plans.

Most of these retirement vehicles will make living with inflation difficult or at least uncomfortable. In order to generate lasting wealth, it wouldn't be prudent to employ financial tools that can only wager a losing battle with inflation. You may win a few battles but you'll never win the war against inflation.

When I was growing up, penny loafers were all the rage. They were leather slip-ons, very comfortable and easy to get in and out of. Everyone wore them!

But here's the best part about these shoes. On top of the shoes, where the leather would cover the bridge of your foot, there was a slit, cut into the leather by the manufacturer, where you could slip in a penny. I had a buddy who used to put two shiny pennies into the slits, one for each shoe. Plenty of others did the same. (That's probably why they are called "penny loafers.")

Pretty soon, my friend found a more functional purpose for the slits in those shoes. He took the pennies out and replaced them with a dime and a nickel. Now he had "emergency phone money"! Soon thereafter, and as a result of inflation, he replaced the nickel with a quarter because the price of phone calls had risen from 15 cents to 35. To make a long story short, eventually he ended up wearing folded dollar bills!

I'm sure you have your own war stories about inflation. But no matter how small, insignificant, and inconsequential the stories may seem, they all underscore the indisputable existence of inflation in our lives.

> Starting your own business will help you cultivate additional sources of revenue, reduce your taxes, and get you back in control of your retirement!

When trading stocks and/or options, you're really investing in a business that will give you a chance to overcome lost purchasing power due to inflation. You'll not only be preserving your capital, but you'll be giving it a chance to grow at a superior rate of return.

Manage Your Investments Like a Business

As you can see, starting your own business will help you cultivate additional sources of revenue, reduce your taxes, and get you back in control of your retirement! But there's an even more important principle at work here. It's not enough to *want* to start your own business; you must also manage your investments *like* a business.

Consider for a moment a typical retail business. It makes money buying wholesale and selling retail – the owner buys in order to sell. Now let's contrast that with what most people have been taught to do in the stock market – buy and hold. It shouldn't come as a surprise, then, that many find it difficult to make any money from their investments.

Don't get me wrong. I'm not saying you should run out and sell all of your investments, nor am I saying that you shouldn't build a nice portfolio for the future. Buying and holding your investments just isn't the most effective or productive use of your resources. Think for a moment what would happen if you ran your business that way!

For example, say you own a retail establishment. Someone walks into your store and wants to make a purchase. You look them straight in the eye and say: "I can't sell you anything. We buy and hold our inventory." Obviously I'm being facetious, but my point is an important one: You don't make a dime until you sell something.

Can you be asset-rich and cash-poor? Sure you can! Many find themselves in that situation. They have plenty of assets that look good on paper, but they still can't pay their bills. As a result, their retirement is on hold. Many are forced to reenter the workforce just to make ends meet.

Furthermore, if you bought a stock at $10 and it's trading at $100 today, have you made any money? No. Granted, your gains look fabulous on paper, but the last time I checked you couldn't put stock certificates in the gas tank or buy groceries on margin. That's what I mean by being asset-rich and cash-poor! Oh, and by the way, what enables you to buy the assets in the first place? Money!

It's creating a reliable source of money that enables you to quit your job. It's money that enables you to take a vacation. It's money that pays for the kid's piano lessons – not your assets.

Take it one step further. Do you currently work for someone else? If you do how long do you think it would be before your income stops if you didn't go to work? Not long!

Even if you own your own business, how long would it be before your business goes out of business if you stopped working? One day? One week?

If this applies to you, it simply means that you are your only money-producing asset. If you don't go to work, the money stops! Consequently, your first order of business is to create an additional source of income, so the money keeps coming in whether or not you go to work.

Do you remember how Domino's Pizza founder Tom Monaghan accomplished this? He created a system for making money whether he went into Domino's Pizza or not. He could be at the beach, by the pool, or fast asleep in bed, and the money didn't stop.

But isn't that everyone's goal? You bet it is! That's the American Dream! Financial independence! Doing what you want, when you want to do it. Have you ever given any thought as to what it means to you? Does becoming financially independent mean spending more time with your kids? Having no debts to worry about? Taking a trip around the world? Perhaps fixing up the antique car in your garage? Whatever it means to you, that becomes your goal!

In order for me to help you reach that goal I need you to change your approach to investing. By doing so, you'll open the window to so many promising financial possibilities that it will blow your mind!

First of all, scrape together whatever amount of money you can. In Chapter Four, "The Quest for Capital," I'll show you how innovation and imagination can unearth all kinds of newfound money. For example, you can have a garage sale or sell some of your homemade crafts on eBay.

Now that you've accumulated a little nest egg it's time to buy a stock or option (according to your game plan). But instead of buying and holding like you've been taught to do, sell it as soon as you can. Buy in order to sell!

> Manage your investments like a business – buy "wholesale" and sell "retail."

If you can do this in three weeks, great! In one day, fantastic! The bottom line is that you need to manage your investments like a business – buy "wholesale" and sell "retail." By doing so, you're creating a cookie-cutter approach to making money. Then repeat the process over and over again, thereby producing an additional stream of income that is independent of you!

By adopting such an approach to trading stocks and options, you'll put yourself in a position to make unbelievable amounts of money. What would it mean to you to make an extra $1,200 to $2,500 a month? How about earning $40,000 a month or more? It's possible if you take the time to learn how to do it. It will be life-changing! But that begs the question: If this is so profitable, why aren't more people doing it? Turn the page and find out.

Key Points to Remember

➤ One of the lost secrets to achieving financial independence is working for yourself.

➤ As a trader, you won't face many of the problems that plague other businesses.

➤ Running and operating your own small business helps protect you and your family from two "American Dream Killers," taxes and inflation.

➤ The biggest household expense for most Americans is taxes. Thus, by reducing your taxes you get an *instant* pay raise!

➤ There are more tax deductions available to a small business than an individual – the second lost secret to financial freedom.

➤ In order to generate additional stream of revenue, generate more write-offs, and secure a better retirement you need to start some type of small business.

➤ Manage your investments *like* a business – buy in order to sell!

➤ The secret to becoming wealthy is repetition and duplication – you find something that makes money and then you do it over and over again. This is the third lost secret to financial freedom.

Three Barriers to Achieving Financial Independence

When you consider the speed with which you can make unbelievable amounts of money buying and selling stocks and options, you may be asking yourself, "Why aren't more people doing this? Why haven't my brokers or financial advisors told me about it?"

Why aren't more people doing it? I love to pose the same question to seminar attendees across the country. As you can imagine, I get varied responses, but ultimately, they revolve around three areas, or "walls," as I like to call them. I call them walls because they act as barriers that prevent you from getting what you want. If you could identify the walls that are holding you back, would that have value? Sure it would. If you knew what they were, you could tear them down. Let's uncover what the three walls are.

Lack of Knowledge

The biggest wall for most people is the lack of *knowledge*. Most people have never been taught anything about the stock market, let alone trading options. Realistically, you can't expect yourself to invest in stocks or options with any degree of success if you don't know how. Can you gain knowledge quickly? Yes, you can. And I don't mean just any kind of knowledge. I mean specialized knowledge. If you dig for oil where there's oil (using specialized knowledge), what will you find? Oil! So, if you specialize in knowledge that makes money, what will you make? Money!

Lack of Confidence

You can have a lot of knowledge about something but what else can hold you back? *Fear.* You don't take action because you don't know what to do, how to do it, or what to say. As a result, fear, or a lack of confidence, becomes another barrier in your life. It prevents you from taking your desired course of action.

What do you think the scariest trade of all will be? That's right your first one. It is the same for everyone. Whether it is the first date, the first day on the job, or the first time riding a bike, everyone lacks confidence at one time or another. For those first times, how did you conquer the fear? By doing it! What makes the task a lot easier is knowing what to do, how to do it, and what to say. Possessing the right knowledge helps your confidence grow.

Lack of Money

You can have a lot of knowledge and overflow with confidence, but what else do you need to get started trading stocks and options? *Money!* The lack of money is the third wall that prevents people from realizing their financial dreams.

As I travel across the country teaching my introductory, two-hour seminars, people consistently tell me they love what they learned, but they just don't have the money to get started. My response is always the same: "If you don't scape some money together, you can't implement what I'm teaching you! And if you continue to do what you've always done, what will you continue to get? Zero, zip, zilch, nada, nothing." Understanding this is critical to getting started. You can't continue to do what you've always done and expect different results!

> You can't continue to do what you've always done and expect different results!

So the question is really not whether you have the money, but how and where are you going to get it? If you don't, you can't get started. If you can't get started, you are left with what you had in the first place. And that's exactly what you're trying to change! You want more out of life, that is, more money and ultimately, more freedom to do as you please. In order to do so, you must take action! But what action should you take?

Let me share a little secret with you. If you take the time to learn how money is made, what's going to happen? You start to make money! If you *don't* take time to learn how money is made, what's the result? *Nothing.* Am I telling you knowledge is the answer? I sure am! Acquiring specialized knowledge is the key to achieving financial independence!

It's knowledge that makes you money. It's knowledge that gives you the confidence (by knowing what to do and when to do it) to take action. The American Dream is alive and well, simply take the time to learn how to obtain it. By doing so, you can tear down the walls preventing you from achieving financial independence.

> Acquiring specialized knowledge is the key to achieving financial independence! It's knowledge that makes you money.

Read the following chapter very carefully. It will help you realize that the money to get started is all around you – you just need to know where to look! As you'll soon see, never underestimate the power of your resources, imagination, and innovation.

Key Points to Remember

➤ The three "walls" that prevent you from getting what you want are: Lack of knowledge, lack of confidence, and lack of money.

➤ If you specialize in knowledge that makes money, you will make money.

➤ Possessing the right knowledge helps your confidence grow.

➤ If you continue to do what you've always done, you will continue to get what you've always got!

➤ If you take the time to learn how money is made, you will start making money!

➤ If you don't take time to learn how money is made, you will end up with nothing.

➤ Acquiring specialized knowledge is the key to achieving financial independence!

CHAPTER 4

The Quest For Capital

Money, the long green
cash, stash, rhino, jack
or just plain dough.

Chock it up, fork it over
shell it out. Watch it
burn holes through pockets.

To be made of it! To have it
to burn! Greenbacks, double eagles
megabucks and Ginnie Maes.

It greases the palm, feathers a nest
holds heads above water,
makes both ends meet.

Money breeds money.
Gathering interest, compounding daily.
Always in circulation.

Money. You don't know where it's been
but you put it where your mouth is.
"Money" by Dana Gioia 1991

Gladstone once observed that not even love had made so many fools of men as pondering over the nature of money. There are many definitions of money from those who have had much of it to those who wish they had more of it. But no matter what "money condition" you're in, I'm sure that you'll agree with what Carl Sandburg had to say about it in his 1936 poem "The People."

To paraphrase Sandburg, money is power, it's a cushion, and it equals freedom. Money is the sum of all blessings. Money is all of these and more. Money can pay for whatever you want – especially if you have enough of it. Money buys food, clothes, houses, land, riches, and jewels. And it notably buys time to be lazy. Money buys everything except love and immortality.

> Remember, all you'll need to get started is a few thousand dollars, if that.

Most of the time, our "money condition" won't allow us to do something extra, a condition commonly known as being strapped for cash. What can you do without a little bit of extra money? Not much. And it's a certainty that you wouldn't be able to invest in or start trading stocks or options without it. Remember, all you'll need to get started is a few thousand dollars, if that. That's not too much money! It certainly won't be that hard to come up with it if you have a plan. Perhaps an example from J. Paul Getty's life can get you started.

J. Paul Getty was the world's first renowned billionaire. He hosted many dinner and social events at his estate. He used such occasions to schmooze friends, sway business associates, and bilk information from competitors. Although he was considered a congenial host, he did display one major hitch in his "party host" etiquette. He became infuriated with individuals who used his phone for local calls.

You see, Mr. Getty couldn't stomach being taken advantage of financially (all of ten cents a call!). He figured that every time he hosted a gala event, he was losing a few extra dollars. To put a stop to it, he had a pay telephone installed in his front hallway! Imagine that!

Biographical experts who have studied the life and times of Getty have suggested that he hated to miss out on any amount, however small, of potential capital. Obviously, Getty knew the value of a dime and wasn't going to lose an opportunity to earn one, if he could afford to.

Even though many people think Getty was nuts, doesn't everyone share a bit of his attitude toward money? For example, if you see a nickel in the street do you pick it up? Do you pick up a dime or a quarter? How about a dollar bill? You may not pick up a penny if you see one, but you probably pick up just about any other amount you may find.

This chapter is about tapping into your resources and imagination so you can get your hands on the initial grubstake required to get you started in your new business of trading stocks and options.

Let me tell you how a mentor of mine earned the money to make his first trade. He didn't earn it. He found it. That's right. He found approximately $1,200 in loose change (pennies, nickels, dimes and quarters) buried in sawdust piles under the monkey bars of elementary schools and public parks all around Seattle, Washington.

How did he do it? He bought a metal detector for around $150 and started to explore the carefree world of going to the playground. Come to think of it, he could have simply taken on a second job for a short while, but he loved to take his niece there after school. Stopping at playgrounds or parks not only seemed like a perfect place to have some fun, but it was also the perfect opportunity to find some lost and long-forgotten change.

He told me that he had read about the J. Paul Getty "pay telephone" story, and even though *he* thought he was the world's biggest penny pincher, his interest in a dime triggered his desire to find some start up capital of his own to invest in options. He knew that he wouldn't need too much money to get started (probably around $1,000).

As you know, it takes money to make money. So when you finally decide to get started, more likely than not, you will come up with an innovative strategy to get your hands on some money.

My friend was extremely excited about trading. He was tremendously motivated to do what he could to scrape together his initial start-up capital. He put his imagination to work and presto – he was in business!

A lot of you probably don't have a lot of extra money right now either. That's okay. As excited and motivated as you may be, you're most likely wondering how you can find some extra money to get started. At this point, let me share with you a couple more stories that demonstrate how innovation and imagination were used by others in their quest for start-up capital.

This same gentleman later shared another story of how a friend of his approached him and asked, "How long did it take you to save up enough money for your initial investment?" He told his friend that he never did save any money out of his regular paycheck for investments. Due to family responsibilities, he really didn't have any extra time to pick up an extra job, either. So what he did was get a little creative. He used a metal detector to find lost coins. In addition, he told him that it took some time to accumulate the capital, but during that period, he was studying and learning all he could about the options market. Basically, he felt as though he had wasted no time.

Within a few months of relating this story, this same friend approached my mentor and said that he had prepared a plan. He was planning an estate sale. Actually, it was just a fancy garage sale, with many friends and extended family participating.

The sale went well but not as successful as he had anticipated. He earned about $600 for a three-day weekend event. But he felt he still needed more money. He was considering taking on a part-time job delivering pizzas for a few months. But he really didn't want the wear and tear on his automobile.

Still totally convinced that he should get into the options business he made one of the biggest decisions in his life. He decided to sell his baseball card collection, including some vintage memorabilia.

Now for those of you who love collecting baseball cards this is a big deal! It's hard to part with cards you may have had since you were a kid. As I recall, the most expensive item in the man's collection was a 1951 World Series Championship ball signed by every member of the New York Yankees. Six signatures on that ball belong to players who are now in the Baseball Hall of Fame. He received $900 for it. To make a long story short, he ended up selling a few cards, a couple of baseballs, and a rare "Colt 45s" baseball hat. (The Colts were the early expansion team name for the Houston Astros.) His total take was somewhere around $1,000.

With this newfound capital, plus his previous garage sale money of $600, he was set to invest. For him $1,600 was more than enough to start trading. He placed his first trade and within six weeks, his investment had tripled. He realized nearly $1,200 in profit.

You should see his baseball collection now! I'm told it's better than he ever anticipated or dreamed it would be. One Christmas, he gave away six Ken Griffey Jr. rookie cards to nephews for stocking stuffers! He has so many other valuable collectibles that the rookie cards were merely "low-priority stuff."

Can you see how his desire to trade options motivated him enough to use his creativity and imagination to secure his initial capital? Boy, was he ever sure about what he wanted to do! He wasn't going to let anything prevent him from fulfilling his dreams of starting his own business. He made his dreams come true!

Though many people would tell you this is a rare and amazing story, his story is not unlike hundreds of others. Trading stocks and options will open a whole new world of wealth to you. At times, you may find yourself wondering why you didn't discover this business earlier.

The story above constantly reminds me about a motto that Chess, another would-be trader, had made his own:

"It's not what happens to you that matters,
but how you react to it that counts."
– Epectetus

A week didn't go by that he didn't allude to this maxim. You see, he loved to turn the negatives in his life into positives. Not only that, he was always suggesting that everyone do the same. He fervently believed that anything bad that happens to anyone can turn out for the better.

"People who lose their jobs only end up putting themselves in a better situation," he used to say. And of heart attack victims, he claimed that they all would say, "This is the best thing that's ever happened to me! I've stopped drinking and smoking. I've changed my eating habits. I eat less fat." Chess believed that out of life's apparent disasters, positive results would and could arise.

At some point, Chess began to take an interest in options. He wasn't an investor, but for years he keenly listened to stories, thoughts, and ideas about trading. He readily picked up on the terminology and strategies and if you didn't know any better, you would have thought he traded options himself.

One eventful day, Chess announced that he was going to open an account with a broker and start trading. This came as no surprise to those who knew him. He certainly knew all the basics about getting started. In fact, he had performed quite well over the years on some "paper trades." But many wanted to know why he had decided, after all this time, to start trading.

He said that he had received notice recently that his pension checks were going to dry up. The company that he had retired from had gone broke. And after having accustomed himself to a certain lifestyle due to the pension, he was going to attempt to fill the void with profits from his trading.

At that point, he was asked how he was going to get the initial capital to trade. "Are you going to take it from your savings?" he was asked. "No," he replied, and at that moment he produced an unusual lightweight metal alloy coin from his pocket. It was scratched, dented and corroded. On one side was a star of David, the date 1943, and the word "ghetto." On the other face of the coin was the inscription "Quittung uber 10 Mark" – translated, that means, "Receipt against 10 marks."

Chess went on to say that ever since he had been liberated from Auschwitz after the end of World War II, he had held on to that coin. Shortly after his liberation, he found the coin in his pocket. For many years he didn't pay much attention to it. And he claimed that he had carried it in his wallet for some time, perhaps attributing some value of good luck to it.

After a while, the coin had found a more permanent resting place in the bottom of his dresser drawer. Recently, however, the Holocaust Museum in Washington, D.C., had advertised that they were looking to purchase personal articles and artifacts from Auschwitz. This was his opportunity.

You see, Chess was willing to part with the coin in order to secure capital for his first trade. In the end, the need for capital persuaded him to sell the rare coin to the museum.

Chess's disaster, good fortune, innovation, and imagination helped him procure his initial capital to invest. He traded for years, living a comfortable but not lavish lifestyle, and that stood as a constant reminder of Epectecus' motto.

These are only a sample of the stories that I have heard of over the years concerning the raising of capital. By relating these inspiring and unusual stories, I hope I've shed some light on what a little creativity can do. The possibilities are endless. It is not required that you have a unique story. Many individuals have worked second jobs to earn the money. I can assure you that plenty of pizza and newspapers have been delivered by those who needed capital to start trading. Others have merely dipped into their savings accounts.

It doesn't matter what method you choose. It only matters that you get started! Remember, it takes money to make money so take some time right now and devise a plan to obtain your initial grubstake. Then put it to work for you and your loved ones in your own trading business!

Never underestimate the power of your resources, imagination, and innovation. But money alone won't propel you to financial independence. Understanding and harnessing the power of the "Eighth Wonder of the World" will! What's that, you ask? Read on and you'll find out.

Key Points to Remember

➤ All it takes to get started trading is a few thousand dollars, if that.

➤ Your initial start-up capital won't be hard to come up with once you have a plan.

➤ Let innovation and imagination guide you in your quest for start-up capital.

➤ It doesn't matter what method you choose. It only matters that you get started!

CHAPTER 5

The Eighth
Wonder of the World

The original Seven Wonders of the Ancient World was a Greek list of notable objects that were built between 3000 B.C. and 476 A.D. In order to qualify for the list, the Greeks determined that the objects had to fulfill two criteria. First, they had to be man-made. Second, the objects had to be considered notable because of their great size. Even though they were the originators of the list, the Romans who followed lent credibility to the Greek list by suggesting the list should only include beautiful, colossal, and memorable things that travelers should see.

Can you list all of the ancient wonders? No? Can you at least name one of them? Yes, that's correct. The pyramids were indeed one of the seven.

The pyramids were built as tombs for Egyptian kings, and they are the oldest and best preserved of all the ancient wonders. They were built around 2500 B.C. One of the largest pyramids was the Great Pyramid, which stood 450 feet high and had a base that occupied 13 square acres. It took decades and thousands of Egyptian workers and slaves, equaling an enormous amount of man-hours, to build it.

Another great wonder was the Hanging Gardens of Babylon, which were built by King Nebuchadnezzar II around 650 B.C. in a desert. As the legend goes, the king built them for his homesick wife, who apparently missed the lush vegetation and more tropical surroundings of her childhood home.

Historical accounts describe the gardens, laid out on brick terraces about 400 feet above the ground, as stunning. They were so immense that in order to irrigate the flowers, lawns, and trees in the gardens, hundreds of gardeners and slaves had to work in shifts, turning water screws 24 hours a day, to lift water from the Euphrates River.

Other ancient wonders included: the Temple of Artemis at Ephesus, the statue of Zeus, the Mausoleum at Halicarnassus, and the Lighthouse of Alexandria.

All were built by hundreds, and sometimes thousands of men. The man-hours required for their construction numbered in the hundreds of thousands.

Rounding out the list of the Seven Wonders of the Ancient World is the Colossus of Rhodes. The Colossus was a huge bronze statue that stood 120 feet tall. (About as high as the Statue of Liberty, if you were wondering.) A legion of sculptors worked 12 years cutting 6.8 metric tons of stone into blocks to support the statue.

What allowed these ancient civilizations to build such awesome structures? Do you know? Can you hazard a guess? Or is it a long-lost secret?

I can tell you that the secret to building such gargantuan structures is as old as civilization itself. If this principle had not been used, such structures would have never been built. It is the primary building block of prosperity and wealth. This secret has been used by mankind for thousands of years. Its power works the same today as it has in centuries past.

The secret's basis is grounded in the discipline of mathematics. The answer is:

MULTIPLICATION

In fact, Albert Einstein, who knew a little about mathematics, referred to multiplying capital as the "Eighth Wonder of the World."

It's no wonder that, if given the chance to multiply your capital, you would take advantage of the opportunity, especially if you could reduce or eliminate your risk.

The pyramid builders knew how to multiply their efforts. They knew what they could accomplish if they could harness the power of hundreds of men. You could literally build mountains if there were enough men. The Seven Wonders of

> Albert Einstein, who knew a little about mathematics, referred to multiplying capital as the "Eighth Wonder of the World."

the Ancient World were built upon the backs of thousands. No one man can accomplish what scores of men can! They had no modern technology in 3000 B.C., yet the building of nations and the building of prosperity centered on the notion of multiplying the efforts of thousands.

Can you see how prosperity and wealth are built today? It's still built by using the same age-old principle of multiplication. Let me give you a more contemporary example.

Ray Kroc, the inventor of the milkshake machine and also one of the founders of McDonald's, noticed that his hamburger joint was doing quite well. So in order to sell more hamburgers, he decided that he would have to recreate his hamburger business in other locations. He did. He expanded. He essentially multiplied his efforts by multiplying the number of his hamburger stores. He eventually franchised his business, blazing a trail that many would follow (like Domino's Pizza), and you know the rest of the story.

There are McDonald's fast-food restaurants all over the world today. Do you think he could have sold 40 billion or even 100 billion hamburgers out of one store? No way. Mr. Kroc didn't get rich by frying burgers himself. He got thousands of others to cook them for him. Remember, the Egyptian pharaohs didn't get those pyramids built by doing it themselves. They had thousands of others do it for them. Mr. Kroc got richer faster by using multiplication. The pharaohs also got the pyramids built faster via multiplication.

Investing uses the principle of multiplication. In future chapters you will learn how to trade stocks and options.

Soon you'll be trading more than one company at a time. You'll be trading multiple shares or contracts! You will be doing what every great prosperous, wealthy, and successful business man/woman has done. You will be multiplying your efforts and multiplying your wealth.

MULTIPLICATION IS AN AWESOME POWER!

It's the key to any wildly successful, money-making endeavor. Let me share with you a classic story, which demonstrates how fast money can grow when the principle of multiplication is applied.

A paperboy asks his boss for an increase in his weekly pay. The boss does not want to pay the increase so the paperboy tricks the boss into agreeing to pay him a penny a day with the condition that the amount be doubled every day for 30 days. "Just pay me a penny today, two tomorrow, four the day after and so on," the paperboy says. So the boss, thinking that pennies won't amount to much, agrees to the "penny-a-day payment program."

Here's what the paperboy was to receive in wages for each day of the month.

Day 1	$0.01
2	0.02
3	0.04
4	0.08
5	0.16
6	0.32
7	0.64

Day 8 $1.28
    9   2.56
    10   5.12
    11   10.24
    12   20.48
    13   40.96
    14   81.92
    15   163.84
    16   327.68
    17   655.36
    18   1,310.72
    19   2,621.44
    20   5,242.88
    21   10,485.76
    22   20,971.52
    23   41,943.04
    24   83,886.08
    25   167,772.16
    26   335,544.32
    27   671,088.64
    28   1,342,177.28
    29   2,684,354.56
    30   5,368,709.12
    31   10,737,418.24

Wow! Can you believe what the paperboy is owed in wages at the end of the month? To say the least, the boss was shocked. You see, the paperboy knew the power of multiplication. He didn't receive just the last day's pay of $10,737,418.24. That amount was his pay for only one day. His total payment would have been the accumulation of all 31 days – more than $20,000,000.00!

Though this example is just a story, it teaches you to never underestimate the value of a penny, nickel, dime, quarter, or dollar when magnified by the "Eighth Wonder of the World," namely multiplication.

Trading options enables you to harness this awesome power and put you on you on the path toward realizing the American Dream. Thus, it's time to introduce you to the wonderful world of options.

> **Trading options enables you to harness this awesome power and put you on the path toward realizing the American Dream.**

Key Points to Remember

➤ Albert Einstein referred to multiplying capital as the "Eighth Wonder of the World."

➤ Multiplication is the primary building block of prosperity and wealth.

➤ When you trade stocks and/or options you will be multiplying your efforts and wealth.

CHAPTER 6

The Wonderful
World of Options

Introduction

Ruins of an architectural nature have always stimulated my imagination. There is something mysterious about them; something evocative about them; but most important, ruins resonate with a lasting and indelible impression of truth. And truth is the bridge that fills the gap between the past and the present.

Ruins give us a point of contact from peoples of the past. And truthful concepts and principles that have been derived from past human endeavors can be used successfully today.

"But," you say, "what do architectural ruins have to do with trading options?" Well, they both share some common but very important characteristics.

Take the Parthenon. The Parthenon is probably the most celebrated building of the entire classical world. It is one of the buildings that forms a complex of ancient buildings known as the Acropolis, which still dominates the skyline of Athens. The basic skeletal structure or backbone of the Parthenon still stands today because Greek classical architects devised a series of guidelines and rules that revolutionized the art of building construction.

The marble footings provided a tolerable stress foundation that would limit the risk of a building collapse. The even number of marble load-bearing columns provided the unlimited potential of creating one of the biggest buildings of its time. And because marble was abundant and could be quarried locally, there was little monetary expenditure in terms of building supplies.

You see, basic, simple guidelines and rules provided the groundwork for a structure that still exists today. A structure that, I might add, was built around 447 B.C. And those same building techniques and characteristics can be applied to building the ideal investment trading opportunity.

> Options are financial instruments that enable you to profit from any situation possible.

I'm sure you would agree that traders must also trade by a series of guidelines and rules that provide for a successful and enduring trading program. In addition, I'm sure you would agree that if you were to build a model of the most ideal investment opportunity, it would have the following characteristics: limited risk, unlimited reward, low stress, and little cash investment to get started. Is there such a durable, versatile investment? There is, and it's called an option.

Options are financial instruments that enable you to profit from any situation possible. Options are available on various stocks, futures, commodities, currencies, and indices. Although the focus of this report will be on equity (stock) options, the general concepts discussed herein apply to all optionable securities.

When considering trading options and/or stocks, you must remember the stock market boils down to three simple scenarios:

Stocks go up

Stocks go down

Stocks can stay the same

What's critical to your success as a trader is learning strategies that will profit from any one of those three situations. When you do, the odds of winning shift dramatically in your favor. This enables you to stay in the market at all times and have the opportunity to make money, regardless of the market's direction.

When you buy stock, you depend on prices climbing higher in order to make money. You have one shot and one shot only – the stock must go up! Keeping that in mind, how would you like to win whether stocks go up or down? You could be totally wrong about market direction, still make money, and reduce your risk to almost zero at the same time! Sound too good to be true? It isn't. Options provide you with more flexibility and limitless trading opportunities. They are a dynamic investment vehicle, enabling you to take your trading to the next level. Consider the following characteristics that options have to offer:

You can participate in the movement of the stock for a fraction of the cost, enabling you to get a bigger bang for your dollar spent!

You can position yourself to capture explosive moves with very little risk.

You can create an endless stream of cash flow, "free money," from current stock holdings.

You can buy your favorite stock below market value!

You can protect your current portfolio against a market disaster and do it inexpensively.

You can reap windfall profits without having to predict market direction!

Over the ensuing chapter, you will be exposed to what options are and how they work. What's more, you will learn how options limit your risk, while at the same time offering explosive profit potential. And to top it all off, you can get started with very little money! So, it is with great pleasure that I welcome you to the wonderful world of options!

Historical Introduction

The Chicago Board Options Exchange (CBOE) opened and traded the first standardized, exchange-listed equity option on April 26, 1973. This first listing contained only call options on sixteen underlying stocks. Just over one million option contracts were traded by the CBOE during that first year – quite modest by today's standards. The CBOE had introduced a revolutionary, new financial product to the world.

Options became so popular over the next couple of years that other securities exchanges began offering them as well. The American Stock Exchange (AMEX) and the Philadelphia Stock

Exchange (PHLX) started trading options in 1975. The Pacific Exchange, Inc. (PCX) introduced option trading in 1976. The New York Stock Exchange, Inc. (NYSE) finally joined the others and began option trading on its floor in June 1985. However, in 1997, the NYSE transferred its option business to the CBOE.

In 1977, the first put options became exchange-listed and expanded the benefits of options. On March 11, 1983, the CBOE introduced another innovative product in the form of index options on the Standard and Poor's 100 Index (OEX). The OEX has become the most actively traded index option in the world. The PHLX's Semiconductor Sector Index Option (SOX) has become the most actively traded sector index option.

In 1990, the CBOE introduced Long-term Equity AnticiPation Securities (LEAPS®). These long-term options give you added flexibility by allowing you to buy an option with up to three years remaining before expiration. In 1997, the CBOE began offering options on two mutual fund indexes – the first of its kind. As you can see, each exchange is continually adding new products, features, and cutting-edge technology to meet the demanding appetite of the modern-day investor.

Spurring this move for cutting-edge technology are new competitors specializing in electronic trading. For example, in 2000 the International Securities Exchange, a screen-based system, began listing the 600 most popular options. As a result, the exchanges are transitioning toward this highly popular, low-cost form of order execution and away from the traditional open-outcry system (in which traders conduct business by calling and gesturing at one another with a series of intricate hand signals).

In addition, to help them remain competitive, the exchanges are slashing customer fees to attract more volume. In fact, in February 1999, the AMEX and the CBOE announced they wouldn't charge customers (clearing firms) for orders of less than 30 contracts. Ultimately, this benefits you as an option trader, since trading becomes more efficient and costs fall, not only in form of commissions but in the spread (the difference between the bid and the offer) as well. It probably won't be too much longer before you see zero-cost execution and market makers paying for order flow like any other institution.

As proof of the popularity of options, the AMEX trades options on 1,400 stocks and 24 indices. The CBOE trades options on more than 1,850 stocks and 33 indices. The PHLX trades options on 922 stocks and 13 indices, and the PCX trades options on more than 800 stocks and four indices.

The option market is experiencing explosive growth across all the exchanges and, in my opinion, will only continue to grow. Consider that in 1998, a little over 138 million individual stock option contracts were traded on the CBOE. By the end of 2000, that had soared to more than 326 million contracts, a far cry from the one million contracts that traded that first year in 1973! In fact, the CBOE averaged 1,271,240 million contracts per day in 2001! On April 16, 2001, a single-day record of 2,726,267 contracts traded on the CBOE.

Additionally, on January 7, 2002, the Options Industry Council (OIC) stated in a press release that for the tenth consecutive year total equity options volume hit record levels (all four exchanges combined). Volume in 2001 reached 722,680,249 equity contracts, a 7.4 percent increase over 2000's record volume of 672,871,757 contracts. Average daily volume in 2001 was 2,914,033 contracts, up from 2000's average daily volume of 2,670,126.

Another indication of the fast-growing options market is the demand for a seat on the floor on the various exchanges. The price of each seat is determined by Economics 101, that is, supply and demand. As a result, prices will fluctuate according to market conditions, economics and so forth. In fact, there is a bid and an offer, just like any marketable security.

For example, a seat on the PCX sold in January 1996 for $82,500. In March 1998, it sold again for $500,000. Not a bad investment! However, in October 2001, a seat sold for only $75,000. In October 1997, a seat on the CBOE sold for $727,500. In October 2001, it went for only $360,000. In 1996, a seat on the AMEX sold for $200,000. In February 1999, it sold for $660,000, and in February 2002 it went for $310,00. All in all, demand remains fairly strong but with the expansion of electronic screen-based trading, trading on the floor isn't as appealing as it once was.

The Options Clearing Corporation

Who keeps track of all the transactions and makes sure everyone gets paid? It's called the Options Clearing Corporation (OCC), which is jointly owned by the participating exchanges. All option contracts traded on the various exchanges are issued, cleared, and guaranteed by the OCC. In effect, the OCC becomes the buyer to every clearing firm representing a seller and the seller to the every clearing firm representing a buyer. Since they are essentially taking the other side of every option traded, the OCC provides an efficient and secure means by which transactions can take place.

The OCC is a registered clearing corporation with the Securities and Exchange Commission (SEC), and has received an "AAA" credit rating from Standard & Poor's Corporation. The rating applies to the OCC's ability to fulfill its obligation as the clearing party.

What Is An Option?

Options are contracts. One contract, the minimum you can buy, controls 100 shares of stock. (Two contracts control 200 shares of stock, eight contracts controls 800 shares and so forth.) As a buyer of an option, you can own from one contract to as many contracts as your trading capital will allow. An option gives you the right, but not the obligation, to buy or sell 100 shares of stock, on or before a certain date (expiration date), at a specified price (strike price). An option is a fixed-time asset. If you run out of time, what becomes the worth of your asset? Zero! A great way to visualize this is when you buy an option, it's like buying an ice cube. When you hold an ice cube in your hand, what starts to happen? It begins to melt – eventually turning to water, or in this case, expiring worthless. That is why many people view options as risky – you can lose your entire initial investment. Time is one of your enemies when it comes to buying options.

> When you buy an option, it's like buying an ice cube.

Two Types of Options

There are two kinds of options you can buy or sell: call options and put options. A call option gives you the right to buy the stock. A put option gives you the right to sell the stock. Whether you invest in calls or puts depends on whether you think the price of the stock will go up or down.

If you purchase a call option, you want the underlying stock to go up. As the stock's price climbs, the value of your call

> So whether a stock goes up or down, options can make you money!

increases – you're making money. If you buy a put, you are betting that the price of the underlying stock will go down. As the stock falls, the value of your put increases – you're making money. So whether a stock goes up or down, options can make you money!

How Are Options Different From Stocks?

As mentioned previously, options have a limited life – they stop trading at expiration. Stocks do not. If an expected move does not occur right away, the investor can hold onto the stock for another week, or indefinitely for that matter. An option buyer does not have that luxury.

An option does not give you, the buyer, any ownership rights, voting rights, or rights to dividends (if any). It only allows you to participate in the movement of the underlying stock.

When you purchase stock, there is physical delivery of a certificate, which is proof of ownership of the shares you have bought. These certificates can be held by you or your broker. If those shares are sold at a later date then the certificate would be delivered, via a transfer agent, to the buyer. As you can imagine, this can be a time-consuming process, not to mention the complications that arise if the certificates are lost, stolen, or destroyed. Options avoid such problems because there are no certificates of ownership. The OCC maintains all records, which are computerized.

Your confirmation slip from your broker will act as your record for the transaction

Finally, you'll frequently hear people refer to the number of shares outstanding in a publicly-traded company. This represents a fixed number of shares available to buy and sell. However, there is not a fixed number of contracts available when it comes to trading options. The number of outstanding contracts, referred to as "open interest," is only limited by the number of willing buyers and sellers.

The Life of an Option

Unlike stocks, an option is a "wasting asset," commonly referred to as *time decay*. You are racing the clock. The "clock" is the *expiration date*. For equity (stock) options, it is the Saturday following the third Friday of a particular month. Since you can't trade on Saturday, the third Friday becomes your focal point. All you need to do is open up a calendar, identify the third Friday, and options for that particular month will expire at market close (4 p.m. EST) on that day. So if you had your choice, would you rather have more time or less time at your disposal? Clearly more. With options, time can act as a safety net. One of the biggest mistakes option traders make, novice and seasoned alike, is they give themselves too little time. As a result, they pick the right stock but run out of time. When in doubt, err on the side of time! So what are your choices?

> One of the biggest mistakes option traders make, novice and seasoned alike, is they give themselves too little time.

There are four months (two near term and two farther out), not including LEAPS®, from which you can choose. The two near-term months include the current month and the following month. The other two months vary depending on which one of three expiration cycles the stock's options are assigned to. The January cycle consists of January, April, July, and October. The February cycle consists of February, May, August, and November. And the March cycle consists of March, June, September, and December.

For example, if the option is assigned to the January cycle and the current month is February, you could choose from February (the current month), March (the next month), April, and July (the next two months available in the January cycle). There's no need to memorize the various cycles, as your broker can tell you which months are available to choose from.

The Strike Price

The price at which you agree to buy or sell the stock at is known as the *strike price*. This is also referred to as the "exercise price," the term used if you decide to actually buy or sell the underlying shares of stock. Strike prices come in the following set increments and are independent of the stock price:

From $5 to $25 they move in $2.50 increments – 5, 7.50, 10, and so forth.
From $25 to $200 they move in $5 increments – 25, 30, 35, and so forth.
Above $200 they move in $10 increments – 200, 210, 220, and so forth.

An exception to this would be if there is a stock split. The strike price would be adjusted to reflect the split, regardless of the aforementioned increments. For example, with a 2-for-1 stock split (as a shareholder, you would receive two shares for every one owned and the stock price would be cut in half) the 75 strike price would split like the stock itself. It would trade, post split, at 37.50; the 70 strike price adjusts down to 35; the 65 strike price adjusts down to 32.50 and so forth.

In that the strike prices are predetermined, as a function of listed options, you always know which strike prices are available to choose from. Let's say you're interested in an option on IBM, and IBM is currently trading at $91. You could choose the 85, 90, 95, 100, and so on for strike prices. If you chose the 95 strike price, you would have the right, but not the obligation, to buy or sell 100 shares of IBM at $95 per share. New strike prices are made available as they become necessary for example, IBM climbs higher and is now trading at $130.

It is the relationship between the strike price and the stock price that determines whether an option is in-the-money, at-the-money, or out-of-the-money.

A call option is said to be *in-the-money* if the stock price is higher than the strike price. This is because the call option becomes more profitable as the stock price climbs above the strike price. Conversely, a call option is considered out-of-the-money if the stock price is less than the strike price.

For example, if IBM is trading at $91, the IBM July 85 call is in-the-money by 6 points, and the IBM July 90 call is in-the-money by only 1 point. However, the IBM July 95 call is out-of-the-money by 4 points.

A put option is said to be in-the-money if the stock price is trading below the strike price. Keep in mind that a put option becomes more profitable when the stock price falls below the strike price. Conversely, a put option is out-of-the-money if the stock price rises above the strike price.

For example, if AT&T is trading at $60, the May 65 put is in-the-money by 5 points, and the AT&T May 55 put is out-of-the-money by 5 points.

At-the-money refers to any option, put or call, where the stock price is the same as the strike price. However, sometimes people refer to the strike price that is closest to the stock price as being at-the-money, although it may be a little in – or out-of-the-money. The table below illustrates this relationship between the stock price and strike price, assuming the stock price is $60:

Call	Strike Price	Put
	40	
In-the-Money	45	Out-of-the-Money
	50	
	55	
At-the-Money	60	At-the-Money
	65	
	70	
Out-of-the-Money	75	In-the-Money
	80	

The Premium

The final piece of the puzzle is known as the "premium," or the price of the option. Remember that options are sold in contracts, and one contract controls 100 shares of stock. Thus, if the price of the option is $1.25, it would cost you $125 ($1.25 x 100 shares) per contract. If the price of the option is $8, it would cost you $800 ($8 x 100) per contract. Once again, one contract is the minimum amount you can buy. As you can see, the cost of buying an option is significantly less than buying the stock. This is one of the many exciting features of options – levereage!

The option price consists of time value and intrinsic value. An option's intrinsic value is equal to the amount a stock trades above (for calls) or below (for puts) the strike price. An option's intrinsic value is the in-the-money portion of the option. The amount remaining is referred to as time value. This is the "ice cube" or decaying portion of an option.

Confused yet? Don't worry - it's just a matter of time before you'll be come familiar with the new terms and concepts. In fact, let's walk through another example to help you tie everything together. Assume for a moment that you are bullish about Procter & Gamble's (PG) prospects going forward – you feel the stock is heading higher.

Q: What kind of option would you buy, a call or a put?
A: A call.

Procter and Gamble is currently trading at $73 and you're interested in an in-the-money option.

Q: Which strike price(s) would you inquire about?
A: Perhaps the 60, 65, or 70.

You call your broker and get a quote for the June 70 calls.
They are currently priced at $7.

Q: How much will it cost you to buy one contract?
A: That would be $700, excluding commissions ($7 x 100
shares per contract).

Q: What does the $7 represent?
A: Intrinsic value and time value.

Q: How much of that $7 is intrinsic value?
A: $3.

Remember, intrinsic value (for call options) is equal to the
amount the stock price is above the strike price, which in
this case is $3 ($73 stock price – $70 strike price = $3).

Q: The option is worth $7. What's the other $4? (price of
the option – intrinsic value = time value, i.e. 7 – 3 = 4)
A: Time value. The $4 represents the ice cube – that portion
of the option that melts as time passes.

Q: At expiration, with no time remaining, what would
your option be worth?
A: It would be worth $3. At expiration, intrinsic value
has tangible worth. Time value, on the other hand, is
gone. When there is no time, there is no time value.
At-the-money and out-of-the-money options initially
consist of only time value.

Q: Who determines the price of an option?

A: The market makers, buyers and sellers.

Q: How do they come up with a price?

A: There are six variables that determine the value of an option: the stock price, strike price, time until expiration, the volatility of the underlying stock, dividends, and short-term interest rates, not to mention demand in the marketplace. (These are discussed at length in Chapter 15, "The Greatest Money-Making Secret in the World.")

You Bought an Option. Now What?

When you buy calls and/or puts, you are betting on stock prices moving either up or down. As a result, the option could expire worthless if the stock does not move in your desired direction before expiration. If it does move in accordance with your wishes, you have two choices: Sell the option and take your profit, or exercise your right to buy or sell the underlying shares of stock. What do you do? To give you a little help, let me ask you a question. If you are going to manage your investments like a business, you would buy options and do what with them? SELL them!

> If you are going to manage your investments like a business, you would buy options and do what with them? SELL them!

As previously stated, a business makes money by buying wholesale and selling retail; they buy in order to sell. The same will hold true in the options market. You buy options in order to sell them – that's how you make money! Now, if you wanted to, could you exercise your right to buy or sell the underlying stock? Yes. But will it take a lot more money to buy the stock? You bet. So why go through all the headache and hassle of buying the stock when you don't need to? Just sell the option and pocket the cash!

When Can You Exercise Your Option?

Once you have bought an option (an opening transaction), you can sell your option (a closing transaction) at any time on or before expiration. Some investors choose to exercise their option by actually buying or selling the underlying stock. The time frame in which you can exercise your option is dependent upon the style of option you have purchased. There are three styles of options available: American, European, and CAPS. Each has a different time frame in which the option can be exercised.

Most options, including all equity options, are American-style options. Being able to exercise your options at any time on or before the expiration date is a feature inherent with American-style options. You have total flexibility.

European-options can be exercised only on the expiration date, which is also known as the *settlement date*. Options on the Standard and Poor's 500 Index (SPX) is an example of a European-style option.

CAPS are European-style options but with an added feature. If the option reaches its cap price (maximum value) it is automatically exercised. CAPS are available on various indices such as the Standard and Poor's 100 Index (OEX).

Exercising An Option

For example, let's say you bought one contract of the Microsoft May 60 call for $8, spending $800 ($8 x 100 shares controlled). Realize that when you bought the option there were two parties to the transaction. At the time you placed your order to buy, your broker, Merrill Lynch, sent the order to the floor of the exchange. At the same time, another firm, Charles Schwab, represented a client looking to sell a call option. There is an agreement on price and the trade takes place. You bought – they sold. The transaction is recorded at the OCC.

In the OCC's "books," Merrill Lynch's account will be credited one call option (your purchase) and debited the purchase price, $800 (which you pay for, of course). So if Merrill Lynch's clients owned 123 of these calls before, the account would now show a total of 124.

Conversely, the Charles Schwab account is reduced one call option and credited the $800. Your name and the seller's name are not on record at the OCC, but your accounts at Merrill Lynch and Charles Schwab would reflect the trade accordingly.

It's now expiration (the third Friday) and Microsoft is trading at $88 a share. You own one May 60 call on Microsoft, in other words, you have the right to buy 100 shares of Microsoft at $60 per share. You decide to buy the stock, thus exercising your option. You notify Merrill Lynch, which in turn sends an exercise notice to the OCC for one Microsoft 60 call. The OCC will then consult its computers to determine how many firms sold this call option. From this list the OCC randomly selects one of the firms and notifies them of the exercise. It doesn't necessarily have to be Charles Schwab. Every firm with that position has an equal chance of being selected. It could be assigned to Goldman Sachs for example. At that time, Goldman Sachs would receive notification to deliver 100 shares of Microsoft stock to Merrill Lynch. They have three business days to deliver the shares.

In addition, recognize that Goldman Sachs may have 60 clients who sold this same option. How do they choose who delivers the shares of stock? They can do it randomly like the OCC, or they can employ the "first in, first out" rule – whichever client sold the call option first will be exercised first. Once an option is exercised, delivery *must* take place.

While exercise can take place any time on or before expiration, most options are exercised at expiration. The majority of investors, as discussed earlier, find it more profitable to sell the option beforehand. I should point out that you can experience what's known as an "automatic exercise." Simply stated, if an option is at least 3/4 (0.75) of a point in-the-money, the OCC will automatically exercise the option unless instructions to the contrary are received from the client's brokerage firm. This procedure was instituted to make sure no one leaves "money on the table" at expiration. Also, most brokerage firms have rules under which options will be automatically exercised so check with your broker to determine which rules may apply to your account.

Are Options a Good Investment Vehicle?

The first and most obvious thing that potential investors notice about options is that they require significantly less cash than stocks to get started. Even if you're just a beginner, you can get your feet wet and learn the ropes, and do so with a small amount of money.

Additionally, you can take advantage of two of the most important features inherent with options – limited risk and leverage. Your risk is limited because the most you can lose is your initial investment. Your downside is capped. And leverage, because you can control a large amount of stock with a small amount of money. Leverage creates fortunes, if used wisely. As a result, options can provide you with a bigger bang for your dollar spent!

> Leverage creates fortunes, if used wisely.

A Case Study

Let's look at a few more examples, but this time in greater detail. I'll ask some questions you're probably wondering about, while at the same time providing the answers you're looking for. (It should be noted that the following examples exclude commissions.)

Let's say you're interested in Home Depot. You feel it's going to go up in price. You call your broker and find out that Home Depot is trading at $52 per share. You'd love to own the stock, but you don't want to spend that much money; maybe you don't have that much money in your brokerage account to begin with.

Nevertheless, you want to invest in Home Depot, so you inquire about buying a call option. You call your broker and ask, "What are the September 55 calls going for on Home Depot?" (Buying Home Depot calls would give you the right, but not the obligation, to buy 100 shares of the stock, on or before the third Friday in September at $55 per share.)

The broker responds, "$2", meaning $2 per share controlled, or $200 per contract. In other words, $200 would give you control over 100 shares of Home Depot.

Q: Do you have to buy 100 shares?
A: No. You have the right, not the obligation, to buy 100 shares.

Q: How much money would you need in your account to buy the option?
A: Only $200 (per contract). You're not responsible for the cost of the underlying stock.

Q: If you were to buy 100 shares of stock, what would that cost you?
A: It would cost $5,200 ($52 x 100 shares). Talk about leverage! $200 for the option vs. $5,200 for the stock. (Less, if done on margin)

Let's say you are very bullish. You want to control 1,000 shares of Home Depot.

Q: How many contracts would you need to buy?
A: 10. (10 x 100 shares per contract = 1,000 shares).

Q: How much money would that cost you?
A: $2,000 ($200 per contract x 10 contracts).

Let's compare that to buying 1,000 shares of stock.

Q: How much would it cost you to buy 1,000 shares of stock at $52 per share?
A: $52,000! (Less, if done on margin)

Q: What would you rather spend – $2,000 or $52,000?
A: Clearly $2,000.

Q: What happens if the stock declines or stays the same? In other words, what happens to your $2,000 worth of options?
A: They expire worthless.

Q: Will your entire $2,000 be lost?
A: Yes. If the stock price is not above the strike price at expiration, the option is worthless.

Q: So you're telling me you're willing to kiss that money goodbye?
A: Absolutely not!

Q: Is that what makes options risky?
A: Yes.

Q: Can you lose your entire investment?
A: You bet!

Q: If the stock moves against you, can you sell your option at any time and cut your losses?
A: Yes. In fact, risk management is critical to your success as an option trader. You want to cut your losses short!

> Options can be used very conservatively to build enormous wealth – if you take time to learn how.

The bottom line is that options can be very risky if you don't know what you are doing. This is why many people avoid options because no one

takes the time to adequately
explain to you what they
are and how they work.

When buying options your risk
is limited at all times, yet your
profit potential is staggering!

Thus, while everyone looks
at options in a negative
light, let me share with you why I absolutely love options! The
fact remains that options can be used very conservatively to build
enormous wealth – if you take time to learn how. Here's why.

Q: When you buy an option, what's the most you can lose?
A: Your initial investment. That is the maximum amount
of money you could lose. Your downside is capped.

Q: What's your potential upside?
A: Infinite! The sky's the limit!

Q: Does an investment vehicle appeal to you where
your downside is capped and your upside is infinite?
A: You better believe it. Sign me up!

Minimal risk and maximum reward is what every investor
looks for and that's exactly what options deliver. When buying
options your risk is limited at all times, yet your profit
potential is staggering! That's why I love options!

Let's go back and take a look at our previously stated figures
and compare them, once again, with owning the stock. Recall
that you purchased 100 shares of stock at $52 per share.

Q: How much could you potentially lose if the stock
goes to zero?
A: $5,200.

Q: Which would you rather lose – $200 or $5,200?
A: $200, that's easy.

But wait a moment. The likelihood of the stock falling to zero is next to nothing.

Q: However, what about the stock dropping from $52 to $48? Can that happen?
A: You bet it can!

Q: How much have you lost on paper?
A: $400.

Q: May it take months, possibly years, for the stock to get back to break-even? Could the stock continue to fall?
A: Yes.

Q: Where do you have more money at risk – stocks or options?
A: Stocks. Your exposure is much greater because you have more money Invested and as a result, at risk.

To make matters worse, your money is tied up, leaving you no access to it unless you sold the stock at a loss. Beyond that, it just takes a lot more money to play the "stock ownership game."

That's why I call it the "wonderful world of options," because your risk is limited and your upside is infinite. You have total flexibility and can make money regardless of market direction. You can get started with a few hundred dollars, and potentially turn it into thousands of dollars. You can realize phenomenal returns, yet at the same time keep your risk low. Which begs the question: How do you make all this incredible money? The answer lies in the relationship between the movement of stock and the movement of the option.

The Explosive Nature of Options

Assume you're bullish on Krispy Kreme (KKD). Let's say the stock is currently trading at $27. You call up your broker and find out it would cost you $1 or $100 per contract to buy the April 30 call. You're trying to decide whether to buy 100 shares of stock or buy the option (one contract). In the table below, notice what happens to the price of the option as the stock goes up in price.

As the stock climbs from $27 to $30, the option goes from $1 to $2. The stock moves up to $32 and the option is worth $3.50. The stock climbs to $35 and the option is worth $6.25. As the stock hits $36, the option is now worth $7. What's going on?

Stock	Option
$27	$1.00
30	2.00
32	3.50
35	6.25
36	7.00

Q: The stock went from $27 to $30; about a 10% move, but what did your option do?
A: It doubled! ($1 – $2)

Q: The stock moved from $27 to $32 – less than a 20% move. How far did your option move?
A: It more than tripled – a 350% return! ($1 – $3.50)

Q: By the way, is that happening over the same time frame?
A: Yes, it is! For the same amount of time that it took the stock to move from $27 to $32, the option moved from $1 to $3.50!

Q: So, where are you getting the biggest bang for your dollar spent – stocks or options?
A: OPTIONS!

What's the reason behind this explosive move in the option? Simply put, a small movement in the stock equates to a magnified movement in the option. The reason is leverage. You control a $3,000 asset (100 shares x the $30 strike price) for only $100 (your cost for one contract)!

Furthermore, buying stock would have required you to tie up a lot more money ($27 x 100 shares = $2,700), thus putting more money at risk. Plus you only saw a 18% return on your investment (32 – 27= 5; 5/27 = 18%). Now, take a look at the option.

With the option, you had very little at risk ($100 = $1.00 x 100 shares), thus very little exposure, and you saw a 100–350% return on your investment. Returns like that will definitely make a difference in your bottom line!

"But wait a second," you say. "I still think someone can make more money by owning the stock." Well, let's run the numbers for both stocks and options and see which one comes out on top.

Using our previous example, you go ahead and decide to buy 100 shares of Krispy Kreme at $27 a share.

Q: How much will that cost you?

A: $2,700. (Keep in mind I'm excluding commissions.)

Using the table above, let's say your stock climbs to $36 per share. You decide to sell your 100 shares of Krispy Kreme for a gross profit of $3,600.

Q: How much did you net?

A: $900. ($3,600 − $2,700 = $900)

That's about a 33% return on your investment (900/2,700 = 33%). Not bad!

Let's see what happens if you buy the option.

Q: If you bought one contract and the price of the option was $1, how much would that of cost you?

A: $100. ($1 x 100 shares per contract = $100)

Q: What's your maximum risk?

A: $100.

Q: Do you have to lose the entire $100?

A: No. You can sell your option at any time. That $100 is the most you could lose.

Q: How many shares do you control?

A: 100.

Q: With the stock at $36 what could you sell your option for? (See table)

A: $7 per share controlled.

Q: What is your gross profit?
A: $700. ($7 x 100 shares controlled)

Q: What's your net profit?
A: $600. ($700 – $100)

Now here's the "$64,000" question!

Q: Where did you make more money – stock or option?
A: Stock. ($900 vs. $600)

Q: Where did you get better use of your money – stock or option?
A: Clearly options – 33% for the stock vs. 600% for the option!

Q: Where did you have greater downside exposure i.e. more money at risk?
A: Stock. ($2,700)

Q: What was your reward again?
A: 33%. (900/2700)

Q: What was your downside exposure in buying the option?
A: $100.

Q: What was your reward?
A: 600% – six times your initial investment!
(600/100 = 600%)

When was the last time you saw returns like that? What makes it even better is that you aren't waiting years to see those phenomenal returns. It can happen in a matter of weeks, if not days! Such astronomical returns can launch your account skyward!

The numbers become even more staggering when you increase the shares of stock and the number of contracts you are buying. If you were to take the above example and use 1,000 shares instead of 100 shares, it really opens your eyes to the amazing leverage of options. Instead of spending $27,000 to buy 1,000 shares of stock, you can control the 1,000 shares of stock for only $1,000 (10 contracts) by buying the options! What does your risk/reward look like now? Buying the stock puts $27,000 at risk, whereas buying the options puts only $1,000 at risk. Your risk is substantially less with the options. What about your reward?

First of all, don't forget your rate of return remains the same, it's just that the dollar amounts get larger. Using the example above, you would net $9,000 investing in the stock and $6,000 investing in the options. Once again, the stock delivers more gross profit, but where do you get a more explosive reward? Options! A whopping 600%! The leverage of options is absolutely fantastic! Why? Because you harness the awesome power of multiplication!

Conclusion

In conclusion, options are an exciting and dynamic investment vehicle if understood and used wisely. Moreover, options employ the four most sought-after traits for any and all investments: limited risk, unlimited reward, low stress, and little cash investment to get started.

Options can be used conservatively to build real wealth. And just like the Greek architects of old, if you follow basic and simple guidelines you can lay the groundwork for an enduring and durable trading program that can last for generations.

> Options employ the four most sought-after traits for any and all investments: limited risk, unlimited reward, low stress, and little cash investment to get started.

What's more, options can generate explosive returns with a relatively smallmove in the underlying stock. That's the beautyof leverage. The flexibilityof options (calls and puts) enables you to profit regardless of market direction. Options allow you to construct a tradewhere you can be totally wrong about market direction andstill make money! As a result, options have and will continueto stand the test of time.

So, you're probably ready to get started, yet at the same time wondering how you can construct your very own "money-making Parthenon." While there are no "crystal balls," there are a few essential tools you'll need in order to help you create a lasting and successful option trading program.

The principles that will be addressed in the remaining chapters are indispensable in helping you formulate a winning strategy. Your ability to construct and follow your very own trading program is absolutely critical to your success as an options trader. By doing so you will dramatically increase your odds of winning and winning BIG!

Key Points to Remember

➤ Calls give you the right, but not the obligation, to buy the underlying stock, on or before the expiration date, at the specified strike price. Calls increase in value as the price of the stock climbs.

➤ Puts give you the right, but not the obligation, to sell the underlying stock, on or before the expiration date, at the specified strike price. Puts increase in value as the price of the stock falls.

➤ Options have a limited life and are referred to as a "wasting asset." Buying an option is like buying an "ice cube." Time is one of your adversaries.

➤ Options expire on the Saturday following the third Friday of a particular month. You can't trade on Saturday, so the third Friday becomes the date to focus on.

➤ When buying an option, you will always have four months from which to choose: two near-term and two farther out. (This doesn't include LEAPS®.)

➤ The price at which you agree to buy or sell the stock at is known as the strike (exercise) price. Strike prices are in increments of 2.50, 5, or 10, depending on the price of the underlying stock.

➤ Options require substantially less money than buying the stock outright. As a result, the amount of money you have at risk is less.

➤ The maximum amount of money you can lose in buying an option is the amount paid for the option. However, you can cut your losses at any time by selling the option.

➤ Options enable you to realize returns of 100%, 300%, 500%, or more – sometimes in a matter of days! This is due to the enormous leverage they provide.

CHAPTER 7

Options,
a Parade of Riches!

"Money is better than poverty, if only for financial reasons."
– Woody Allen

"In the late twentieth century, no one – with the possible exception
of a few as yet undiscovered tribes people – is wholly exempt
from the rule of money. It is the atmosphere we all breathe."
– Kevin Jackson

The preceding quotes say it all. Don't they? Face it, to make it
in this world you'll need more than your current job can
provide. You'll need to start your own business. Preferably
your own business of buying and selling stocks and options!

Now is a perfect time to briefly review what you have learned
so far.

1. Make "time" to change your life financially. Start your
financial make over by treating time as a valuable asset.

You can learn from the past, but more important, make future learning opportunities a priority.

2. Weigh the risk and reward of your own business. Use the Franklin scale. It will help you ascertain exactly what you should do. If you haven't created a Franklin scale yet please, for your own sake, do it NOW!

3. Business capitalization and overhead shouldn't prevent you from getting into the options business. If you must, use your imagination and innovation to raise your business capital. Remember, you can invest in your own options business with as little as a few thousand dollars.

4. Learn how to harness the Eighth Wonder of World – *multiplication.* Through the use of options you can multiply your profits manifold, with limited risk and unlimited upside.

The Promising Parade of Profits

As a child, growing up in the suburbs, I eagerly awaited the annual visit by the circus that would come to Portland or Seattle every autumn. There's nothing better than watching all the circus performers parade around inside the big tent because they always did it with an extraordinary amount of pomp and circumstance. But the indisputable marvel of any parade is that something unusual, bizarre and unexpected, that can't always be anticipated, happens.

For example, most parades feature all the colossal main stay attractions like the big animal celebrities. Lions, tigers, bears and elephants are the marquee players. Sometimes they sleep in their cages. Oftentimes they appear dead, hardly moving at all. Yet, if prompted or provoked, they will excite and delight the crowd with frightening roars and admirable tricks. You see circus animals are really entertainers who, most assuredly, perform on cue.

Other common attractions are "The Human Oddities" who stroll amid the animal cages and other circus performers. They too are performers, acting on cues and in response to each other and the crowd. Though their performances are peculiar and bizarre their antics are curiously delightful.

The bearded woman, the sword swallower, the fire-eater and the man who walks on stilts are more than crowd pleasers. They create excitement and command attention. When they interact with each other or take their act into the crowd they most definitely become standouts and leave parade-goers with unforgettable memories.

There's nothing more exciting than a fire-eater spitting flames all about your head while you watch in awe holding your soda pop, waiting to dowse the blaze in case things get out of control. Or how about a sword swallower who thrusts five feet of shiny saber down his throat right in front of your face!

Never have I witnessed the animals and performers in a circus parade disappoint. They'll never let you down nor fail to fulfill the promise to provide crowds with thrills. More often than not, the parade keeps moving along at a pace that is intended to excite, delight and enchant. Circus parades are truly crowd pleasers!

You see, the stock and option markets are like a circus parade. Even though they do not deliver roars, tricks and hilarious antics they provide similar excitement, delight and enchantment in terms of potential financial profit. The option market can be just as big a crowd pleaser for investors. Just as the animals and performers flow past you in a constant stream of anticipated activity so do the markets. Both the circus and the market promise to thrill and electrify you. It is truly mesmerizing.

There are many unusual, explosive and exciting moves and performances among a myriad of stocks. However, the key to cashing in on this parade of riches and promising profits is to avoid getting caught up in the excitement. While it's wonderful to lose yourself in the excitement of the circus, doing so in the stock market will cost you dearly.

Stocks will constantly move along in front of you. Like a parade, markets are constantly changing and exciting. There's always something to see, something unique and unusual happening, and something that will thrill you. Trading options will provide you with a constant parade of promising profit opportunities.

But remember, in order for you to experience a stock's "roar," that is, catch an explosive move, you must train yourself to be patient and disciplined. The real secret to trading successfully lies in mastering your emotions. To do so, you must understand the psychology of trading.

CHAPTER 8

The Psychology of Trading

When you talk about stocks, it's easy to get caught up in the numbers. You want to know whether your favorite stock has gone up or down. Analysts dissect a company's balance sheet to predict future growth and the sustainability of current earnings. Numbers dominate the landscape, but there is another aspect of Wall Street that people rarely acknowledge. It's more critical to your success than any other element associated with trading. It revolves around the psychology of trading i.e., your mental mindset before, during, and after every trade you place.

It's rarely emphasized, yet it is the deciding factor between success and failure. Without a clear understanding of psychology's role in trading, you may become just another "fatality" on your way down Wall Street. The next two chapters are dedicated to taking a look at the psychological and emotional side of trading and how you can better deal with their inevitable impact.

In this chapter, you'll specifically discover a "psychological trap" that seduces traders more than any other. More importantly, you'll earn what can be done to protect yourself from its costly influence, ensuring your survival as an investor.

> Don't undermine your own success by pursuing a path that is in direct conflict with your psychological make-up.

Before you read any further, I should mention that it is of the utmost importance that you trade within the comforts of your personality and lifestyle. Don't undermine your own success by pursuing a path that is in direct conflict with your psychological make-up. Ultimately, it behooves you to better understand what makes you "tick."

First and foremost, you need to determine your strengths and weaknesses. Does the stock market have an uncanny way of finding out your weaknesses? Yes! And unfortunately, it gets very, very expensive when it does so. Why not take care of that right from the get-go? Why not find out what your strengths and weaknesses are so you can shore up your weaknesses and build upon your strengths. You need to determine what your personality is, so you can determine what kind of trader you are. Knowing this is critical to your success. It will help you find out what trading style is best for you.

Having taught and trained thousands of investors from all walks of life, what I have noticed over and over is that people pursue strategies that do not fit their personality. And then they wonder why the stock market is so difficult. "Why am I having such a hard time making money?" they ask me. It's because they have personalities incongruent with the strategies they have chosen. Let me give you a couple of examples.

Perhaps you're intrigued by the day-trading concept. The fact that you can buy in the morning, sell in the afternoon, and make a living sounds wonderful. But once you put on those short-term trades, you find that your pager is going off, the cell phone is ringing, the kids need to be taken to school etc. Life is getting in the way of your trading! You're drawn away from computer screen and you miss trading opportunities because you weren't there to take advantage of them. Frustration and losses mount because of those missed opportunities, and to make matters worse, you can't cut your losses when a trade moves against you. You wonder why you're having a hard time making money. In fact, you're getting pretty good at losing money! The problem is simple: Your lifestyle doesn't mesh with such short-term strategies.

Let's look at another example. By nature you're a totally conservative investor. Up to this point, mutual funds, bonds, and a few blue chip stocks made up your portfolio. It took you two months to convince your broker that they should approve you to trade options. They sat there trying to talk you out of it. Finally, you were given the green light. You're happy as can be and now you start buying options that expire in three weeks. They seem so cheap. You're really attracted to those that expire in three days, so you try those. Now you own short-term options and you're wondering why you can't sleep at night. You wonder why you have more gray hairs? You wonder why you're tense all the time and why the kids avoid you when the market is open?

The answer, in a nutshell, is that you have a conservative, that is, a "long-term" personality and you're using short-term strategies. Your personality and your strategies are butting heads. Because of that, it doesn't matter how hard you try, you're going to have a hard time making money. Trading should flow easily and naturally. If it feels laborious, stressful or difficult, then most likely you're employing strategies and techniques that run counter to your personality.

> Trading should flow easily and naturally. If it feels laborious, stressful or difficult, then most likely you're employing strategies and techniques that run counter to your personality.

A person who wants to generate money immediately would find trading LEAPS® (Long Term Equity AnticiPation Securities) frustrating. For people like that, it's like watching paint dry. They would be much better suited to buying shorter-term options so they could be in and out within a matter of weeks or days. In this case, they possess a short-term mentality but are pursuing a long-term strategy.

What's the bottom line? If you have a short-term mentality, you have to focus on short-term option strategies. If you have a conservative personality, focus on longer-term strategies. If you're somewhere in the middle, choose options that expire at least three or four months from when you buy them.

What I'll be sharing with you throughout this book has my personality written all over it. It exudes my trading style. You'll soon see that I have more of a relaxed approach to trading. I do not like to be on edge. As a result, I don't day trade or buy a lot of short-term options. In fact, I usually give myself two to four months of time when I buy an option (two to four months before expiration). Yet on average, my holding time may only be a matter of weeks, if not days.

What's your purpose when you buy an option? To sell it! If you can sell it in a day or two, go for it. If you need more time, then you have it. It's far better to have time and not need it than need it and not have it. That approach will serve you well.

Once you determine what trading style fits your personality and lifestyle, trade accordingly. You will

> It's far better to have time and not need it than need it and not have it.

find your trading to be less stressed and more in harmony with your state of mind. Since there are so many different ways to make money you need to determine what works best for you. Don't become the "jack of all trades and master of none." Become the master of one. Then as you see fit, add and augment your game plan with additional strategies.

You may be surprised to see the emphasis placed on acquiring your own identity as a trader. Why, you ask? Because you want to develop confidence in your own decision-making process so you can avoid one of the most common traps of new traders. It's commonly referred to as the "herd mentality." In fact, it's rooted in human nature - people want to feel accepted and loved by their peers. They want to fit in. Thus they act, dress and talk like they do.

Sadly, investors are no different. They want to own the "hottest" and most "fashionable" stock. They want a "trendy" portfolio chock full of the sexiest investments just like their peers. Unfortunately, this approach is hazardous to your financial health. By joining the herd you stop thinking for yourself and you buy and sell at the same time everyone else does. That's why the majority of investors buy at the top and sell at the bottom.

Do you recall the "lemming legend" from your studies of natural sciences? Well, as an analogy to the herd mentality let's review the lemmings. Lemmings are rodents closely related to meadow mice. They live in grasslands and tundra in Arctic regions. In order to adapt to their harsh snowy environment and to perpetuate their long-term existence lemmings have adopted a mating season that lasts from spring to autumn, a full three seasons of the year (much longer than other animal species).

However, because of this extended mating season, lemmings force themselves to migrate periodically from their homes when their population begins to exceed their food supply. A death march results as thousands drown in the sea, rivers, and streams attempting to find land with more abundant food sources.

Can the herd mentality create a problem? For lemmings it sure can! You see these rodents aren't making their own independent decisions. They exit en masse, predicated on what the herd chooses to do, and it costs them their lives. While joining the herd isn't life threatening, it can destroy your trading account if you're not careful.

In fact, in a later chapter you'll see that one of the keys to racking up big-time profits is making the trend your friend. In other words, you're going to learn how to ride the herd all the way to the bank! The secret lies in knowing when to walk away.

The problem is, once you join the herd you'll find yourself making decisions that you otherwise wouldn't have made. Think about it. When masses of people get together, dangerous things start to happen e.g., riots unfold, things are set on fire, and people are trampled to death. The herd is a powerful force, and it can have negative effects on the most even-tempered person. The herd can provoke you to act differently.

You only need to look at history for examples of how the herd mentality can lead to irrational financial decisions. In 1841, Charles Mackay wrote a book called *Extraordinary Popular Delusions and the Madness of Crowds*. In it, he describes several mass manias. One example I found intriguing was the Tulip Mania in Holland in 1634.

The tulip craze in Holland induced the Dutch to abandon their jobs and businesses to grow tulips, broker them, and trade them. In fact, banks even accepted them as collateral. Speculators made a fortune. Unfortunately, this mania collapsed in waves of panic selling, leaving many financially ruined, and a nation in disarray.

You can find many other examples throughout history, such as the oil boom and consequent bust. Even the Cabbage Patch Doll, Beanie Baby, and Pokemon phenomena demonstrate how easy it is to get caught up in the hype and hoopla. How about the Pet Rock craze? People paid outrageous prices for something they could find in their own backyards!

Another more recent example is the great boom and bust cycle of the Internet. Since the market's peak, more than $4 trillion of investor wealth has been wiped out! According to *USA Today*, 493 Internet companies have gone out of business in 2000-01 (as of May 2001). You only need to look at the charts of AMZN and YHOO to see how costly such bubbles can be.

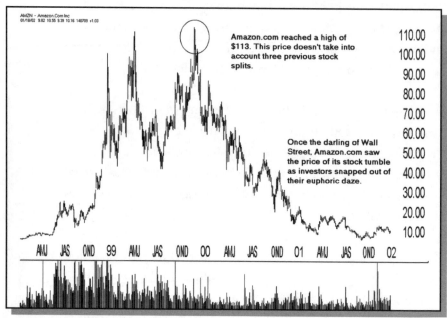

AMZN - Amazon.Com Inc
01/18/02 9.82 10.55 9.39 10.16 140709 +1.03

Amazon.com reached a high of $113. This price doesn't take into account three previous stock splits.

Once the darling of Wall Street, Amazon.com saw the price of its stock tumble as investors snapped out of their euphoric daze.

Courtesy of TC2000®.

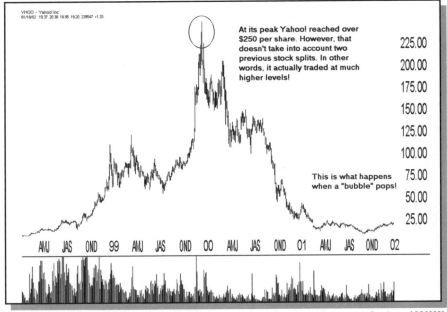

YHOO - Yahoo! Inc
01/18/02 19.37 20.38 18.95 19.20 239547 +1.33

At its peak Yahoo! reached over
$250 per share. However, that
doesn't take into account two
previous stock splits. In other
words, it actually traded at much
higher levels!

This is what happens
when a "bubble" pops!

225.00
200.00
175.00
150.00
125.00
100.00
75.00
50.00
25.00

AMJ JAS OND 99 AMJ JAS OND 00 AMJ JAS OND 01 AMJ JAS OND 02

Courtesy of TC2000®.

Speaking of bubbles and YHOO, here's another good example:
"One 28-year-old Yahoo! Inc. exec who had spent two years
searching for the perfect mansion not only bought his
$2.5-million house, but also paid his taxes with margin
loans...When Yahoo's stock began to collapse, the man was
forced to sell the house before he moved in" (*Business Week*
e.biz, April 16, 2001, Rochelle Sharpe). I bet that "humble
pie" didn't taste too good.

Investors' arrogance in the face of flawed business plans and
money-losing operations made it clear that investors found
themselves in one of the biggest speculative excesses of all time.
To say the least, the days of gaining 100% to 300% in Internet
stocks are most likely gone. Common sense was trampled
under a stampede of greed as investors lost all sense of reality.
Everyone wanted in on the action. Stocks became America's

favorite pastime. According to the Investment Company Institute, by the end of 1999 nearly 80 million Americans owned stock, compared with a little over 42 million in 1983.

So how did it happen? Simple. People fell victim to the deadly herd mentality – buying and selling the same stocks as everyone else. Why? Because it appears to be the right thing to do – it must be, everyone else is doing it! CNBC is talking about it, the analysts are mentioning it, and the financial newspapers and magazines are touting it. Unfortunately, this tends to cloud your judgment, hindering your ability to make sound decisions in the process.

You're not the one making the decision anymore. You've lost control. You're buying and selling because someone is telling you to. To be successful, you must analyze the herd, but act independently. That's why I stress finding a trading style that fits your personality. If you don't, you're more susceptible to adopting the herd mentality.

How many times have you bought a stock or an option, only to watch it turn on a dime and move in the opposite direction? And here you didn't think you had the power to move the markets. "Hey, the market's got my number!" you say. You feel as if there's a conspiracy to prevent you from making money!

The same thing can happen in the opposite direction. How many times have you sold a stock or option, only to watch it reverse course and head higher? "Unbelievable! I sold at the absolute bottom," you scream in exasperation. Sound familiar?

It sounds all-too familiar to plenty of traders. The reason is simple; if everyone is buying/selling, then at some point there's no one left to buy/sell. Sellers/buyers step back in and send the market back in the opposite direction. Members of the herd act in sync with one another. They buy and sell alike. That's why you must think and act for yourself.

What are some warning signs you're losing your independence and becoming a part of the herd? One of the most obvious is seeking the advice of others before you buy or sell. Anxiously awaiting the arrival of a daily e-mail or fax advisory service so you know what you should buy or sell that day is also a red flag. It's fine to use such resources to help you generate your own trading

> If you make or lose money, you want to know why.

ideas, but if you mimic what they say to do, then you're setting yourself up for disaster. Think about it. If you make money with such tips, what will you continue to do? Follow their recommendations. If you lose money, will you know why? No. If you make or lose money, you want to know why. That way, you can replicate your success and rid yourself of your mistakes. If you don't know why, then it's impossible to do.

Viewership in CNBC, CNNfn, or Bloomberg TV has risen over the last few years as interest in the stock market has exploded. What do you think are the most popular segments on those networks? Typically, it's when a guest analyst comes on the show and shares his or her opinion about where the market is headed. Then people can call in and ask whether they should buy, sell, or hold a particular stock. People want to be told what to do instead of thinking for themselves. Remember, this is dangerous to your financial health! If you seek the opinions of others, what does that demonstrate you lack? Confidence.

If you know why you own a particular stock or option, does it really matter what an analyst on CNBC says about it? No. If you knew why you wanted to buy, does it really matter what they think? No. If you have a game plan that dictates when you should buy and sell a position, why ask your broker what they think? Remember, no one will look out for your money the way you will. Good old-fashioned common sense will serve you well.

> Remember, no one will look out for your money the way you will.

So, do you find yourself calling up your broker and saying, "Hey, what do you think about XYZ? I really like those $80 calls." *Don't place the trade.* You're already in trouble. If you begin to seek out the opinions of others, you're losing confidence in yourself and your game plan. There's nothing wrong with that. Simply view it as a warning sign to stop and review your intentions. The key to your success is developing confidence in your own decision-making process. Opinions are a dime a dozen!

> The key to your success is developing confidence in your own decision-making process.

Here's a little couplet to help keep you out of trouble: "When in doubt, stay out, or when in doubt, get out!" If you begin to question yourself about putting on a trade don't do it. If you begin to ask others what they think about a particular position you own, close it out. That couplet will not only save you a lot of money by helping you

> "When in doubt, stay out, or when in doubt, get out!"

avoid bad trades, it will also make you a lot of money because it teaches you to trust your instincts.

By understanding the psychology of the market, you can maintain your independence and objectivity. Don't make your trading decisions on the fly. That's why staring at real-time quotes can be so dangerous. You start to feel every tick ripple through your body and soon you find yourself trading impulsively. You climb aboard an emotional roller coaster. That's why it is so important that you develop a plan, a system, or way to know when to buy and sell. If you knew when to buy or sell would that be useful? Of course it would! You'd have the cat by the tail. Soon I'll share with you how to develop such a game plan and what it should consist of. If you have such a plan then there is no reason to seek the opinions of others – no matter who they are!

The herd has power to create trends. The trend is your friend. You don't *have* to trade with the trend, but by all means don't fight it! Trying to pick tops or bottoms in a trending market is foolish. When you start making trades based on emotion instead of a rational game plan, you'll find yourself on a one-way trip to the poorhouse.

So let's address the two deadliest emotions that every trader must deal with and what can be done to keep them in check.

Key Points to Remember

➤ Trade in accordance with your personality and comfort level.

➤ Analyze your strengths and weaknesses before you begin trading.

➤ Avoid the herd mentality at all costs! The key to your success is developing confidence in your own decision-making process.

➤ If you begin seeking the opinions of others it's a clear indication that you lack confidence in your position. When in doubt get out, when in doubt stay out!

➤ No one will look out for your money like you will.

CHAPTER 9

The Achilles Heel of Every Trader

Believe it or not, you are the weakest link of any trading plan. Your emotions are going to be your worst enemy and most likely the reason behind any mistakes. They are your "Achilles heel." While you can't control the emotions of the herd, you can and must learn to control your own. This is essential to your survival.

Is the stock market an emotional place? You bet it is. A good friend of mine showed me why:

> "Steve, have you ever bought an stock or option, then sold it at a profit, only to see it continue higher?"
>
> "Sure," I said.
>
> "How did that make you feel?"
>
> "I was mad and frustrated that I sold too soon," I replied.
>
> Then he asked, "Have you ever bought a stock or option and it went down, forcing you to take a loss. But as soon as you sold it, it fell even further?"

"Yes, I have. I got out just at the right time for a change,"
I responded.

"How did that make you feel?"

"Great! My timing was perfect," I said.

"So let me get this straight," he says. "You made money and
felt bad but when you lost money, you felt good?"

This exchange is a good illustration of how emotions can turn
you upside down when it comes to the stock market. Every
single day the market becomes a melting pot of various human emotions, for example, joy, euphoria, pain, frustration, anger, and feelings of inferiority. It is this collision of emotions that creates opportunity for those who

> There are two emotions that wreak more havoc in your life as a trader than any others. They can and will put you out of business if left unchecked. They are fear and greed.

know what to look for. By learning how to read the "emotional
thermostat" of the market you will have a huge advantage
in making effective and profitable trading decisions. There are
two emotions that wreak more havoc in your life as a trader
than any others. They can and will put you out of business
if left unchecked. They are fear and greed.

Fear

When it comes to the stock market there are two kinds of fear
that you should be aware of:

1. Fear of taking a loss.
2. Fear of losing a profit.

First of all, let's analyze the fear of taking a loss. Is it tough to lose money? You bet it is! When faced with a losing position you have to admit to yourself, your broker, your family, and the world that you were wrong. On top of that, you may end up losing some of your hard-earned money. As a result, instead of cutting your losses (the way you know you should), you slip into the "hope and dream phase." You "hope" the stock turns around and you "dream" of a big payday! You begin suffering from denial.

For example, let's say you originally bought some options for $800. Now they're worth $600 and you quickly find yourself down a few hundred bucks. Your instincts tell you something is wrong and that you should to get out. However, the fear of taking a loss overrides such thoughts and induces you into thinking, "I'll get out on the first rally back to my break-even point." As a result, you don't exit the trade.

Pretty soon you find yourself down $500. The scene replays again, but you still don't exit the losing position. This time you tell yourself, "I'll exit as soon as it rallies back to the price it was at yesterday." Beginning to sound familiar?

As you know, this story rarely has a happy ending. The point of "no return" is hit and all your money is lost. Sadly, you had multiple opportunities to exit the trade, but you didn't. Why didn't you? The fear of taking a loss prevented you from taking action.

Also keep in mind that a losing position becomes an emotional "ball and chain." Every single day it sits in your account it reminds you of your mistake. It wears you down emotionally. Struggling traders always believe that tomorrow will provide a better opportunity to exit rather than today. Such thinking will lead to financial ruin! Remember, your first loss is your best loss.

Furthermore, by holding onto a losing position you're losing much more than you think. Consider the *opportunity cost* involved. The money that is languishing in a losing position could be invested elsewhere. If that money could be doubling or

> Remember, your first loss is your best loss.

tripling in another position, the true cost to you is substantial! The fear of taking a loss prevents you from letting your money work harder for you. Don't forget your mission statement: buy in order to sell!

Now you're angry and frustrated that you let yourself make such a costly mistake. "How could I have been so stupid? Look at all that money I let go down the drain," you mutter to yourself. Your emotions come roiling to the surface and you decide to make all your money back on the next trade. So you double up on your next position, risking more money than before, hoping to avenge your previous loss.

Just when you need to be more cautious, you increase the stakes and your risk. Why? You feel angry, guilty, and frustrated. Your emotions are tossing you around like a rag doll. Unfortunately, this process tends to spiral out of control and your decisions become more and more irrational. Losses begin to mount.

It doesn't take long before you lose confidence in your decision-making ability. Your game plan is long forgotten Now you find yourself in an environment of apprehension and doubt, making it difficult to trade. It's as if you're frozen, like a deer caught in the midst of headlights. As a result, you miss out on numerous opportunities because you can't pull the trigger and the cycle of frustration, pain, and anger begins anew. It's safe to say that you should avoid this psychological trap, the fear of taking a loss, at all costs.

Fear of Losing a Profit

Now let's turn our attention to the second type of fear, namely the fear of losing a profit. Assume for a moment that you currently own four positions and you are losing money on three of them. Let's also say that you "bite the bullet" and take the loss on all three. At this point, how do you feel? Most likely dejected and depressed.

However, just when it seems like it can't get any worse, you notice your fourth position is becoming profitable. You bought the option at $6 and now you can sell it for $8.75. So now what do you want to do? Most likely, part of you wants to hold on, while the other part is itching to sell. In fact, if you're like most traders, you will sell. Why? For starters, you just took the loss on three trades and there's no way you're going to lose again. Hey, you're finally in a position to ring the cash register! Secondly, you remember

> Exiting trades too early will be a major stumbling block for you and most every trader.

the adage, "You can never go broke taking a profit." Regrettably, that's exactly how you will go broke – by taking profits early.

Exiting trades too early will be a major stumbling block for you and most every trader. Why does it happen? Because in the previous example you fear losing that $2.75 profit (particularly on the heels of a loss). Your fear of losing that profit, based purely on emotion and not logic (which your game plan is based upon), induces you to sell. Yes, you still made money but as soon as you sell, what invariably happens? The stock moves higher! You watch helplessly as the option becomes worth much more than what you sold it for. "I left so much money on the table," you lament. Then you start mentally "kicking" yourself again, but this time for selling too early.

> "Cut your losses short and let your profits run."

Fear of taking a loss and fear of losing a profit are very real. The quicker you learn to neutralize those psychological traps, the more money you will make and trading will be less stressful. You will be able to execute trades more efficiently and with more confidence. Fear won't dictate your actions anymore.

As you know, the adage on Wall Street that you want to embrace is, "Cut your losses short and let your profits run." However, if you let emotion creep into your trading, you'll end up letting your losses run and cutting your profits short – a one-way ticket to the poor-house! This is exactly what many traders fall victim to, that is, a bunch of small gains and a few big losses.

> When you're right, make as much money as you possibly can.

From now on you must cut your losses short, keeping your losses small. When you win, maximize your gains. In other words, when you're right, make as much money as you possibly can. Milk it for all it's worth! A bunch of small losses can easily be overcome by just one big gain. As soon as you adopt that mindset, your results will dramatically improve. However, won't such an approach make you too greedy? Let's find out.

Greed

To begin with, consider the following story of a limousine company owner: "At one point he was nearly a millionaire, having watched his $100,000-plus bet on the Net and tech stocks skyrocket 800%. He became addicted to the market. He started talking to his broker five times a day and became glued to CNBC. For a while, his obsession made him feel great. 'I began to feel like a guru,' he says. He would talk excitedly to friends about his latest successes. On his best day, he was up more than $45,000. 'I felt like I was almost cutting edge,' he says. Ultimately, he lost about $700,000 in paper gains. He went on to say, 'I feel absolutely devastated by my lack of good financial judgment.'" (*Business Week* e.biz, April 16, 2001, Rochelle Sharpe)

You see, this man's mistake wasn't in making 800% on his investment. His mistake was letting his success cloud his judgment. As the previous story so poignantly pointed out, as soon as you begin making money there's a tendency to be swept off your feet with feelings of joy, infallibility, arrogance, and euphoria. It's at such moments that you feel you can do no wrong! Unfortunately, such moments sow the seeds of your downfall.

Don't Bite Off More than You Can Chew

Let's walk through another example so you can learn to recognize and avoid this treacherous, psychological trap. Assume that you double your money, turning an investment of $1,000 into

$2,000. How do you feel? Great! Nevertheless, like most people, when you're making money you always wish you had invested more! You think, "$20,000 would have made me $40,000!" And it's exactly that line of thinking that leads to ruin. The very success you so desperately crave is now leading you down a forbidden path of greed.

Remember those feelings of infallibility? They've now become your enemy, seducing you into committing too much money on your next trade. You've become "intoxicated" with your own success, clouding your judgment in the process and leading you to make irrational decisions. That is my definition of greed! It has nothing to do with how much you make and everything to do with how much you buy!

> Greed! It has nothing to do with how much you make and everything to do with how much you buy!

You see, concentrating too much capital into too few deals invariably leads to disastrous results. Not only is there less room for error but cutting your losses becomes much more difficult since the amount of the loss is that much bigger! As a result, you end up taking one step forward and three steps back. Talk about demoralizing!

Could you win six, seven, or eight times out of every ten trades but still lose money? Of course you can. If you let too much money ride on those two or three losing positions, a large portion of your trading account can be wiped out in a hurry! Just consider the plight of a young man who lost 60% of his $1,000,000 inheritance in just two weeks! To say the least, if he had it to do all over again I'm sure he would have invested a lot less.

So here's a simple little formula to keep you on the right track: big gains, small losses, less money, and more deals!

You Snooze, You Lose

Another aspect of greed is remaining in a position for too long. You try to squeeze every last dime out of every single trade you put on. As you'll learn

> So here's a simple little formula to keep you on the right track: big gains, small losses, less money, and more deals!

later, selling tops is a losing proposition. More often than not, you'll end up watching a profitable position move back to break-even or worse yet, turning into a loser. (I definitely learned *that* lesson a few times!)

Thus, knowing when to take profits is critical to your success as well. In fact, before you place a trade, you should already know exactly what point you're going to sell at. This not only applies to cutting your losses but taking profits as well. Rest assured, in later chapters you'll learn simple guidelines that will help you know exactly when to sell. This will keep fear and greed in check and enable you to make sound trading decisions. Otherwise they'll get the best of you, creating too much stress in the process.

Stress – exactly what you *don't* need more of in your life! How would you like to be able to trade stress free? Wouldn't it be nice to be able to invest in the stock market and still sleep like a baby? Well, you can. That's exactly what this book is about – taking the emotion out of trading!

Don't forget, the whole purpose of why you want to trade is to realize the American Dream and financial independence – being able to do what you want, when you want to do it. If you let your emotions get in the way, it can quickly become the "American Nightmare."

So how can you achieve a trading environment that's stress-free? How do you conquer fear, greed and stress? The solution is very simple. You learned about it in Chapter 2 namely, you need a plan, system, or way to help you know when to buy and sell.

If you knew when to buy and sell would that have value? Sure it would. Well, by the time you're done reading this book, you'll be in a position to create a well-crafted game plan that's just right for you.

You'll know exactly how to maximize your gains and minimize your losses. By anchoring yourself with a reliable game plan, you can withstand the "emotional waves" of Wall Street. You'll know precisely what to do and when to do it. So let's discuss what your game plan should consist of.

Key Points to Remember

➤ If left unchecked, your emotions will wreak havoc with your decision-making process and ultimately, your bottom line.

➤ Emotions represent the Achilles Heel of every trader, particularly fear and greed.

➤ There are two types of fear: Taking a loss and losing a profit.

➤ Holding onto a losing position costs more than just the amount you're losing in the trade – you're also losing the opportunity to put that money to work harder elsewhere.

➤ Cut your losses short, let your profits run!

➤ Committing too much capital into too few deals puts tremendous pressure on you to be right, making it difficult to cut your losses.

➤ Don't look a gift horse in the mouth – always know when you'll sell a winning trade.

CHAPTER 10

Three Pillars of a Successful Trading Program

As you learned in Chapter 8, you can't control the emotions of other traders (the herd) on Wall Street, but you *can* control your own. Ultimately, your goal is to learn how to trade without emotion. So if someone were watching you trade they should have a hard time determining whether you are making or losing money. You must become insensitive to the daily gyrations of the stock market. Is that a tall order to fill? You bet it is. However, your success in becoming a consistent and effective trader depends on your ability to triumph over your Achilles heel. The secret lies in following a simple, three-step formula:

1. Create a game plan.
2. Write it down.
3. Keep a trading diary.

Did you realize that step 1, creating a game plan, begins in your wallet? That's right, a $1 bill provides some keen insight into the purpose of a game plan.

Have ever really closely inspected the back of a U.S. dollar? Have you ever really looked and learned something from the good old American buck? Look at the back of a dollar. What do you see? By any chance, do you see a pyramid?

I've mentioned pyramids before. Remember, they were considered one of, and perhaps the greatest of all the wonders of the ancient world.

Have you ever wondered *why* there is a pyramid on the dollar? I sure did. After extensive research I found out that in 1782 the U.S. Congress approved the use of the symbol because pyramids represent strength, durability, endurance, and timelessness. The U.S. dollar bill (for more than 200 years) and the pyramid (for well over 3,000 years) are still symbols representative of strength.

The purpose in sharing this is my attempt to have you, as a trader, associate the pyramid with making money. Just as the pyramids have a strong foundation, you too need to build your game plan upon a similar strong foundation in order for your trading to withstand the test of time. It must be composed of durable and effective principles and strategies.

Many people *think* they have a game plan, but out of the thousands upon thousands of investors I've taught and trained, many did not. There should never be any doubt in your mind as to what you're going to do and when you're going to do it, regardless of market conditions. So what should a strong and reliable game plan be built upon?

There are three pillars upon which to build a successful trading program. If the foundation of your trading program is built upon these three pillars, you will minimize your losses and maximize your gains. They are:

1. Correctly identify the trend.
2. Choosing the appropriate strategy.
3. Implementing a comprehensive, disciplined risk and money management program.

Let's take a look at each one of these.

Correctly Identifying the Trend

To become an effective trader, you need to be able to tell whether a stock is trending higher or lower. Let's face it, if you can tell which direction a stock is headed, you'll definitely put some money in your pocket! As the adage goes,

"The trend is your friend."

"The trend is your friend." Unfortunately, too many investors let themselves get distracted by less important matters. As a result, they don't make the trend their friend.

One of the biggest misconceptions among beginning traders is that success is predicated upon buying at the bottom and selling at the top. Nothing could be further from the truth! That requires perfection, and no one is perfect! Thus, trying to pick tops and bottoms is a losing game at best. Don't think for a moment that you're going to capture 100% of the move.

Why put that kind of pressure on yourself? Instead, focus on capturing 50% to 60% of an existing trend. Get in late and get out early!

> Focus on capturing 50% to 60% of an existing trend. Get in late and get out early!

For example, if a stock runs from $20 to $100, get in at $35 and get out at $85. If you learn to do that on a consistent basis, do you think you'll make a few dollars along the way? Of course you will! Let perfection be someone else's burden and not yours.

Don't forget, the herd creates powerful trends, and riding their "coattails" will make you a lot of money. Where you will get into trouble is trying to outsmart the market, that is, buying puts on stocks in strong up trends or buying calls on stocks in strong downtrends. That's like standing in front of a runaway freight train – you'll get crushed! Let the trend be your friend – don't fight it. By correctly identifying the trend, you will tilt the odds dramatically in your favor.

Choose the Appropriate Strategy

If you correctly identify the trend but pick the wrong strategy, will you lose money? Guaranteed! It doesn't really matter how good you are at identifying the trend, if you don't choose the appropriate strategy, you're going to have a difficult time making money.

> It doesn't really matter how good you are at identifying the trend, if you don't choose the appropriate strategy, you're going to have a difficult time making money.

What makes a strategy appropriate or not depends upon the amount of money you have in your account, your experience level, your lifestyle, and how the option is priced (cheap or expensive).

Choosing strategies that are suitable for your account and experience level are essential. Don't "run" before you learn how to "walk." Pursuing overly aggressive strategies that don't meet your level of expertise will only lead to headache and heartache. Besides, you'll have a hard time gaining approval for such strategies from your broker.

If you are starting out with a smaller account, strategies that are margin- or capital-intensive are not realistic. Don't bite off more than you can chew.

Second, choose strategies that enable you to lead your desired lifestyle. For example, it wouldn't make sense to engage in short-term trading strategies if you travel a lot or prefer to be on the golf course.

Finally, once you determine if the option is cheap, fairly priced, or expensive you will know whether to buy or sell it. You'll learn exactly how to do this in Chapter 15.

Overall, don't make trading more complicated than it is. Let the trend be your friend and stick with the basic "chocolate" and "vanilla" strategies, such as buying calls, puts or the stock.

Risk and Money Management

Last but not least is managing your risk and money wisely. You need to protect your nest egg. In Chapter 16, you'll be

> Focus on protecting what you have instead of focusing on what you want to make.

taught this invaluable principle in depth. You can easily "crash and burn" if you don't pay attention to the amount of risk and money involved in any one trade. Take a defensive stance every time you put on a trade. Focus on protecting what you have instead of focusing on what you want to make. If you do so, the money will take care of itself.

> Take a look at a dollar bill often! By building your game plan upon these three pillars you will, like the pyramid, have a solid foundation from which to trade.

Take a look at a dollar bill often! By building your game plan upon these three pillars you will, like the pyramid, have a solid foundation from which to trade. But creating a game plan is not enough. The second step is just as important. You need to write your game plan down.

Write Down Your Game Plan

By writing your game plan down, you can constantly refer to it, thereby internalizing it. This can be on a 3 x 5 card or sheet of paper. When we have the opportunity to meet at a workshop or conference, I want you to be able to walk up to me and say: "Steve, here is my game plan. This is how I trade. These criteria dictate when I buy and sell. This is how much I risk per trade."

Without a doubt, knowing what you're going to do and when you're going to do it will help you become a more effective trader. Plus, it will simplify your life immensely. Don't make the stock and options market more difficult than it needs to be by "trading by the seat of your pants." By taking time to write down your game plan, you create an easy-to-follow roadmap that fosters stress-free trading.

> By taking time to write down your game plan, you create an easy-to-follow roadmap that fosters stress-free trading.

Maintain a Trading Diary

The third step entails keeping a trading diary. Write down your thoughts and impressions of the market on a daily basis. Make note of seasonal tendencies, patterns, and marketing-moving news.

I also keep track of various market statistics such as, advancing issues, declining issues, new highs, new lows, and so forth. In fact, as you read my updates on **www.mytradingdiary.com** you'll see that information and more.

If you place any trades jot down the reason why. Review your performance regularly. Learn from your mistakes and duplicate your successes.

For example, entries in your trading diary may look like this:

"I bought IBM $100 calls because the stock broke out above resistance."
"I bought puts on KLAC because it broke through its 40-day moving average on heavy volume."
"I sold the QQQs today because it traded below the 10 day moving average."

"CSCO announced worse-than-expected earnings today, but the stock finished higher. It seems as if it just doesn't want to go down any more."

Why is maintaining a trading diary so important? First of all, writing down the reasons behind your decision to enter or exit a particular trade will automatically force you to reexamine your premise for doing so. If your reasons appear flawed, then you can avoid placing the trade. In other words, it functions like a personal version of "checks and balances."

Moreover, it provides you with the opportunity to review and analyze your past trades. By reviewing your performance, you'll learn to identify why you are making or losing money. You'll come to recognize and fix deficiencies in your game plan. How can you correct your mistakes or duplicate your successes if you don't know what you've done? When performance is measured and tracked, it improves! Above all, by keeping a diary you'll better understand the psychology of the market.

> **When performance is measured and tracked, it improves!**

Key Points to Remember

➤ Your game plan should be built upon three pillars: identify the trend, choose the appropriate strategy, and implement a rigorous risk and money management program.

➤ Write your game plan down, maintain a trading diary, and review it often.

➤ When you buy or sell a stock and/or option write down the reason why.

➤ Be realistic – choose strategies that are conducive to your lifestyle and experience level.

CHAPTER 11

The Psychology of the Market

If you listen to the terminology commonly used to describe investors (bulls, bears, hogs, and sheep) you may think you have wandered into a zoo or farm. You see, Wall Street was originally named after a wall that kept farm animals from leaving a settlement at the tip of Manhattan Island. As a result, a day won't pass without you hearing the terms "bulls" and "bears" bantered about. So what do they mean?

A bull is a buyer, a person who profits from prices going higher.

A bear is a seller, a person who profits from prices going lower.

Every single trading day, Wall Street is the battleground between bulls and bears – a tug-of-war between buyers and sellers. Correctly identifying and aligning yourself with the winning team will help you reap consistent profits.

Keep in mind that just because a stock finishes the trading day at $85 doesn't necessarily mean it will open up at that same price the following day. If news comes out after the market closes or before the market opens regarding a new product release, a $1 billion contract, or an earnings shortfall, it will undoubtedly impact the market's view about the worth of that company's stock.

As you watch the price of a stock fluctuate throughout the trading day, recognize that each trade represents what two parties were willing to buy and sell at. If no one wanted to buy or sell at that price, then no trade would take place.

Thus, if a stock opens at $78 after closing at $85 the day before, it's because no one was willing to pay more for it. Remember, a trade takes place between a willing buyer and seller. If there were never any willing buyers, a stock's price would fall to zero! Think of it as an auction: "Will somebody give me $86 for XYZ? Do I hear $83? How about $81? Any takers at $78?" Then finally the auctioneer yells "Sold!" pointing to the buyer who offered $78. As soon as that willing buyer steps forward, a trade takes place. Until then, however, the price continues to fall.

What if no one wants to sell? Demand bids up the price of the stock. "Will you sell it to me for $86? How about $88? $90? $92? $94? $95? Sold!" Until there is a willing seller, the price continues to climb.

> The price of a stock simply reflects supply and demand.

As you can see, the price of a stock simply reflects supply and demand. The greater the demand, the higher the price. The greater the supply, the lower the price.

If you want to buy an option, someone must sell it to you. If you sell a stock, someone must buy it from you. For every buyer there is a seller and for every seller there is a buyer.

As you know, at the end of the day it's fear and greed that drive prices higher or lower. You buy a stock or option because you believe prices will move higher. In your mind, the "train" has left the station and you don't want to be left behind. Conversely, you sell because you believe prices are heading lower. Otherwise, you would hold on to your position.

Sometimes, stocks climb or fall extremely quickly as traders buy or sell at any price. Such panic is indicative of the herd mentality as investors lose control over their emotions and succumb to the opinions of others. To avoid falling into the same trap, you need tools to help you determine which direction a stock and/or the market is headed. The most important one of these tools is a chart.

Charts

Charts are like footprints in the sand – they enable you to see where the price of a stock has been and anticipate which direction it may be headed. Charts provide a snapshot of market psychology, enabling you to interpret the behavior of other traders. It is such analysis that

> Charts are like footprints in the sand – they enable you to see where the price of a stock has been and anticipate which direction it may be headed.

helps you identify trends, uncovering shifts in the balance of power between bulls and bears in the process.

Most importantly, having access to this information enables you to make sound and logical trading decisions. Not using charts in your decision-making process is like driving blindfolded – confusing and dangerous!

In spite of the costly consequences, most investors don't look at a chart before they buy or sell. Surprisingly, many still buy and sell based upon someone else's recommendation.

Think about it. If you can't "see" what's going on, could you be buying right when you should be selling? Could you be selling right when you should be buying? Unfortunately, it happens all the time. Thus, far too many people get "lost" when it comes to investing.

Would you go hiking without a compass? No. Does a pilot take to the air without a flight plan? Of course not. Would you travel in a foreign country without a map? No! It would be foolish, not to mention a waste of your time and money (and even dangerous). Accordingly, don't buy or sell without looking at a chart. Navigating the stock market becomes much easier if you have a roadmap to guide you.

> A chart is your
> roadmap to riches!

At the same time, there are no guarantees that a stock's future price action will mirror what it's done in the past. Stocks sometimes take an abrupt right turn without any warning! Unfortunately, such surprises come with the territory. Hence the importance of risk management, something you'll learn about in Chapter 16.

Nonetheless, looking at a chart will help you make far superior buying and selling decisions than investing without one. A chart is your roadmap to riches!

Two Types of Charts

Two types of charts that investors most often employ are the line chart and the bar chart. A line chart is composed of a smooth, continuous line connecting the closing prices of each trading day.

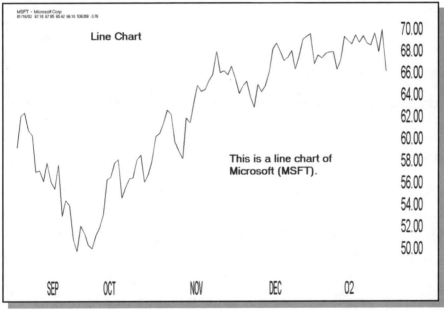

MSFT - Microsoft Corp
01/18/02 67.10 67.95 65.42 66.10 536358 -3.76

Line Chart

This is a line chart of Microsoft (MSFT).

70.00
68.00
66.00
64.00
62.00
60.00
58.00
56.00
54.00
52.00
50.00

SEP   OCT   NOV   DEC   02

Courtesy of TC2000®.

A bar chart is made up of single vertical bars, each depicting the opening, high, low, and closing prices for a particular trading day. The top of the vertical bar represents the high of the day. The bottom of the vertical bar represents the low of the day. The notch to the left represents the opening price and the notch to the right represents the closing price.

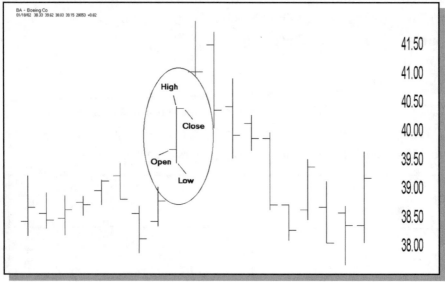

Courtesy of TC2000®.

In addition, you can look at a line or bar chart on an intraday (for example, one, five, ten, 30- or 60-minute bars), daily, weekly, or monthly basis. All this simply means is that every vertical bar represents one 60-minute interval, one day, one week, or one month's worth of data.

MSFT - Microsoft Corp
01/18/02 67.10 67.95 65.42 66.10 536358 -3.76

Bar Chart

This is a daily bar chart of Microsoft (MSFT). Each bar represents one trading day.

Courtesy of TC2000®.

By looking at multiple bars strung together you can determine the prevailing trend of a stock over these various time frames. You can also glean some important clues by just looking at a single vertical bar.

That's why most traders prefer bar charts instead of line charts because they provide more information about what happened during a specific trading day. With a line chart you can only see where a stock closed, whereas a bar chart enables you to see the open, high, low, and close. As a result, you can clearly identify subtle shifts or major reversals in momentum.

> With a line chart you can only see where a stock closed, whereas a bar chart enables you to see the open, high, low, and close.

What You Can Learn from a Single Vertical Bar

First of all, the height of the bar reveals the intensity behind that day's battle. A tall vertical bar indicates dominance by the bulls or bears. They bought or sold with passion, causing the stock to move decisively in their favor. A short vertical bar tells you trading was listless and uneventful. The day's action was void of emotion.

Pay close attention to where the stock closed. Why? It tells you who won! You can also determine how powerful the victory was by comparing the closing price to the stock's intraday range.

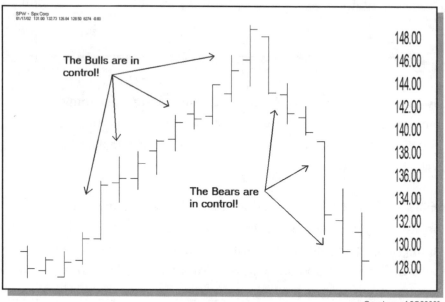

Courtesy of TC2000®.

In looking at this chart, you can clearly see who's winning at any given time. When the closing price is at or near the high of the day, the bulls won. If the closing price is at or near the low of the day, the bears won. Also take note of where the stock opened. If a stock opens at or near the low of the day but finishes at or near the high of the day, what does this tell you about the "quality" of the bulls' victory? It was impressive. They won, hands down! The same holds true for the bears as well – the stock opens at or near the high of the day and closes at or near its low.

Not only that, paying attention to where a stock opens and then trades during the day in relationship to where it closes can help you identify dynamic shifts in momentum. This can prove invaluable, helping you uncover reversals in the prevailing trend.

For example, if a stock opens up, trades higher during the day but then closes down, is that bullish or bearish? It's bearish. It depicts a massive reversal of momentum as the bulls, for whatever reason, ran for cover. In this case, the sellers are back in control.

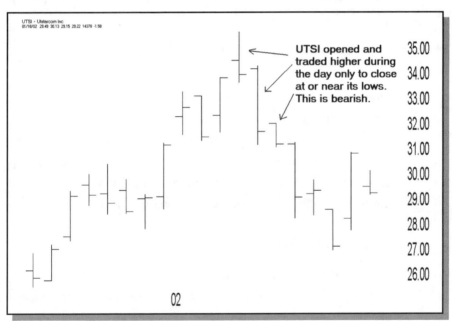

UTSI - Utstarcom Inc
01/18/02 29.49 30.13 29.15 29.22 14376 -1.59

UTSI opened and traded higher during the day only to close at or near its lows. This is bearish.

Courtesy of TC2000®.

Conversely, if a stock opens down, trades lower during the day but then closes higher, it would be bullish. The bears lost control and the bulls regained the upper hand, rallying the stock back the other direction.

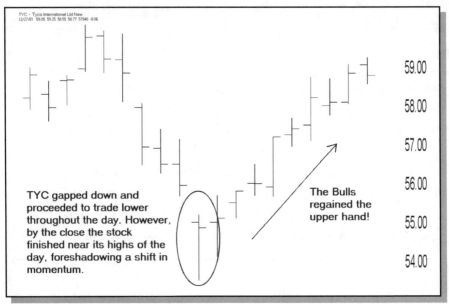

TYC - Tyco International Ltd New
12/27/01 59.05 59.25 58.55 58.77 57940 -0.06

TYC gapped down and proceeded to trade lower throughout the day. However, by the close the stock finished near its highs of the day, foreshadowing a shift in momentum.

The Bulls regained the upper hand!

59.00

58.00

57.00

56.00

55.00

54.00

Courtesy of TC2000®.

Finally, pay attention to the closing price in relationship to the height of the vertical bar, that is, the price range the stock covered during that trading day. This will also help you determine who has momentum on their side. It helps you better position yourself on the side of the winning "team." If the bulls are in control go long. If the bears are stronger go short.

A Time to Place Trades

Another reason why you should place more emphasis on closing instead of opening prices is your desire to trade with and not against the "smart" money, such as: hedge funds, pension funds, mutual funds etc. Their buying and selling creates the chart patterns you see!

Retail customers (you) have a bigger impact on opening prices than you think. The reason? Most people make their buying and selling

> Trade with and not against the "smart" money, such as: hedge funds, pension funds, mutual funds etc.

decisions in the evening or before they leave for work in the morning. Unlike professionals, they don't have the luxury of watching the market all day long. They can't buy situations that look cheap or sell those that appear expensive during the trading day. As a result, they place their "buy" or "sell" orders while the market is closed.

Thus, opening prices merely reflect pent up supply or demand. Once the market opens, orders get filled on a first-come, first-served basis. Herein lies a potentially costly situation.

As mentioned, news can affect the price of a stock. Imagine for a moment that while doing your "homework" one evening, you identify a chart that looks very bullish. After further research, making sure the stock fits your game plan, you decide to buy it. Realizing you'll be too busy the following morning to place the trade you enter the order via your online broker. You place a market order (buy at best available price) to buy 100 shares of ABC. So as soon as the stock begins trading the following trading day your order will be filled.

Now fast forward to the following morning. Unbeknownst to you, before the market opens, ABC announces a negative earnings report. The stock gaps down $6 on the open. Your order gets filled. Yes, you bought the stock at a much lower price than the day before, but it's hardly something to get excited about. You bought a "lemon!" Had you waited for the market to open, you wouldn't have placed the trade.

The reverse is also true. You could end up paying a much higher price than makes sense. This happened a lot with the red-hot IPO (initial public offering) market over the past few years. People wanted a piece of the action so badly that they placed a "market order" on the open.

As you can imagine, many an individual ended up buying at the highs of the day. Basically, they were getting in as the smart money was getting out. In some cases, the difference between where they bought and the price the stock closed at was huge. So

> Don't place market orders overnight to buy on the open.

what's the lesson to be learned? Don't place market orders overnight to buy on the open. It can get ugly. Trade with the professionals, not against them.

So when should you place your trades? First of all, you should do your homework in the evening, away from the noise of the market. This is what I do. This prevents the herd mentality from creeping into your decision-making process. However, never place your orders before the market opens. My preference is to place my trades later in the day, typically within the last hour of trading. This way, you can see if the smart money is selling or buying into the close. It helps you determine whether supply or demand is for real. That's not to say stocks that finish up won't open down the following day or vice versa. You're simply trying to tilt the odds of momentum in your favor.

I will place trades earlier in the day, particularly if there's a clearly defined trend. Regardless of how strong or weak stocks look on the open, let stocks trade for the first 30 to 45

> Regardless of how strong or weak stocks look on the open, let stocks trade for the first 30 to 45 minutes before placing a trade.

minutes before placing a trade. This is a very emotional time, as traders try to make sense of news reports and worldwide events. Thus, stocks can experience huge price swings within a short period. You don't want to step onto that battlefield!

Furthermore, it allows time for all the retail market orders to get filled and out of the way. Now you can sit back and gauge where the true equilibrium of the market is, that is, let natural supply and demand take over before wading in. As you can imagine, the busiest times of the day are typically the first and last hours of trading.

Resistance and Support

Wall Street is a battleground where bulls and bear fight for each other's money. They both have "bunkers" from which they can attack. These "bunkers" are referred to as *support* and *resistance*. The bulls are stationed at support and the bears at resistance. By understanding why such levels exist, you can cash-in when these strongholds give way. This shift in market psychology creates both bullish and bearish opportunities.

The chart below is an example of support and resistance.

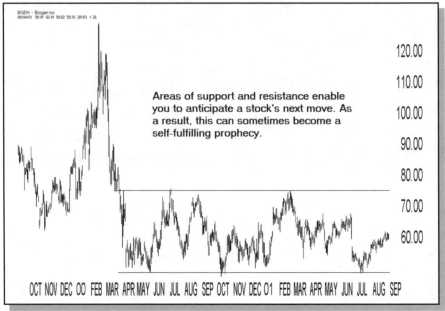

Areas of support and resistance enable you to anticipate a stock's next move. As a result, this can sometimes become a self-fulfilling prophecy.

Courtesy of TC2000®.

Support and resistance represent monetary and emotional commitment. The stronger the commitment is, the stronger the levels of support and resistance.

In some respects, you could say that support and resistance are a byproduct of a self-fulfilling prophecy. Think about it. Do your expectations sometimes become reality? Sure they do. How do you think the market would behave if no one had a chart to look at? Let's say for one or two months no one could use any charts whatsoever. Would that affect people's buying and selling decisions? Clearly it would, particularly if you depend upon them. I sure do! I can't place a trade without looking at a chart first. I need a roadmap. I need to see where to buy and sell.

To begin with, approach it from a psychological standpoint. How do you become "programmed" to buy support and sell resistance? Actually, it's quite easy. Let's say you've been watching a stock for some time. Soon you realize that every time it gets around $35 it reverses and moves higher. How many times do you need to watch this before you want to jump in? Probably just twice! Why? You have confidence the stock will do it again. You feel in control because the pattern helps you anticipate what will happen next. It becomes predictable. Now consider how powerful this becomes when you realize everyone is looking at the same thing.

So when it does return to that level, what are you going to do? What is everyone going to do? You're going to buy! This is a slam-dunk, isn't it? You've made up your mind beforehand: "I'm going to buy the next time it hits support." The pattern has conditioned you and everyone else to buy at that price.

Pavlov's Dogs

As I'm sure you remember from your psychology class, classical conditioning is the pairing of an action or response to a stimulus. Ivan Pavlov was a Russian physiologist best known for his discovery and work in the area of conditioned reflexes. Early in the 1900's Pavlov accidentally discovered classical conditioning. You see, he noticed that the dogs on which he had performed digestion experiments salivated when they heard food being brought to them. He later discovered that if he rang a bell each time they were fed, the dogs would salivate at the sound of the bell even when food was not present.

Eventually, the bell became the conditioned stimulus that triggered the salivation or the conditioned response. Traders, like Pavlov's dogs, can become programmed to buy support and sell resistance in much the same way.

For example, let's look at resistance. Let's say that you want to buy a stock but it is approaching resistance. In looking at the chart you notice that every time the stock approaches $45 it tends to lose momentum and reverse direction. Are you going to buy at $45? No way. You'll wait for lower prices before jumping in. Thus, resistance creates an absence of buyers.

Moreover, let's say that you already own the stock, having bought it at $35. As the stock rallies back up to $45, what action will you most likely take? You will sell. Why? Because by looking at the chart you notice the stock has a tendency to hit a "ceiling" around $45 and fall back down. Thus, resistance induces selling.

Ultimately, your expectations become reality, or shall I say, the herd's expectations become reality! There's a "buyers' club" at support and a "sellers' club" at resistance.

Buy the Breakout

Where this really gets exciting and profitable is when a stock finally breaks out above resistance or below support. In fact, it is my favorite time to buy calls or puts. As a result, I call these patterns "cash-in-the-boxes"!

> Where this really gets exciting and profitable is when a stock finally breaks out above resistance or below support.

A breakout denotes a major shift in market psychology and can be quite lucrative if you learn to recognize and exploit it. Clearly, something you'll be able to do once you finish this book.

When you identify a stock channeling between support and resistance, be patient and wait for the stock to break out. Once it does, you have a green light to implement bullish or bearish strategies, depending on the direction of the move.

Keep in mind that sometimes stocks break out to the upside but can't follow through, returning to where they just were. Stocks will also break down below support but then quickly rally back to their initial area of failure. However, it doesn't necessarily mean the play is over.

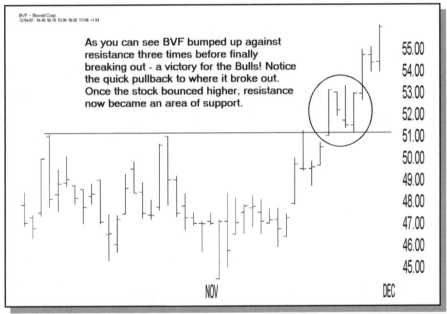

Courtesy of TC2000®.

There still may be another wonderful opportunity to capture an explosive move. It depends on what happens once the stock moves back to the point of the initial breakout. Will these areas of support and resistance give way, or will they reverse rolls? Let me explain.

When stocks break out of a trading range, there may be a few days where traders lack conviction. The key is whether support becomes resistance, or resistance becomes support. If they do, you'll be presented with another opportunity to enter the trade.

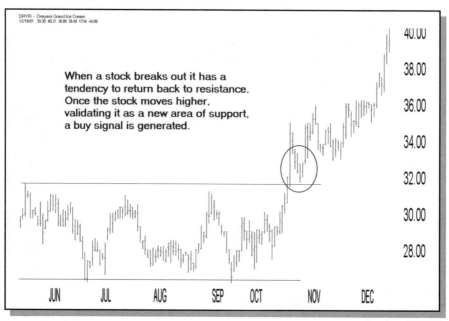

When a stock breaks out it has a
tendency to return back to resistance.
Once the stock moves higher,
validating it as a new area of support,
a buy signal is generated.

Courtesy of TC2000®.

In this example below, the first entry can be made when the stock breaks out above resistance for the first time. If it pulls back to where it broke out, finds support, and then bounces higher, that is your second buying opportunity. Resistance became support. If you missed buying the initial breakout, don't let the second opportunity pass you by.

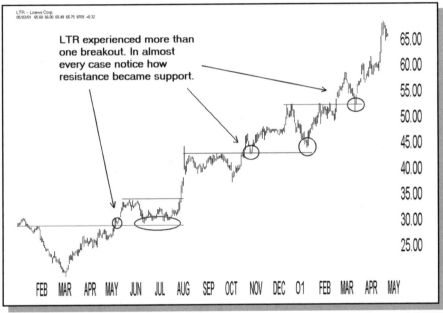

LTR - Loews Corp
05/03/01 65.60 66.00 65.49 65.75 8709 +0.32

LTR experienced more than one breakout. In almost every case notice how resistance became support.

Courtesy of TC2000®.

If a stock breaks down through support, you buy puts. Likewise, if you miss the initial breakout, a second buying opportunity is created when the stock rallies back up to support and stalls. Once it rolls over, validating what was once support as resistance, you have the green light to implement bearish strategies – short the stock, buy puts, and so on.

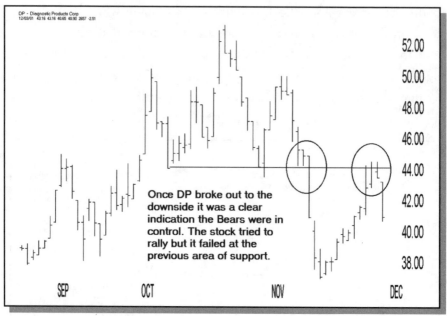

DP - Diagnostic Products Corp
12/03/01 43.16 43.16 40.65 40.90 2657 -2.51

52.00
50.00
48.00
46.00
44.00
42.00
40.00
38.00

Once DP broke out to the downside it was a clear indication the Bears were in control. The stock tried to rally but it failed at the previous area of support.

SEP   OCT   NOV   DEC

Courtesy of TC2000®.

What makes this approach such a low-risk strategy is that you let the stock prove itself to you before you enter the trade. Namely, you wait for the stock to bounce before entering a bullish trade or you wait for the stock to roll over before entering a bearish trade. You let support become resistance or resistance become support before spending a dime.

> What makes this approach such a low-risk strategy is that you let the stock prove itself to you before you enter the trade.

Rest assured, there will be stocks that break out that will fail. False breakouts occur so remember to practice good risk management – if a breakout fails, cut your losses quickly!

Key Points to Remember

➤ Charts give you great insight into who is winning the battle between the bulls and the bears.

➤ The height of the bar tells you how intense that day's battle was.

➤ Avoid the first 30 to 45 minutes of the trading day.

➤ Trade with professionals, not against them.

➤ Support and resistance are sometimes a byproduct of a self-fulfilling prophecy.

➤ Buy the breakout. If you miss it, wait for resistance to become support or support to become resistance.

➤ If a breakout fails, cut your losses quickly.

➤ The key to your success is trading with charts and without emotion.

CHAPTER 12

A Canary in the Coal Mine

Don't Get Caught Unprepared by the Next Market Selloff!!

You have already been exposed to the concept of maintaining your independence as a trader. If you don't develop your own trading style within the realms of your comfort level and personality, you'll have a difficult time trading with any consistency. Furthermore, if you drift from your game plan you'll become more susceptible to the herd mentality. As a result, when the trend changes you will not be able to recognize it. You could end up buying when you should be selling and vice versa – just like everyone else in the herd. This can prove quite costly.

If you don't trade according to your game plan, you'll find it difficult to trade with any confidence, buying and selling recklessly. Crushed by the emotional waves of Wall Street, you're easily swept away in the undercurrent of a powerful trend.

If you don't believe me, just take a look at the unbelievable rallies that began in technology stocks and the Internet sector at the end of 1999. The *last* thing you want to do is fight the prevailing trend. If you get caught looking the wrong way, you can be wiped out at the drop of a hat. Thus, the key to your success lies in your ability to get the most out of the prevailing trend but remaining independent at the same time. You need to know when to walk away.

Frankly, the biggest problem you will face is recognizing when to walk away. Too often the herd drives stocks and the market in general beyond their "natural" limits. As a result, you will get yourself in trouble when the trend changes and reverses course – *if* you don't know what to look for.

> Frankly, the biggest problem you will face is recognizing when to walk away.

Most of the time, the masses get it right. That's why it pays to make the trend your friend. But the masses are notorious for being wrong at the turning points when trends reverse. That's why you often hear the phrase "the wrong-way crowd". It pays, literally, to head in the opposite direction. It is the purpose of this chapter to help you identify when the herd has gone too far in one direction. The basic premise is that if everyone is doing it, then it's wise to move in the opposite direction. This is what it means to be a contrarian: You take the road less traveled.

One of the greatest contrarians of all time (even though he wasn't an options trader) was Hannibal, general of Carthage, an ancient North African city (247-183 B.C.). Because of his excellent military strategies and tactics, which always involved doing the exact opposite of what his enemies thought he would do, he repeatedly overcame great handicaps and defeated armies much larger than his own.

Hannibal's most famous victory embodied the contrarian strategy of taking the road less traveled. You see, just after Rome declared war on Carthage in 218 B.C., Hannibal astonished the Romans with a very daring military maneuver. With 60,000 troops, 6,000 horses, and countless African elephants, he crossed the Pyrenees mountain range in France, and braved the snow and fierce cold of the Alps and entered Roman Italy.

Can you imagine? African elephants in the snow-capped Alps! Well, the Romans had been expecting a Carthaginian attack by sea, but Hannibal reached Rome by a means contrary to everyone's expectations – through the mountains! He entered Rome via the "back door," completely unexpectedly.

After the Carthaginian invasion of Rome Hannibal maneuvered, for many years, virtually uncontested throughout northern, central, and southern Italy. Repeatedly, he handed the Roman army the worst defeats they had ever historically recorded.

History has treated Hannibal as a contrarian. His approach to war served him and his country well. This analogy should be used by all options traders, not only as a reminder of how powerful being a contrarian can be, but also of the importance of crafting a well-thought-out game plan.

Keep in mind that being a contrarian doesn't mean buying beaten-down stocks just because they are out of favor (they are out of favor for a reason!) or selling stocks just because they've doubled or tripled in price. What you want to determine is if investors have become too bullish or bearish. When this occurs, it foreshadows a tremendous price shock in the not-too-distant future.

It is absolutely critical you learn to spot the early warning signs of such impending danger. Not only can you mitigate the damage to your portfolio, but you can also take advantage of the situation, reaping enormous profits in the process.

You need a reliable, early-warning system to alert you when the trend is about to reverse. What you need is a canary in the coalmine. Let me explain.

In the early 1700s, coal mining rapidly developed in North America as society changed from an agrarian culture to an industrialized one. As a result, a small fragile bird (the canary) became a major role player in an industry whose product (coal) would initially drive American industrialization.

Of course, it's important to remember that mining was fraught with dangers. It was discovered – belatedly – that noxious gases were produced and trapped within mine shafts and tunnels during coal extraction. Many a mine explosion occurred when certain gases, such as methane, ignited from candles worn on miners' caps. Many unsuspecting miners would perish due to their inability to predict when they were approaching danger.

"Getting shafted" is exactly what happened to thousands of miners throughout history. In addition, carbon monoxide and the lack of oxygen put miners at peril in the ill-ventilated environment of the mines.

In order to remedy the hazards connected with "foul air," many mine companies discovered that they could use canaries to detect carbon monoxide and methane. You see, canary heart rates are so high and their respiratory system so simple that they would die or pass-out very quickly when exposed to only the slightest hint of a harmful gas. Canaries would die long before the miners were in harm's way. As a result, this unfortunate tragedy for the birds allowed miners to avoid catastrophe themselves.

Canaries were caged and placed in strategic locations along the mine tunnel and watched to see if and when they would fall off their perches. The canary became a literal "life saver" – an early-warning signal for the unpredictable and ever-present danger in the coalmines.

In much the same way, you need an early-warning system to forewarn you of imminent danger in the stock market. Otherwise, you may find yourself crushed by a market reversal.

Fortunately, there are some simple indicators that will not only keep you apprised of the "wrong-way crowd," but they'll also act as the canary in the coal mine of Wall Street. The indicators include: *CBOE's Volatility Index (VIX)*, *equity-only put/call ratio*, *surveys*, and the *days to cover or short ratio*.

CBOE's Volatility Index (VIX)

The VIX is a tool you can use to measure optimism or pessimism in the marketplace. It is taken from eight different OEX options, typically at-the-money (the closest strike prices to where the index currently trades), with around 30 days remaining before expiration. Since the OEX is a broad-based index and representative of the market in general, many feel the

VIX is an excellent indicator of how investors feel about the prospects of the market going forward. It measures whether they're fearful or complacent.

Accordingly, the VIX is a good predictor of overall stock market movement. This is a simple but powerful tool that has become widely used in predicting market direction.

Essentially, the concept is a contrarian one. When the market falls, people begin to panic and buy puts. The further the market falls the greater the fear, resulting in higher demand for protection. This ever-increasing demand for puts causes implied volatility to rapidly climb. As you can imagine, implied volatility is greatest in a falling market. Thus, the VIX, which is a numerical measure of implied volatility (see Chapter 15), rises to higher and higher levels, forcing investors to overpay for the options.

Basically investors are willing to buy "insurance," that is, they're buying puts against stock they own, at any cost. They can't take the financial pain anymore and are willing to pay top dollar to protect their portfolios from further losses. As you already learned in a previous chapter, when emotion takes over the decision-making process, things can spiral out o control very quickly. It's at this juncture, when everyone expects the market to fall further, that extreme levels of fear are present. This is when you need to become bullish.

> When the VIX peaks and begins to roll over, it presents an awesome buying opportunity!

When the VIX peaks and begins to roll over, it presents an awesome buying opportunity! It usually marks a short-term trading bottom. So right when everyone is fearful and overly bearish is the time you want to be bullish. Is that tough to do? You bet your bottom dollar it is! That's what being a contrarian is all about.

Consequently, the VIX is a great predictor of market direction. In fact, if you overlay the VIX on top of a chart of the Dow Jones Industrial Average (DJIA), OEX, or SPX, you'll find that virtually every great rally was foreshadowed by a spike in the VIX.

To illustrate this, I've placed a chart of the VIX (bar chart) and the DJIA (smoothed line) on the same graph. (The numbers down the right of the chart refer to the value of the VIX.) It's uncanny how predictable the VIX is!

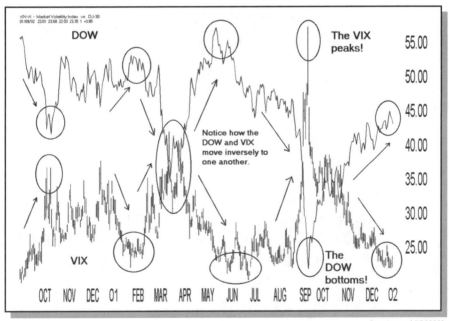

Courtesy of TC2000®.

Typically, you'll see declining volatility in a rising market and increasing volatility in a falling market. It should also be noted that when volatility is low the market is priming itself for an explosive move. This can occur to the downside, but not always. Later in this chapter, you'll see there have been plenty of instances when the VIX was at extremely low levels and the market rallied strongly.

As mentioned, a falling VIX accompanies a rising market, so it seems logical to conclude that as the market climbs higher, fear will naturally begin to subside. When implied volatility is low, denoted by a low VIX reading, it represents a high level of complacency amid market participants. More and more people are becoming comfortable with the "peaceful" state of the market and aren't paying up for options. They think the market is going nowhere. From a contrarian point of view, this means the exact opposite will happen – the market *will* become volatile!

> When implied volatility is low, denoted by a low VIX reading, it represents a high level of complacency amid market participants.

While there is really no absolute number that denotes a buy or sell signal, you can look at a chart of the VIX for guidance. What you are looking for are extremes – peaks and valleys. A peak, or spike in the VIX, and then a downturn is usually a great buy signal. A valley, or low VIX reading, more often than not leads to a selloff of some kind. You can easily see these peaks and valleys by looking at a chart of the VIX.

To show you what I'm talking about, let me walk you through a few examples.

Back in 1994 and 1995, peaks in VIX occurred in the 16% to 20% range. You can see a much bigger spike in early 1994 above 24 – definitely an extreme!

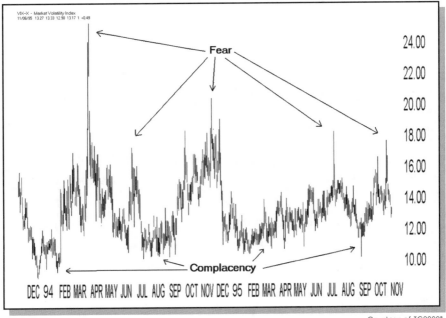

Courtesy of TC2000®.

However, since volatility has steadily increased over the years, peaks in the VIX now occur at levels well above 30%.

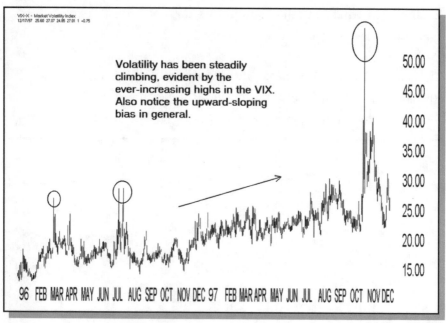

VIX-X - Market Volatility Index
12/17/97 25.60 27.07 24.95 27.01 1 +0.75

Volatility has been steadily climbing, evident by the ever-increasing highs in the VIX. Also notice the upward-sloping bias in general.

50.00
45.00
40.00
35.00
30.00
25.00
20.00
15.00

96 FEB MAR APR MAY JUN JUL AUG SEP OCT NOV DEC 97 FEB MAR APR MAY JUN JUL AUG SEP OCT NOV DEC

Courtesy of TC2000®.

This is a good reminder of why a dynamic approach is best, rather than using fixed levels as buy or sell signals. Volatility is always changing; what was once high may now be low and vice versa. As a result, it is very useful to use the chart to gain the proper perspective.

Note that the peaks in VIX are rather pointy. They occur quickly. This is because they represent panic, which can quickly disappear when the market begins to rally. Also notice that the explosive moves, which follow such spikes in fear, can be rather large. This provides you with an incredible trading opportunity!

Interpreting the VIX in this manner is a contrarian method of investing. When the average person is panicking and buying puts, you (as a contrarian) are thinking about going long (bullish). Of course, now that more and more people are becoming aware of this phenomenon, there is a chance that the signals can become distorted. In any case, it is obvious from the chart that peaks in VIX are still awesome buy signals.

Take a look at the spikes in the VIX in September and October 1997. On October 27, 1997, the VIX spiked to its highest levels since the 1987 crash when the market plunged 554 points. That also marked a bottom, creating a wonderful buying opportunity as well.

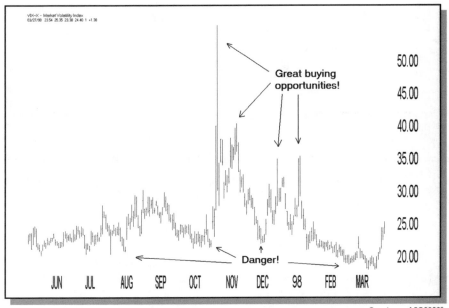

Courtesy of TC2000®.

The spike in January 1998 preceded the huge rally the market enjoyed from February through April. Such spikes have worked like clockwork as contrarian buy signals, since they are indicative of extreme fear by the wrong-way crowd.

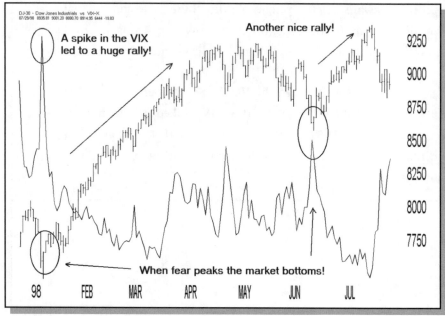

DJ-30 - Dow Jones Industrials vs VIX-X
07/29/98 8935.81 9001.20 8690.70 8914.95 6444 -19.83

A spike in the VIX led to a huge rally!

Another nice rally!

9250
9000
8750
8500
8250
8000
7750

When fear peaks the market bottoms!

98   FEB   MAR   APR   MAY   JUN   JUL

Courtesy of TC2000®.

If you take a look at a chart of the VIX back in October 1998 you'll notice the extremely high reading, spiking over 60 on an intraday basis. That's huge!

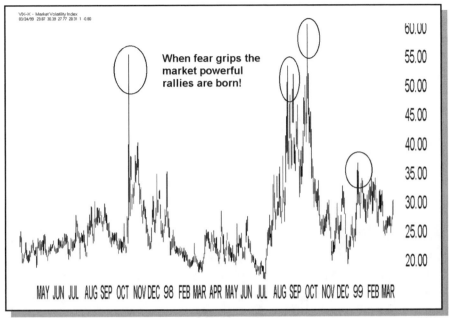

When fear grips the
market powerful
rallies are born!

VIX-X - Market Volatility Index
03/24/99 29.87 30.39 27.77 28.31 1 -0.80

60.00
55.00
50.00
45.00
40.00
35.00
30.00
25.00
20.00

MAY JUN JUL AUG SEP OCT NOV DEC 98 FEB MAR APR MAY JUN JUL AUG SEP OCT NOV DEC 99 FEB MAR

Courtesy of TC2000®.

Why? Well, in 1998 there were various economic crises taking place around the world, not to mention the near collapse of Long Term Capital Management, a very large, highly leveraged hedge fund based in the U.S.

As a result, the markets plunged, sending the bulls running for cover. Everyone was in a state of massive pessimism – capitalism was on its deathbed! It's at such moments of extreme bearishness that a very bullish opportunity presents itself – if you're a contrarian, that is.

Take a look at the chart of the VIX below and you'll see that on both April 14, 2000, and March 22, 2001, the VIX spiked to its highest level since 1998's meltdown. Holy cow!

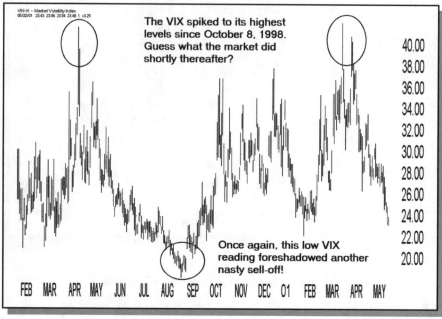

The VIX spiked to its highest levels since October 8, 1998. Guess what the market did shortly thereafter?

Once again, this low VIX reading foreshadowed another nasty sell-off!

Courtesy of TC2000®.

Did you miss it? If you did, from now on you'll see exactly how you can reap the enormous benefits by knowing what to look for.

Back on April 14, 2000 the DJIA tumbled 617 points, while the NASDAQ fell 355 points. Talk about a nasty day! The VIX spiked to 41.53 on an intraday basis. What followed was even more amazing. The DJIA rallied 817 points (net) over the next seven trading days and the NASDAQ soared 13% in just two days! What would have helped you position yourself in front of such an explosive rally? Why, the VIX, of course. Are you sensing a pattern yet? I hope so.

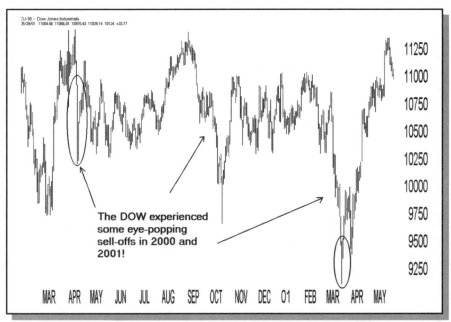

DJ-30 - Dow Jones Industrials
35/29/01 11004.66 11066.01 10970.43 11039.14 10124 +33.77

11250
11000
10750
10500
10250
10000
9750
9500
9250

The DOW experienced
some eye-popping
sell-offs in 2000 and
2001!

MAR APR MAY JUN JUL AUG SEP OCT NOV DEC 01 FEB MAR APR MAY

Courtesy of TC2000®.

Now let's fast forward to March 22, 2001. Stocks are caught in a nasty downtrend. Earnings warnings are littering the landscape. Internet and tech companies are blowing up right and left (just check out the charts of VERT, ARBA, LU, CMGI, and YHOO. Yikes!) Layoffs were soaring. Fear was in the air.

The DJIA fell almost 400 points at the lows of the day, sending the VIX soaring to 41.99 on an intraday basis. However, by the close the DJIA finished down only 97 points. Once again, a spike in fear (VIX) was a prelude to a powerful rally.

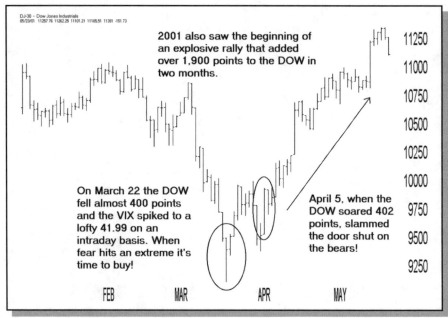

DJ-30 – Dow Jones Industrials
05/23/01 11257.76 11262.25 11101.21 11105.51 11391 -151.73

2001 also saw the beginning of an explosive rally that added over 1,900 points to the DOW in two months.

11250

11000

10750

10500

10250

10000

On March 22 the DOW fell almost 400 points and the VIX spiked to a lofty 41.99 on an intraday basis. When fear hits an extreme it's time to buy!

April 5, when the DOW soared 402 points, slammed the door shut on the bears!

9750

9500

9250

FEB   MAR   APR   MAY

Courtesy of TC2000®.

From the lows of that day, 9106, the DJIA rocketed higher to close at 9947 just three days later! Unbelievable! What tipped you off that such a rally was in store? You got it – the VIX. Can this indicator make you money? You bet it can. Once again, the key is knowing what to look for. But it got even better as the market gave you another fabulous buy signal on April 3.

To say the least, April 3 was an ugly day on Wall Street! The DJIA fell 292 points and the NASDAQ tumbled 109 points. Fear was running high as the VIX closed that day at 39.33, clearly at the higher and extreme end of its range. A buying opportunity was developing! The following day stocks ended mixed, with the NASDAQ falling 34 points and the DJIA gaining 29 – the calm before the storm!

On April 5 the DJIA soared 402 points and the NASDAQ rocketed higher by 146 points – a one-day gain of 8.9%! And as they say, the rest is history. Through the close of May 25 the NASDAQ had gained 35% from the close of April 3 – the day the VIX spiked to an extremely lofty level. The DJIA added an impressive 16% during that same time frame. Both indexes took out critical areas of resistance as well.

Now let's take a brief look at sentiment leading up to the market's major bottom in September 2001.

September 7 marked a wicked end to the previous week's trading as the DJIA fell 234 points and the NASDAQ stumbled 17. So many were hoping for the bulls to wave a white flag of capitulation during Monday's trading session. But unfortunately, they were sorely disappointed.

Yes, both the DJIA and NASDAQ traded lower early on, but it wasn't the gut-wrenching free-fall that everyone had been looking for. Besides, with so many people looking for this so-called capitulation, the market is rarely that accommodating. In fact, the market's unbelievably good at making the herd look downright foolish.

Additionally, the September 10 cover story in the "Money" section of *USA Today* provided another perfect example of why a true bottom hadn't been established. The story was entitled, "Brutal selloff may signal beginning of end for bear: Market bottom could be near as investors wave white flag."

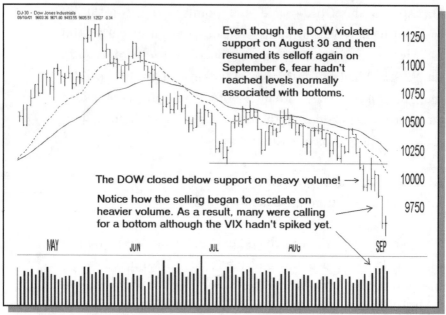

DJ-30 - Dow Jones Industrials
09/10/01 9603.36 9671.80 9493.55 9605.51 12527 -0.34

Even though the DOW violated support on August 30 and then resumed its selloff again on September 6, fear hadn't reached levels normally associated with bottoms.

The DOW closed below support on heavy volume! →

Notice how the selling began to escalate on heavier volume. As a result, many were calling for a bottom although the VIX hadn't spiked yet.

11250
11000
10750
10500
10250
10000
9750

MAY   JUN   JUL   AUG   SEP

Courtesy of TC2000®.

Huh? Were they looking at the same action I was? I didn't want to be a party-pooper, but I didn't see many white flags being waved. Despite the breakdowns in the major indexes, many market participants still appeared more afraid of missing the bottom instead of losing more money. That same cover story described investors maintaining their bullish posture and buying into the tech sector. Scary!

That's why I didn't see any overwhelming evidence to support their headline. By the way, anytime you have a major media outlet touting that a bottom is near, it's not. It's that simple.

Based on historical precedence, there wasn't the extreme level of fear, panic, and bearishness that typically accompanies bottoms.

Just take a look at the chart of the VIX. Granted, the VIX spiked over 35 before closing at 33.87, but the lows of March/April of 2001 saw the VIX spike above 41. In 1998 it spiked above 60! While this was a positive development did it represent the level of fear necessary for a bottom? In my opinion, it hadn't.

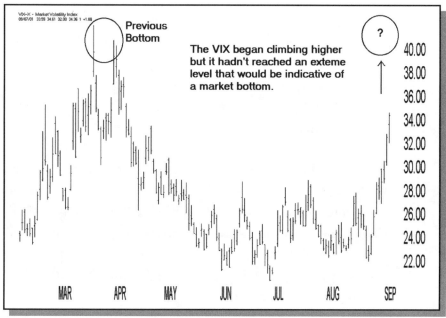

Courtesy of TC2000®.

Little did anyone know what awaited the United States and innocent citizens on the morning of September 11 when terrorists launched their insidious attack on America.

While the U.S. markets remained closed the following week, other world markets were open and their reaction was, not surprisingly, negative. The London's FTSE fell 5.7% before closing early. France's CAC 40 fell 7.4% and Germany's DAX plummeted 8.5%. Asian and Latin were also sharply lower, falling anywhere from 5% to 12%.

On September 17, almost a week after the most horrific and bone-chilling terrorist attack in American history, U.S. markets reopened for business. The market had been closed since the September 11th tragedy, the longest shutdown since the early 1900's.

On September 17, the DJIA fell 684 points (7.1%), its largest point drop in history. It also came on a day when the the NYSE saw its heaviest volume ever – approximately 2.4 billion shares! The NASDAQ didn't fare much better as it crumbled to a 115-point loss or 6.8% – its second-largest percentage drop in history.

As you might imagine, fear and panic started spreading like wildfire (just what the bulls ordered!)! The VIX closed at 44.94 after hitting an intraday high of 47.7. However, it didn't peak until later that Friday, September 21, when it closed at 48.27, having touched 57.31 on an intraday basis! This came extremely close to eclipsing the highs (60.63) established back in October 1998 – the last major market bottom.

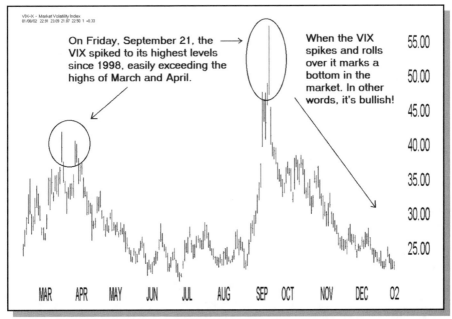

VIX-X - Market Volatility Index
01/08/02 22.91 23.09 21.87 22.50 1 +0.33

On Friday, September 21, the ⟶
VIX spiked to its highest levels
since 1998, easily exceeding the
highs of March and April.

When the VIX
spikes and rolls
over it marks a
bottom in the
market. In other
words, it's bullish!

55.00

50.00

45.00

40.00

35.00

30.00

25.00

MAR   APR   MAY   JUN   JUL   AUG   SEP   OCT   NOV   DEC   02

Courtesy of TC2000®.

When you look at previous selloffs of 500 points or more, higher prices have unfolded shortly thereafter, which should come as no surprise, since fear invariably accompanies such vicious selloffs!

After the terrifying crash of 1987, where the DJIA fell 508 points on October 19, less than a month later the index had risen 12%. By year's end it gained 20.5%. Looking back at August 1998's meltdown, the DJIA lost 512 points, but the index managed to finish the year almost 27% higher. And on April 14, 2000 the DOW fell 616 points, but within 30 days it scrambled to finish 5% higher.

The crash of 2001 delivered in similar fashion! The DJIA soared 9.7% and the NASDAQ rocketed higher by 8% in a matter of days from the lows of September 21. Furthermore, from the intraday lows of September 21, 2001 (8,062), to the intraday highs of January 7, 2002, the DJIA exploded for a 28% gain!

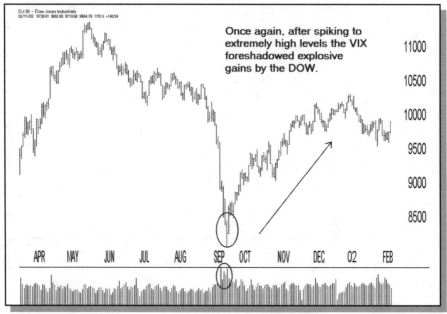

Having established that extreme peaks in VIX are good buy signals, can we then conclude that extreme low readings are good sell signals? The answer is less definitive.

Lows in the VIX occur when complacency is high and implied volatility is low. Market participants believe the market is going nowhere. As a result, low VIX readings typically precede an explosive move by the market, but that move can occur in either direction. Sometimes that move is to the downside, but there have been plenty of spectacular moves to the upside following low VIX readings as well. Thus, the proper strategy to establish when VIX is extremely low is a straddle (buy both a put and a call with the same terms – something you'll learn in, High Octane Options). Straddles benefit regardless of the direction of the move – as long as it's big enough!

Once again, you want to look for low points on the VIX chart on a relative basis, not an absolute level. For example, back in 1994 and 1995, troughs occurred with VIX down around 10% to 11%. In 1996 low VIX readings were more commonly in the 15% to 16% area. In 1997 low readings were in the 19% to 22% range. In 1998 the VIX fell into the 17% to 20% area.

Low VIX readings preceded large rallies by the market in February and September 1995, August 1996, May 1997, March 1998, December 1998, April 1999, and November 1999. In fact, the smallest gain from this list, was 6.8% (based upon the OEX), following the low VIX reading in November 1999.

The message is loud and clear – a low VIX reading foreshadows an explosive move, but it can occur in either direction! So don't be lulled into thinking

> A low VIX reading foreshadows an explosive move, but it can occur in either direction!

that a low VIX reading guarantees a selloff. Nonetheless, there have been some severe selloffs following a low VIX reading.

As you'll remember, going into July 1998 the market had another record-breaking run to new highs but it also pushed the VIX down to two-year lows. Complacency reigned supreme!

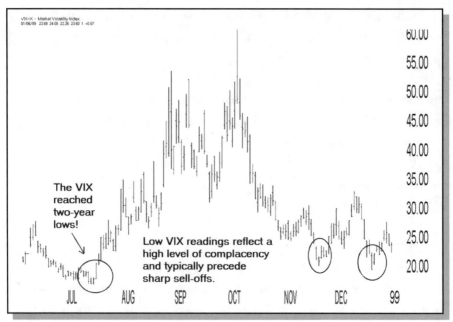

VIX–X - Market Volatility Index
01/06/99 23.68 24.08 22.36 23.60 1 +0.07

The VIX reached two-year lows!

Low VIX readings reflect a high level of complacency and typically precede sharp sell-offs.

60.00
55.00
50.00
45.00
40.00
35.00
30.00
25.00
20.00

JUL   AUG   SEP   OCT   NOV   DEC   99

Courtesy of TC2000®.

To be even more specific, the DJIA closed at all-time high on July 17, finishing at 9337. On the same day, the VIX closed at a two-year low of 16.88 – a clear indication an explosive move was right around the corner! By September 1, less than two months later, the DOW fell more than 1,900 points, touching 7400 on an intraday basis.

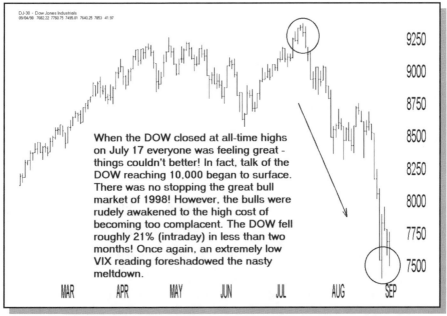

DJ-30 - Dow Jones Industrials
09/04/98 7682.22 7760.75 7495.81 7640.25 7953 41.97

When the DOW closed at all-time highs on July 17 everyone was feeling great - things couldn't better! In fact, talk of the DOW reaching 10,000 began to surface. There was no stopping the great bull market of 1998! However, the bulls were rudely awakened to the high cost of becoming too complacent. The DOW fell roughly 21% (intraday) in less than two months! Once again, an extremely low VIX reading foreshadowed the nasty meltdown.

MAR   APR   MAY   JUN   JUL   AUG   SEP

9250
9000
8750
8500
8250
8000
7750
7500

Courtesy of TC2000®.

To say that most investors were caught off-guard would be an understatement! However, had you been watching the VIX, you would have known an explosive move was brewing and you could of planned accordingly.

Just remember, when such an environment of extreme complacency exists you should substantially reduce, if not eliminate, any use of margin. Rid your portfolio of any exposure you might have to potentially devastating losses. Bulletproof your account through the use of puts or cost-free "insurance policies" (see *High Octane Options*). Consider implementing straddles and stick to trading the strongest stocks, not the speculative ones.

Equity-Only Put/Call Ratio

You buy calls when you feel stock prices are going higher and you buy puts when you think prices are heading lower. Knowing the quantity of calls and puts being bought on stocks at any given time can give you insight into the bullishness and/or bearishness of option traders.

If an excessive amount of calls are being bought on underlying stocks, it means people are too bullish. As a contrarian, you would view that as a red flag. The reason is simple. If investors are excessively bullish about the stocks then most likely they have already acted and are fully invested. If you thought the market was going higher, you wouldn't wait for it to happen, but you would want to participate as it happens.

Now what? Well, clearly your buying power has been depleted and you begin looking for a reason to sell. Additionally, if the majority of investors are doing the same thing as you, namely buying, who is left over to push prices higher? No one! Everyone is already invested! As a result, buying power begins to fade. Sellers (bears) begin to gain the upperhand over the remaining bulls, pushing the market lower.

If you are bearish, then most likely you have taking a defensive posture in the market, such as selling your stocks and/or buying puts. If the majority of investors are also doing the same thing, then pretty soon the strength of the selling will begin to fade. There's no one left over to sell! If an excessive number of puts are being bought, then it indicates people are becoming too bearish. Now the buyers (bulls) come in and start buying, easily overwhelming the remaining bears. The result? A market rally.

What makes this concept so easy to use is that you can easily measure the bearishness or bullishness of investors by using the equity put/call ratio. It's calculated on a daily basis by taking the number of puts divided by the number of calls traded that day. The resulting ratio helps uncover whether investors are too bearish or bullish. A savvy contrarian will look for opportunities when the herd has reached an extreme. What's considered an extreme?

Consistent daily readings above 0.65 are bullish from a contrarian standpoint (normally, daily readings would be around 0.45 - 0.55). Keep in mind this is the *equity put/call ratio* and *not* the total put/call ratio, which combines equity and index options. What this tells you is that 65 puts are being bought for every 100 calls. It tells you people are bearish toward stocks. They are purchasing more and more puts, a bet that stock prices will decline. This is bullish, since too much pessimism exists.

For example, on September 10, 2001 the equity-only put/call ratio registered an impressive 0.89. More importantly, recent readings included: 0.70, 0.82, 0.85, 0.71, 0.62, and 0.74. This indicator was clearly supporting the bulls' argument for a rally. However, given the events of September 11, these reading were about to change dramatically!

Going into the close of September 21, the equity-only put/call ratio had been posting *extremely high* readings the entire week. Beginning with Monday's close, the week went as follows: 1.10, 1.03, 0.71, 1.21, and 1.14. In a word, amazing! Very rarely do you see such readings above 1.00, let alone multiple daily readings all in the same week! This was quite bullish from a contrarian point of view.

This, combined with the extremely high VIX readings, let you know that a rally was in the offing. Too many people had become too bearish!

A bearish indicator would be consistent readings of 0.35 or lower. What this tells you is that only 35 puts were purchased for every 100 calls. Since a lot more calls are being bought than puts, people are betting that stock prices will rise. As a contrarian you would view that as bearish, since there's too much optimism.

As the market was making its record-breaking run to new highs in July 1997, the equity-only put/call ratio was posting readings below 0.35 for some time. Investors had become too bullish.

Once again, at such times it's best to play "defense." Either you eat a little humble pie on your own or the market will end up force-feeding it to you. Oh, and by the way, guess who picks up the tab? You do!

> As a contrarian when investors are too bullish, you turn bearish and if they're too bearish, you turn bullish.

As a contrarian when investors are too bullish, you turn bearish and if they're too bearish, you turn bullish.

You can check this reading on a daily basis by clicking on the "VIX & Put/Call" link at **www.planetcash.com.**

Surveys

Various investment surveys are taken that measure the attitudes and opinions of professional traders, advisors, industry insiders and investors on a number of different issues. While some of these may seem unimportant, there is one that you should pay very close attention to as an individual trader.

There is a survey conducted by *Investors Intelligence* that measures the bullishness or bearishness of more than 140 independent stock market newsletter writers and advisors. For more than 30 years, the results have shown that high bullish and low bearish readings coincide with market tops, while high bearish and low bullish readings coincide with market bottoms.

This is due to the inevitable impact newsletter writers and advisors have on those who read their commentary. What they think influences the thoughts and ultimately the actions of their subscribers. It promotes the herd mentality!

If you pay someone money for their newsletter or advice then, most likely, you will hold their opinion and insights in high regard. As such, you're investment decisions will be influenced by what they think. If they're bullish, you'll be bullish and vice versa.

That's why this survey is such a great contrarian indicator – the greater the number of bears, the bigger the upside potential. The more bulls that exist, the greater the risk of a market decline.

For example, even though both the DJIA and NASDAQ had been enjoying sizeable gains the entire month of April 2001, sentiment remained muted. Investors Intelligence reported that 43.9% were bullish and 41.8% were bearish.

What's interesting is that the percentage of bulls continued to decline, even though the market had been rallying. From a contrarian standpoint that's exactly what you like to see – if you're a bull, that is.

Keep in mind these were the same people that back in February 2001 were unbelievably bullish when the market was still in a freefall! In fact,the percentage of investment advisors that were bullish hit new five-year highs, yet the market didn't bottom until the third week of March!

DJ-30 - Dow Jones Industrials
09/25/01 9605.59 9696.54 9506.36 9659.97 15798 +56.11

The market continued to slide in the face of overly bullish Investment Advisors.

The percentage of bullish Investment Advisors continued to climb even though the market was breaking down. As a result, you knew the bottom hadn't been reached yet.

As you might expect, on the market did bottom in March the percentage of bullish Investment Advisors had fallen dramatically!

11000
10500
10000
9500
9000
8500

DEC   01   FEB   MAR   APR   MAY   JUN   JUL   AUG   SEP

Courtesy of TC2000®.

Remember, excessive bullishness in the face of deteriorating technicals and fundamentals is bearish. Consequently, at that time you knew the market had further to fall.

However, excessive bearishness in the face of improving technicals and fundamentals is bullish.

Later, in May 2001, complacency began to be reflected in polls. The percentage of bullish investment advisors, as measured by Investor's

> Remember, excessive bullishness in the face of deteriorating technicals and fundamentals is bearish.

Intelligence's survey, had climbed to 50% while 35.4% were bearish. The trend only continued because in July the percentage of bullish investment advisors climbed above 50% while less than 24% were bearish.

Well, you know what the results were. The market continued down its slippery slope before beginning its breathtaking plunge at the beginning of September.

The reverse was true, leading into latter part of September, coinciding with the bottom of September 21. The week before,

> Excessive bearishness in the face of improving technicals and fundamentals is bullish.

only 35.7% of those surveyed were bullish and 37.6% were bearish. That was a tremendous drop in the percentage of bulls and around a 7% jump in the percentage of bears – definitely bullish. And it got even better!

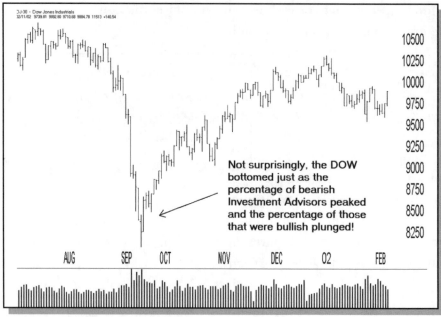

DJ-30 - Dow Jones Industrials
12/11/02 9739.81 9892.90 9710.68 9884.78 11513 +140.54

Not surprisingly, the DOW bottomed just as the percentage of bearish Investment Advisors peaked and the percentage of those that were bullish plunged!

Courtesy of TC2000®.

The same week the market bottomed, the percentage of bullish investment advisors fell to 33.7%. To put that in perspective, the lowest reading in the last five years is 31.9%. The percentage of those that were bearish jumped to 42.1%. The highest percentage of bears in the last five years is 47.5%. So just as the DJIA bottomed the percentage of bulls fell to very low levels and the percentage of bears spiked. It's amazing how predictable these indicators are! It pays to be a contrarian!

Selling Short

As you already know, bulls buy stocks and/or implement option strategies with the expectations that stock prices will rise. Conversely, bears sell stocks short or implement option strategies with the hope that stock prices will fall. Both ways can be very profitable. By better understanding short selling, you can gain an edge that will go a long way in helping you trade from the long side.

Selling stock short involves selling stock that you do not own. So how can you sell something you don't own? Easy, you borrow it. Once borrowed (not all stocks can be borrowed), you sell it in the open market. As a bear you want the price of the stock to drop so you can buy back the shares at a lower price and pocket the difference. You want to sell high and buy low.

While some view this as an unsavory approach to making money, you can use it to profit handsomely-predominantly by taking a contrarian point of view.

There are two things to keep in mind with respect to short selling. First of all, if you short a stock you have unlimited risk. Shares that you sold at $45, for example, could theoretically rally indefinitely. Thus, your exposure is unlimited.

Conversely, your upside or profit potential is capped. If the shares drop in price you'll make money, but the most that you can make is the difference between the price you sold at ($45) and $0. Therefore, $45 per share would be the most you could profit. It is for these reasons-unlimited risk and limited reward–that many frown upon short selling as a viable strategy.

A better strategy would be an option strategy involving puts where your risk is capped (the most you could lose is the amount paid for the put), yet your upside can also be quite profitable. So if you don't necessarily want to short stocks as a way of making money in the stock market, how can you use the above-mentioned factors to our advantage?

You are going to look at the amount of short selling taking place in a particular issue, thereby measuring the sentiment of traders with respect to that particular issue. Once again, you will use this as a contrarian indicator.

One measure you can use is known as *days to cover*, also known as the *short ratio*. Cover is just another word for buying the stock back. You calculate this by taking the total number of shares held short on a particular stock and divide it by the average daily number of shares traded in that particular stock over the last 50 days. The result is the "days to cover" – the minimum number of days it would take (based on the average of current daily volume) for all the shorted shares to be bought back in the open market.

Obviously volume changes from day to day but nonetheless it's a good number to use. Furthermore, keep in mind that investors will continue to buy the stock because they're bullish. This further reduces the quantity of shares available to those who would like to cover, and as a result, the days to cover tends to be on the low side. To help you better understand how this happens, let's take a look at an example.

First of all, assume XYZ Company has 250,000 shares that have been sold short. The average number of shares traded on a daily basis in XYZ's stock is 50,000. The days to cover would be five. You take 250,000 and divide it by the average daily volume, which is 50,000. The result is 5. This means that if all those people who sold XYZ's stock short wanted to buy back the stock, it would take five days to do so.

The larger the number, the more pessimism surrounding the stock. Bears feel the stock is overvalued and there are a lot of them. So how can you use this information to your advantage?

Let's say prices start falling – just what the bears ordered. In order to lock in their profits and close out the position, those who are short the stock will have to buy the same number of shares to replace that which they borrowed. If they sold 1,000 shares short at $55, then they would need to buy 1,000 shares. If they did so at $46, then they would make $9 per share profit (excluding commissions).

But look at what else is happening. In that shorts are buying to lock in their gains, *short-covering* acts as a buffer against falling prices. In other words, you have a guaranteed "buyers club." This is why in a downtrend you will see prices try to rally. That's why it's so difficult to call a bottom in a stock that's in a downtrend. Too many people get suckered into a rally thinking it's new buying coming into the market, but it may very well just represent short covering. While a few brave bulls may be entering the market the majority may ultimately be short sellers.

> Thus, a very large short position can support the price of the stock to a certain extent, but once the covering is done, then natural selling drives the stock down further.

Thus, a very large short position can support the price of the stock to a certain extent, but once the covering is done, then natural selling drives the stock down further. However, if bad news comes out, then the stock could very well get hammered. Bears will stand on the sideline, watching the stock freefall before they start buying to lock in their gains.

The flip side of the coin is when the news starts getting better – exactly what the bears *didn't* order. Things get very interesting at this point and quite possibly very profitable.

What happens as the stock price starts to rise? Bears start feeling some pain. If prices rise, short sellers start losing money. In order for them to cut their losses, they will have to buy back the shares they sold short, at a higher price. If they sold the stock short at $55 but the stock rises to $57, $61, $64, and so on, they will have to decide at what point to cut their losses. This is what is typically referred to as a "short squeeze" – the short sellers are getting squeezed financially and have to run for the exits!

The key is that in order for them to cut their losses they have to buy the stock. If there is a huge short position, it means that there are going to be a lot of new buyers coming back into the market and buying. This drives the stock even higher, and in some cases can be like throwing gasoline on an open fire. Prices jump hard and fast. Their rise becomes nearly vertical as short sellers panic to cover their positions and cut their losses.

By paying attention to the days to cover, you can measure the future buying pressure in a particular stock. As a contrarian you can use this information to see which stocks people are betting against. If the news starts turning positive, then you will see a lot of buyers entering the market, not only from the bullish camp, but also from the bearish one who are forced to cut their losses – and in a hurry!

With stocks that are technically in good shape, you like to see the number of shares shorted increase as it indicates rising pessimism. This can help sustain an uptrend. Conversely, if the number of shares shorted drops considerably, it is a bearish indicator. Our guaranteed buyers' club is diminishing in strength. This can prove troubling since new sellers will eventually enter the market and drive prices lower. You always want a healthy dose of pessimism.

In Summary:

1. In the absence of bad news or no news, a large short position can "hold" a stock up against downward selling pressure.
2. With bad news the "dam" inherent in short-covering will most likely give way. This happens as short sellers ride the wave of pessimism downward as far as they can.
3. As news turns positive and prices rise, short sellers will be forced to cut their losses and buy the stock back at higher prices. This can add fuel to an already uptrending market.
4. As a contrarian you like to see an increase in the number of shares shorted in a particular stock. If the number falls off dramatically you lose your guaranteed buyers club. One would prefer to have buying pressure in reserve and not selling pressure.

In order to profit as a contrarian you need to determine the days to cover. You can get this from your broker or at **www.planetcash.com.**

The website provides a nice shortcut, in that it's already calculated for you. Simply click on "News" found in the left hand column. Enter the ticker symbol of the stock you're interested in the space provided. Now click on "Profile" listed to the right of "More Info." Once the page is displayed, simply scroll down to the bottom of the page and on the right handside you'll find the *short ratio*, also know as the aforementioned *days to cover.*

If all those people who have already shorted the stock wanted to buy it back, how many days would it take to accomplish? The higher the number, the more bullish it is. It tells you how much buying pressure is out there in the marketplace and how long it could theoretically last. If you have a bullish opinion on the stock, this will bode well.

Since a lot of traders don't expect much from the stock, you can benefit on the long side as the tide turns. Better news will drive prices higher and force short sellers to cut their losses. This can cause prices to move vertically as panic sets in amid the bears. Another thing to consider is if the number of days to cover drops off. It lets you know short sellers have locked in profits and feel things may turn positive. As a result, any good news may have already been discounted into the current price of the stock. It has a dampening effect on the stock as no new buyers are forced into the marketplace. Buying pressure dries up.

In conclusion, by thinking like a contrarian you can profit handsomely by knowing when to walk away or trade in the opposite direction. To that end, the *VIX, equity-only put/call ratio, Investor's Intelligence survey,* and d*ays to cover* or *short ratio* will help you not only measure market sentiment, but can act as canaries in the coal mine.

By looking for extreme levels of bullishness and/or bearishness as measured by these indicators you can avoid the *wrong-way crowd*. While there are no guarantees, using this information will keep you out of trouble more often than not. When an extreme is reached, it provides you with an excellent opportunity to take the road less traveled. If history is any indication, such opportunities will continue to present themselves. The reality is that the stock market is driven by emotions and emotions are not going away any time soon.

But how do you know when to buy or sell a stock when sentiment isn't at an extreme? How do you know whether a stock is in an uptrend or downtrend? The secret lies in identifying and harnessing explosive trading opportunities – exactly what you'll learn in the next two chapters.

Key Points to Remember

➤ Market participants are often referred to as the "herd" or "crowd." Crowds create powerful trends. As a result, you don't want to fight them. Make the trend your friend.

➤ The key to being a successful investor/trader is milking the prevailing trend for all its worth and then knowing when to walk away.

➤ The crowd is right most of the time. It's when the trend changes that they get it wrong. This often occurs because they become either too bullish or too bearish. Savvy traders learn how to identify when such extremes take place, capturing huge money making opportunities in the process.

➤ This is what it means to be a contrarian. You take the road less traveled – you head in the opposite direction.

➤ Surveys can be used to measure market sentiment. High bullish readings and low bearish readings coincide with market tops, while high bearish and low bullish readings occur at market bottoms.

➤ Knowing the quantity of calls and puts being bought at any given time can give you insight into the bullishness and/or bearishness of option traders. This is known as the *equity-only put/call ratio*. High readings denote too much bearishness, which is bullish as a contrarian. Low readings denote too much bullishness, which is bearish as a contrarian.

➤ The *VIX* is a tool you can use to measure optimism or pessimism in the marketplace. As a contrarian indicator, the VIX has been uncanny in predicting market tops and bottoms. Too much fear (a spike in the VIX) is bullish, while complacency (a low VIX reading) foreshadows an explosive move is near. However, that move can be in either direction.

➤ You can look at the amount of short selling in a particular stock and determine the *days to cover* or *short ratio*. High readings can be bullish, as buyers may be forced back into the market. Low readings diminish buying pressure, which can be bearish.

CHAPTER 13

A Day Late
and a Dollar Richer

"Riches have wings, and sometimes they fly away of themselves, and sometimes they must be set flying to bring in more."
– Francis Bacon

Wow! Did Francis Bacon ever have a handle on the nature of money! He certainly was a man whose thinking was well ahead of his time. Speaking of money and time, have you ever felt as if you can't make money in the stock market because you're never in the right place at the right time? Perhaps you've been led to believe that the "window of opportunity" is small and as a result, your timing needs to be perfect. Or maybe you've heard that the opportunities to make money in the market are too brief or sporadic, making it nearly impossible for the "little guy" to succeed. Well, take heart, because nothing could be further from the truth! In fact, at times, it actually pays to be late on recognizing a new opportunity. Consider the case of Elston Howard.

As late as the early 1970s professional baseball players were not being paid the astronomical sums of money they are being paid today. In fact, many "star" players were forced to seek off-season employment to supplement their incomes. One such player was Elston Howard, the great, unheralded catcher for the New York Yankees in the 1960's. (Elston Howard replaced the Hall-of-Fame catcher Yogi Berra behind the plate. He ultimately was involved in numerous World Series appearances with other Yankee greats and Hall-of-Famer's such as Mickey Mantle and Whitey Ford.)

Howard played in an era where baseball salaries were not driven by television revenue, advertising, or endorsement deals. Today, many players of that era are quite outspoken about those times. They believe they weren't in the right place at the right time; they believe that the opportunity to make money from playing baseball just didn't exist then.

But this couldn't have been farther from the truth for Elston Howard. Instead of feeling as though he had been cheated (in terms of salary), Howard became more and more focused during his long playing career on developing a tool that would simply help him become a better player. He wasn't concerned with his plight; rather, he believed that his playing opportunity would, in the long run, create other opportunities for him.

To make a long story short, Howard invented the weighted "batting doughnut." It's actually a lead ring that's slipped onto a baseball bat to help develop stronger, quicker hands that will eventually help a batter with his bat speed and swing. Today the batting doughnut is a common tool used by baseball players, of all skill levels, across a myriad of countries worldwide. (In fact, the next time you're at the ballpark, you can't help but notice the ubiquitous baseball doughnut.)

Though it took years to develop, Elston finally spotted an opportunity that enabled him to realize unbelievable financial rewards. An opportunity, I might add, that created wealth for him long after his playing career was over.

Have you ever overlooked some profitable opportunities in the past? Have you looked back and realized, in retrospect, that you had a chance to change your financial situation but didn't? Have you kicked yourself for not making a move when you could have? Everyone has. So take a second look at your current financial situation and see if you've been missing any promising opportunities that may be right under your nose.

By constantly searching for such opportunities, the most promising ones may present themselves when least expected. Elston Howard spotted a lucrative opportunity and seized it. That's what you need to do. In fact, some of the greater financial rewards in life do come "a day late and a dollar richer."

Promising Money-Making Opportunities Should Capture and Arouse Your Attention!

So when it comes to the stock market, how do you recognize a promising money making opportunity? And more importantly, how do you determine which direction a stock is headed? Actually, the answers to both these questions are quite simple.

There's a timeless adage found on Wall Street that says, "The trend is your friend." While this may sound overly simplistic or cliché, it is the foundation of many a fortune. The key to striking it rich on Wall Street has nothing to do with being in the right place at the right time, but simply identifying and harnessing the unbelievable power of an established trend. Accordingly, you can be a day or two late and many dollars richer.

> The key to striking it rich on Wall Street has nothing to do with being in the right place at the right time, but simply identifying and harnessing the unbelievable power of an established trend.

The Windows of Opportunity are Often Quite Large When Powerful Trends Exist!

When such trends are seized upon, you're in a position to maximize your gains and strike it rich! Remember, all you're interested in is capturing 50% to 60% of the prevailing trend. If you try to capture 100% of the trend you're forcing yourself to pick the exact top and bottom – a nearly impossible task. You see, that requires perfection, and unfortunately, the stock market is not for perfectionists.

Even trying to pick up a point or two, here and there, is tough to do. What's more, such an approach ultimately leads to financial headache and heartache.

This chapter will introduce you to three basic, yet powerful tools to help you determine the direction and the strength of the trend. They are: trendlines, moving averages, and volume.

All three are easy to implement, enabling you to identify the trend more quickly and accurately. Above all, these tools will prevent you from trying to pick market tops and/or bottoms – a losing game at best!

If you could forecast which way stock prices were headed, how much money do you think you could make? A lot! That's why so many brokerage houses, hedge funds, and mutual funds spend so much time and money trying to predict a stock's future. In fact, there are two schools of thought to help in this cause, *fundamental analysis and technical analysis.* Let's look at both.

The Story

Fundamental analysis takes a look at the "story" of a company – profits, revenues, management, products, growth rate, debt, P/E ratio, book value, net asset value, and so forth. Now, I don't know about you, but just the thought of trying to understand all these things puts me to sleep. Seriously, are you confused by all this "mumbo-jumbo?" When I'm confused, I find it hard to take action. It induces "paralysis of analysis."

During my live trainings, I often take a look at the charts of various companies. Students will often ask:

> "Steve, what is the company's earnings per share for the last quarter?"
> I don't know.
> "What is the P/E ratio?"
> I don't care.
> "What's the book value?"
> I have no idea.

To say the least, they look at me and they're a little perplexed. Frankly, I've never made a selling or buying decision based on any of these components. Why?

The answer lies in the following statement by a student: "Steve, I don't get it! The stock has good earnings, a good management team, a great product, a low P/E ratio, and their debt seems to be under control. But the stock keeps going down." *Bingo!* That's why I don't use fundamental analysis. It tells me nothing about whether people are currently buying or selling the stock!

You see, Wall Street is based upon perception and not reality. Traders drive down the street looking through their windshield and not in their rear-view mirror. They're not as concerned with what a company has done as much as what a company will do. They're focused on the stock's future potential, not its past results.

> Wall Street is based upon perception and not reality.

That's why a company can have terrible fundamentals but still go up in price. If Wall Street believes earnings will be great in the future, they will buy today. They buy the stock in anticipation of good news down the road.

The Internet craze is a perfect example of this. Investors paid astronomical amounts for companies, even though those companies were losing huge sums of money and they weren't projected to be profitable for years to come. Those investors were buying in anticipation of these companies making lots of money in the future. In fact, it was actually "fashionable" to lose money – at least before the bubble burst!

When trading, avoid basing your buying and selling decisions on the story alone. Why? You are marrying a short-term tactic (options) with a long-term strategy (fundamentals). The time horizons are different. As a result, you'll find it much more difficult to make money. Fundamentals may take months or years to play out. Eventually, good fundamentals will be rewarded, but what good does that do you if you own a two-month option? You would have been better off purchasing LEAPS®!

Consequently, as a shorter-term trader you will, for the most part, find fundamental analysis useless! If anything, use a blending of both.

Charts Don't Lie

When you hear the term technical analysis, think in terms of pictures. Perhaps a better term to use would be "chart analysis." Numbers can be confusing but pictures are, after all, worth a thousand words!

Technical analysis looks at price patterns and indicators such as: volume, RSI, stochastics, moving averages, Bollinger bands, and MACD, to name only a few. You can find all these indicators, and more, on any charting program. However, using too many can prevent you from taking action, so keep it simple! The more you can simplify your trading plan, the more effective and profitable you'll be. Don't make it more complicated than it already is.

The purpose of looking at a chart is to know when you should buy or sell a particular stock. It's that simple!

Make the Trend Your Friend

One of the easiest ways to harness the predictability of charts is to make the trend your friend. This one principle will make you more money than anything else I can teach you in this book. Trading against the prevailing trend is a very costly mistake and should be avoided at all costs!

> Trading against the prevailing trend is a very costly mistake and should be avoided at all costs! A trend in motion tends to stay in motion.

An important fact to remember is that a trend in motion tends to stay in motion. Hey, I bet that sounds like something you learned in physics. That same truth can be found in the stock market as well.

Don't forget, "herds" are powerful. They are an awesome force, so it doesn't pay to buck the trend. Just because it has gone up over an extended period of time is not a good reason to start shorting or buying puts on a particular stock. Plenty of traders have been crushed trying to bet against a powerful trend. As you will find out later, there are safer ways to anticipate and identify reversals.

So, what is a trend? Well, there are basically three types of trends to look for:

An *uptrend* consists of higher highs and higher lows. The bulls are stronger than the bears and their buying forces prices higher.

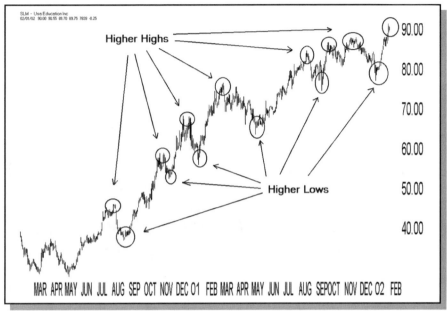

Courtesy of TC2000®.

A *downtrend* is marked by lower highs and lower lows. The bears are stronger than the bulls and drag prices lower.

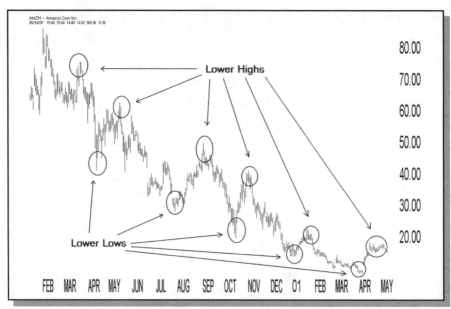

Courtesy of TC2000®.

A *trendless* stock is in a standoff between the bulls and bears. No discernible trend is evident. The stock is stuck in a trading range.

Courtesy of TC2000®.

If you buy a stock that is stuck in a trading range, frustration is sure to follow. Consequently, your success as a trader ultimately depends on your ability to correctly identify which type of trend exists.

After experiencing an impressive 75% gain from its August lows, FNM has been stuck in a trading range since the beginning of 2001.

Courtesy of TC2000®.

Take a look at the chart of **Cardinal Health.** Do you see the trend? It really depends upon the time frame I'm referring to, doesn't it? Overall, the stock is in a nice uptrend over the span of the chart pictured. However, there was a period of time when the stock was trendless.

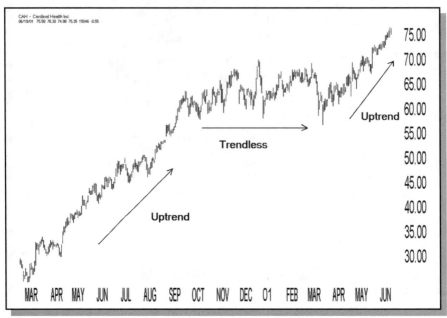

Courtesy of TC2000®.

As a result, trends can be expressed in terms of days, weeks, months, and years. I like to put them into three general categories:

Short term – a few weeks to a few months.
Intermediate – a few months to around six months.
Long term – six months or more.

The longer a specific trend lasts the more important it is. For example, what a stock has done over the last year is far more significant than where it trades over the next ten minutes, yet both can make you money. It depends on how quickly you want to buy or sell.

If you trade using hourly charts, it pays to look at the daily chart. If you use daily charts, make sure you consult a weekly chart. If you use weekly charts, take a look at the monthly chart. This keeps you focused on the "big picture."

> The longer a specific trend lasts the more important it is.

An important point to remember is that different time frames may also present conflicting signals. For example, what looks like a downtrend on a daily chart may be a minor pullback in an uptrend on a weekly chart. Always defer to the longer time frame, since it carries more significance. When in doubt, trade in the direction of the long-term trend.

> When in doubt, trade in the direction of the long-term trend.

Trendlines

Besides looking at different time frames, making use of a trendline is key to your being able to see prevailing trends. There are two you will use: horizontal trendlines and moving averages. Trendlines are used when a stock is trendless and moving averages are used when a stock is trending.

How do you draw a trendline? Just draw a straight, horizontal line that connects at least two points. This enables you to identify support and resistance. Keep in mind that these are areas and not specific price points. For example, support may be 53 to about 55. Resistance may be at 75 to 77.

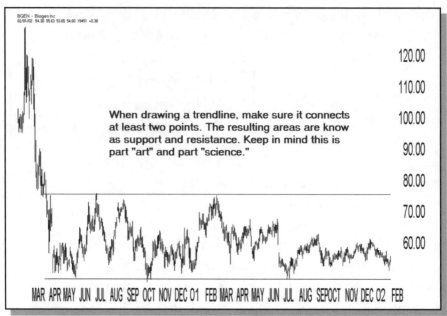

When drawing a trendline, make sure it connects at least two points. The resulting areas are know as support and resistance. Keep in mind this is part "art" and part "science."

Courtesy of TC2000®.

Basically, all the tools you need are a pencil, paper (chart), and a ruler. It doesn't get much easier than that!

Moving Averages

When a stock is trending, moving averages are the tool of choice. A moving average is an average of closing prices over a specified period. All you need to do is specify your desired moving average and the charting program (web-based or stand-alone software) does the rest, that is, it plots a smoothed line on the chart for you. Now you can ascertain the trend and in which direction it is heading. How?

All you need to do is ask yourself two simple questions:

1. Is the moving average rising, falling, or moving sideways?
2. Is the price of the stock above or below the moving average?

> If the moving average is rising and the price of the stock is above it, then the stock is in an uptrend. If the moving average is falling and the price of the stock is below it, then the stock is in a downtrend.

If the moving average is rising and the price of the stock is above it, then the stock is in an uptrend. If the moving average is falling and the price of the stock is below it, then the stock is in a downtrend. As you can see, this is fairly elementary. Making money becomes a lot easier when you simplify your decision-making process. You avoid the dreaded "paralysis of analysis." You can use this technique to determine the direction of the three phases of trend (short-, intermediate-, and long-term).

To do so, it will be necessary to use a different moving average for the specific trend you're trying to identify. For the short-term trend, use an eight to ten-day moving average. For the intermediate trend, use an eighteen to 21-day moving average. For the long-term trend, use the 40- to 50-day moving average. Make sure you only select one from each category.

Now, you can plot one or more moving averages on a given chart. I have found that using two moving averages is ideal, enabling you to quickly and easily determine the strength and the direction of the trend. They will also help you refine your entry and exit points.

For example, when the shorter is above the longer moving average, and both lines are rising, a strong uptrend is underway. Since I'm more of an intermediate- to long-term trader I favor using the eighteen- and 40-day moving averages. Moreover, in order for me to consider using bullish strategies, a stock must also be trading above the 40-day moving average.

Notice how the eighteen-day is above the 40-day moving average on the chart of Deluxe Corp (DLX), and both lines are rising. The price is also above the 40-day moving average. The stock is in a nice, strong uptrend. A trend in motion tends to stay in motion.

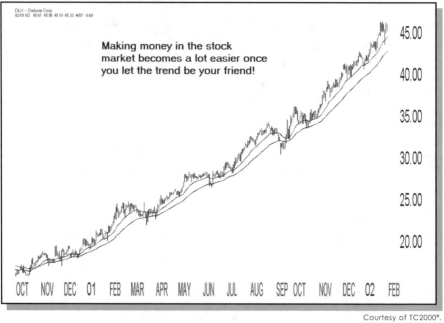

Courtesy of TC2000®.

Conversely, if the shorter moving average is below the longer moving average and both lines are falling, the stock is in a downtrend. To consider bearish strategies, the price of the stock must also be, at a minimum, below the 40-day moving average. So, if the eighteen-day is below the 40-day moving average and both lines are falling, and the price of the stock is below the 40-day moving average, a downtrend is in place. You can clearly see this looking at the chart of JDS Uniphase (JDSU) below.

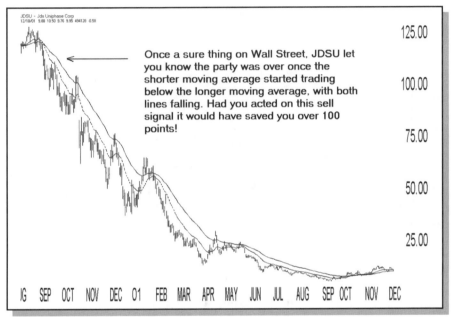

JDSU - Jds Uniphase Corp
12/10/01 9.88 10.50 9.76 9.95 494128 -0.59

Once a sure thing on Wall Street, JDSU let you know the party was over once the shorter moving average started trading below the longer moving average, with both lines falling. Had you acted on this sell signal it would have saved you over 100 points!

125.00
100.00
75.00
50.00
25.00

IG   SEP   OCT   NOV   DEC   01   FEB   MAR   APR   MAY   JUN   JUL   AUG   SEP OCT   NOV   DEC

Courtesy of TC2000®.

Remember, when all phases of a trend are in sync, it gives you the highest probability that the current trend will stay in place. Don't fight it! The trend is your friend! If you stick with this simple rule of thumb, you will stay out of trouble.

I should point out that moving averages work great in a trending environment but they are useless when stocks are in trading ranges. As you can see from the Biogen (BGEN) chart below, it becomes impossible to determine where prices are headed.

This is why horizontal trendlines are superior in such instances. In addition, the more times a stock bounces off support or fails at resistance, the stronger those areas become.

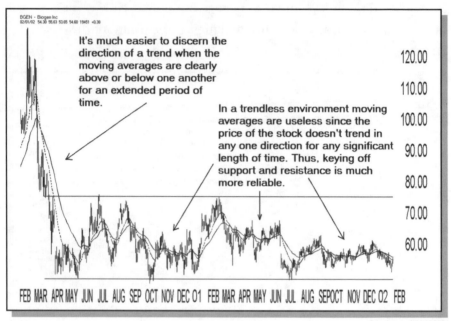

It's much easier to discern the direction of a trend when the moving averages are clearly above or below one another for an extended period of time.

In a trendless environment moving averages are useless since the price of the stock doesn't trend in any one direction for any significant length of time. Thus, keying off support and resistance is much more reliable.

Courtesy of TC2000®.

Now that you have learned how to determine the direction and strength of the prevailing trend, how can you use moving averages to refine your timing? When should you buy or sell?

Whether you use trendlines or moving averages, how a stock reacts around them will dictate your timing. For example, you learned earlier that when a stock breaks out above resistance or below support, you have a green light to buy the breakout. In addition, if a stock pulls back and bounces off support or rallies and rolls over at resistance, you can enter a trade.

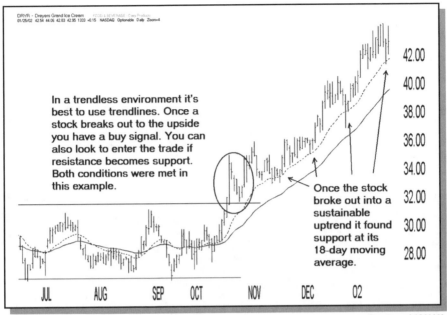

In a trendless environment it's best to use trendlines. Once a stock breaks out to the upside you have a buy signal. You can also look to enter the trade if resistance becomes support. Both conditions were met in this example.

Once the stock broke out into a sustainable uptrend it found support at its 18-day moving average.

Courtesy of TC2000®.

What's more, moving averages can act as support in uptrends or resistance in downtrends. A bullish signal is given when prices pull back to the rising moving average and bounce off. Do not buy as the stock is pulling back. Wait for it to find support and bounce higher before entering the trade. Otherwise, how do you know the stock isn't headed for a deeper correction? Realize that some stocks will find support at their intermediate moving average while others may find support at the long-term moving average. How can you tell? Look at the chart and see what it has done in the past.

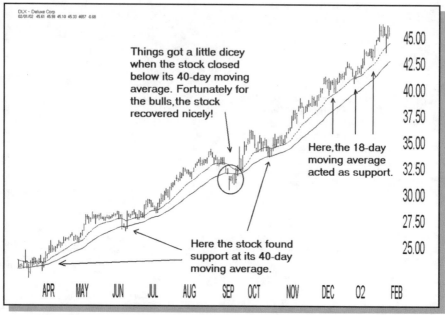

DLX - Deluxe Corp
02/01/02 45.61 45.98 45.10 45.33 4657 -0.68

Things got a little dicey
when the stock closed
below its 40-day moving
average. Fortunately for
the bulls, the stock
recovered nicely!

Here, the 18-day
moving average
acted as support.

Here the stock found
support at its 40-day
moving average.

45.00
42.50
40.00
37.50
35.00
32.50
30.00
27.50
25.00

APR   MAY   JUN   JUL   AUG   SEP   OCT   NOV   DEC   02   FEB

Courtesy of TC2000®.

The reverse is true in a downtrend. The intermediate- or long-term moving averages will act as resistance. If prices rally back to the declining moving average and then fall away, you can implement your choice of bearish strategies. Avoid putting the trade on as the stock is rallying. By waiting for the stock to reverse you'll avoid fighting the trend. As always, be patient.

You can also use a moving average to prevent you from chasing stocks in the midst of an explosive move. Have you ever bought an option on a red-hot stock, only to watch it experience a sharp reversal thereafter? Or perhaps you bought a put on a stock in a precipitous freefall, only to see it turn on a dime and head higher? Been there, done that! So here's a tip to help you avoid that in the future.

Pay attention to how quickly the stock is rising or falling. The steeper the climb or descent, the more unsustainable it becomes. Why? A good analogy would be a sprinter. Sprinters will run as hard as they can, but only for a short distance. They can't sustain the pace over a longer period of time.

The same is true for stocks. As prices make a dramatic rise or fall, the stock will need to stop and catch its breath. The stock needs to

> The steeper the climb or descent, the more unsustainable it becomes.

consolidate before another up- or down-leg can resume. If it doesn't, the trend tends to reverse just as fast.

You can determine whether a stock is rising or falling too sharp, too fast by comparing the stock's price in relation to the intermediate (eighteen- to 21-day) moving average. The further prices get away from the moving average, the more cautious

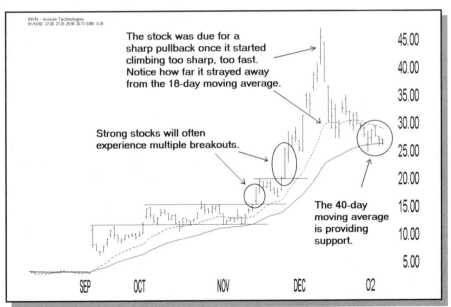

INVN - Invision Technologies
01/10/02 27.00 27.20 25.90 26.73 6360 -0.28

The stock was due for a sharp pullback once it started climbing too sharp, too fast. Notice how far it strayed away from the 18-day moving average.

Strong stocks will often experience multiple breakouts.

The 40-day moving average is providing support.

SEP   OCT   NOV   DEC   02

Courtesy of TC2000®.

you need to become. By all means, don't chase the stock! Wait for it to pull back to support or rally into resistance before placing a trade.

If you find yourself holding such a position, it would be wise to take your money off the table – "don't look a gift horse in the mouth." The sheer velocity of the move dictates it can't be sustained indefinitely

Such moves are usually marked by sharp reversals, particularly parabolic moves to the upside. It typically falls under its own weight. And when they fall this way, they fall hard and fast! Take a look at Rare Medium Group (RRRR) and you'll see how too sharp a rise can end in ruin.

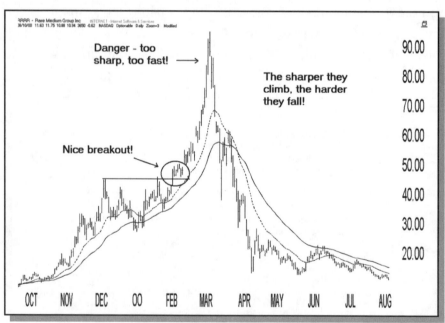

Courtesy of TC2000®.

Another powerful use of the moving average is to combine two moving averages to help identify bullish and bearish entry signals. The signals are as follows: a *bullish signal* is triggered when the shorter moving average crosses up through the longer moving average. A *bearish signal* is triggered when the shorter moving average crosses down through the longer moving average.

For example, a bullish signal is given when the eighteen- crosses up through the 40-day moving average or the ten- crosses up through the 20-day moving average. A bearish signal is given if the eighteen- crosses down through the 40-day moving average or the ten- crosses down through the 20-day moving average.

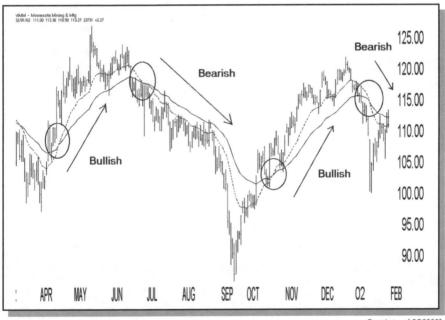

Courtesy of TC2000®.

It should be noted that a moving average is a lagging indicator and is not predictive in nature. As a result, the signals will always be late. Nonetheless, this approach can still be used profitably. You see, when a shorter moving average crosses a longer moving average, it denotes a reversal in trend. In that the signal lags, the new trend will already be underway by the time you find out about it.

> A moving average is a lagging indicator and is not predictive in nature.

This prevents you from picking tops and bottoms, and the new trend is most likely in its early stages.

You can also anticipate a change of trend by looking at the distance between two moving averages. When a stock is in a strong uptrend, the shorter moving average will maintain a constant distance away from the longer moving average. When they narrow and come together, the stock is losing momentum.

Volume

Volume is the final piece of the puzzle that should be used to provide a clearer picture of a stock's trend and price action. As I told you previously, price is a function of supply and demand. Volume reflects the number of shares that trade on a daily basis. By taking a look at price in conjunction with volume, you can determine whether supply is overwhelming demand (bearish) or demand is outstripping supply (bullish).

By the way, this is the only other indicator I use besides moving averages when analyzing a stock. By using just a few indicators, I can make my buying and selling decisions quicker and more efficiently. Keep it simple!

Another reason why volume is so important is because it lets you take the pulse of the market. Does anybody care about the stock going down? Is anyone panicking? If the stock price is heading higher, are traders jumping in or indifferent? What's the level of emotion? So how do you determine whether volume is heavy or light for any stock?

An easy way to measure buying and selling interest is to pay attention to the height of the volume bars. The vertical bars are displayed at the bottom of a chart's window. If the height of those bars is getting progressively larger, volume is increasing. If they are getting progressively smaller, volume is shrinking.

Here are some rules of thumb to help you interpret volume and price action:

Trading volume in relation to a stock's price action indicates whether it is being accumulated or distributed by institutional traders, hedge funds, and mutual funds. As you can imagine, accumulation and distribution often lead to major price movement.

> An easy way to measure buying and selling interest is to pay attention to the height of the volume bars.

A stock that closes higher on heavier volume than the previous day, is said to be under *accumulation*. If you're looking for bullish opportunities, these are the ones you want to focus on. An early clue is a narrowing of the daily price range accompanied by an increase in volume – big buyers have begun to arrive. The stock is primed to explode higher if heavy demand continues.

If volume rises in the direction of the trend, it validates the legitimacy of the move. It tells you the bulls don't want to be left behind. They want in *now!*

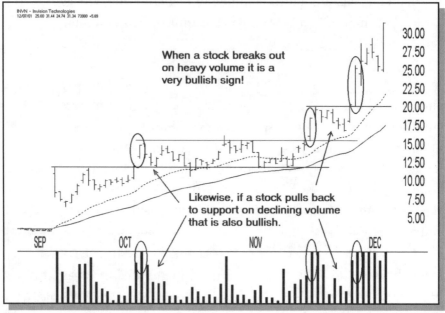

Courtesy of TC2000®.

If a stock breaks out above resistance on heavy volume, the probability of a stock continuing in the direction of the breakout is much higher than if it takes place on lighter volume.

If volume contracts as the stock pulls back to support, it lets you know that the bulls aren't too concerned with the pullback. Otherwise, they'd be panicking and dumping their positions. Since volume is tapering off, they still believe in their position. If the stock bounces off support, you want to see volume expand. A lack of volume would indicate a lack of interest and the rally is suspect.

Finally, it is bullish if a stock finishes in the higher part of its daily range on heavy volume.

If a stock closes lower on heavier volume than the previous day, it is said to be under *distribution*. Bearish opportunities should be your focus. As supply increases, prices fall. Stocks under distribution will often fall for some time after the selling begins.

If after a sustained move higher you begin to see narrow daily bars, with little or no price gains, and heavy volume, it represents churning or topping action. The odds of a decline increase if this occurs over a number of days. The "smart money" is getting out.

If prices break down through support and volume swells, it tells you sellers want out at any price! The probability of a stock continuing in the direction of the breakout is much higher

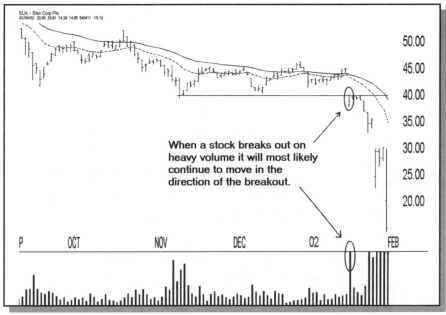

When a stock breaks out on heavy volume it will most likely continue to move in the direction of the breakout.

Courtesy of TC2000®.

if it takes place on heavy rather than light volume. The bears are in control and the bulls are running for cover!

Additionally, it is more bearish if the stock finishes in the lower part of its daily range on heavy volume.

The same could be said of rallies back to resistance. If the rally is accompanied by lighter volume, it is bearish in nature. Light volume is typically a precursor to a reversal. If buyers were really interested in taking advantage of the uptrend, then they would be buying with much more fervor. They don't believe the stock can sustain its climb. If the stock stalls at resistance and rolls over, volume should increase before you implement bearish strategies

Sharp rallies and declines require the irrational and emotional participation of the crowd. When a rally runs out of new participants, a stock can easily reverse. After long rallies or declines, watch for a day of very high volume. This is typically climactic in nature and signifies "exhaustion". Reversals generally follow.

> I recommend you avoid stocks that don't trade at least 100,000 shares on a daily basis.

You can also use volume to assess whether a stock is thinly traded. Such stocks can be easily manipulated since there aren't a lot of buyers and sellers participating on a regular basis. As a result, they can experience explosive price moves when there is higher volume. Thus, you can quickly find yourself on the wrong side of a very volatile stock.

For these reasons, I recommend you avoid stocks that don't trade at least 100,000 shares on a daily basis. You may even want to bump the number of shares higher so as to focus on what are commonly referred to as the "Generals" – blue-chip stocks that are favorites of institutional investors, such as MSFT, CSCO, IBM, INTC, and HD – to name a few.

Putting it all Together

Let's tie all these principles together by looking at a chart of Rambus Inc. (RMBS). In February you have a nice breakout followed by a sharp vertical climb. Until that time the stock was meandering in a tight trading range. Then, all of a sudden the stock broke out and it climbed too sharp, too fast. What did volume do? Look at the height of the vertical bar. It was substantially higher. That is very positive. You love to see stocks breaking out to new highs on heavier volume.

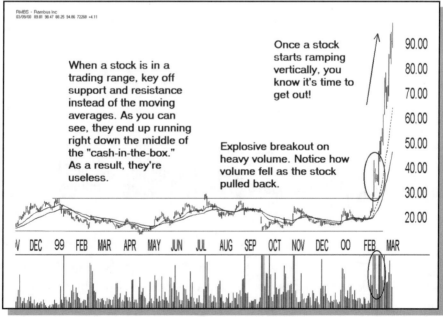

Courtesy of TC2000®.

Now look at the point where prices went too fast, too far. What happened to volume? It dried up. RMBS pulled back and volume dried up. Is this positive or negative for the stock? Positive. As prices started breaking out again, what did volume do? Volume skyrocketed again – another good sign.

However, as prices continued to go higher and higher, volume got lower and lower. This was very negative. Not only was the stock climbing too sharp, too fast, but then it continued higher on lighter volume. Now you had two red flags warning you to take the money and run!

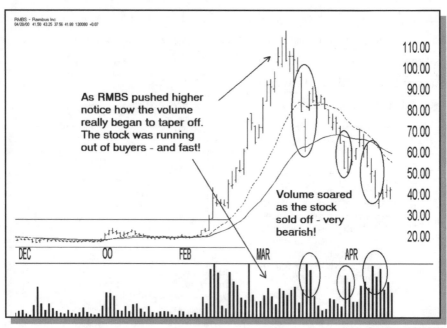

Courtesy of TC2000®.

As prices started collapsing, volume skyrocketed. This was very negative. If you were a put buyer, this is what you would be looking for. If you were long the stock or had a bullish option strategy in place, this would not be a good development for you. The stock's price collapsed on heavy volume.

After a brief rally, prices started collapsing again. Notice how the height of the volume bars started expanding, indicating the sellers weren't done. This told you know the downtrend wasn't over.

RMBS is a perfect example of where you have both bullish and bearish scenarios unfolding on the same chart. Remember, you're using volume to tell you whether anybody cares. It confirms trend. So whether you're bullish or bearish you can use it to your advantage.

The chart of InVision Technologies (INVN) also does a great job of tying all these principles together. In fact, the picture speaks volumes by itself! Nonetheless, let's take a quick look at what you can learn from looking at the chart.

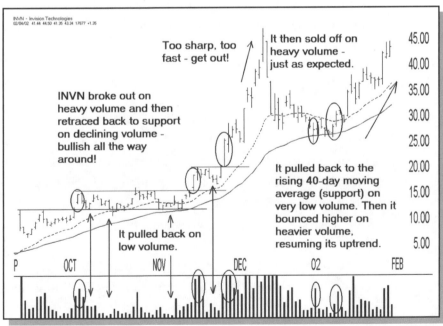

Courtesy of TC2000®.

First of all, note the multiple breakouts on heavy volume – a sign of a strong stock!

Second, see how the trendlines provided support when the stock was trading sideways (trendless) and then the 40-day moving average provided support once the stock was in an uptrend.

Finally, volume enabled you to see that the bulls were mostly in control except for the sharp selloff after the stock climbed too sharp, too fast. Prices contracted and INVN pulled back to the rising moving average. Bulls were champing at the bit to buy, indicative of the spikes in volume as the stock surged higher, bouncing off the 40-day moving average in the process. To say the least, this was a textbook example of how to use trendlines, moving averages and volume.

In summary, by monitoring the price action and volume of a stock, you can better time your buying and selling decisions with greater precision and accuracy.

Wings of Eagles

You often hear that you should buy on weakness and sell on strength. That's a dynamite strategy for stocks in trading ranges or if you're day trading. But other than that, you should adopt a different mindset. You want to buy high and sell higher. If you buy "dogs" you own "dogs." Weak stocks stay weak. I like buying "eagles" so I can soar with them.

Where do you find such stocks? Right in the newspaper under "New 52 Week Highs." Looking for stocks hitting new

52-week highs will give you a myriad of stocks to take a look at. It's awesome! Stocks hitting new 52-week highs tend to trend higher still. When you pull up stocks that are at new 52-week highs, you have two things going for you:

> Regardless of which approach you choose, the key is to buy strong stocks and avoid weak ones.

1. Historically, it has been proven that these stocks tend to be top performers (you have the odds in your favor).

2. The shorter will be above the longer moving average and both lines will be rising. Hence, these stocks are already in strong uptrends.

You can also look for stocks that are breaking out to new 60-day highs.

Regardless of which approach you choose, the key is to buy strong stocks and avoid weak ones. By harnessing the predictable power of chart patterns you'll be in a better position to identify the "cream of the crop." As you'll see in the next chapter, a picture is not only worth a thousand words, but thousands of dollars as well!

Key Points to Remember

➤ The trend is your friend – avoid picking tops or bottoms.

➤ Strong stocks get stronger while weak stocks get weaker.

➤ When all phases of trend (short-, intermediate-, and long-term) are in sync with another it provides you the highest probability that the trend will continue.

➤ A trend in motion tends to stay in motion – stick with it until it is neutralized.

➤ By using two moving averages, you can identify the direction of the trend. In an uptrend, the shorter will be above the longer and both lines will be rising. In a downtrend, the shorter will be below the longer and both lines will be falling.

➤ Pay attention to volume to validate the trend. Heavier volume on breakouts is a must!

CHAPTER 14

A Picture Is Worth Thousands of Dollars

I'm sure you're familiar with the saying, "A picture is worth a thousand words." Well, in this business, a picture is worth thousands of dollars! The picture I'm referring to is a chart. It enables you to see the "footprints" of the bulls and the bears, helping you determine the direction a stock is headed.

By the way, if you knew which direction a stock was headed, would that help you make more money? Of course it would! For that reason, charts will literally become your roadmap to riches!

> Charts will literally become your roadmap to riches!

However, having a map is one thing, understanding what it's telling you is another. The purpose of this chapter is to help you understand and harness the predictability of chart patterns, enabling you to enjoy the riches found in the stock market. In fact, you're going to look at charts in much the same way an athlete looks at game films.

Watch the Game Film

Why do you think athletes watch game films? Because they are trying to learn from the past! By studying the performances of others, as well as their own, athletes are able to identify specific strengths, weaknesses, and predictable patterns of behavior.

You see, all great athletes are constantly looking for ways to improve their game and at the same time discover the "Achilles heel" of their opponents. And if it weren't for game film, they wouldn't be in a position to uncover this invaluable information.

Past performances on film present athletes with two learning opportunities. First, they can analyze their own performance. This, in turn, will help them avoid repeating the same mistakes in the future. Additionally, players can review how they reacted to specific situations, enabling them to improve their response in the future.

Second, and perhaps just as important, they can learn the moves and tendencies of other players. This will not only enhance their own athletic repertoire, but it will provide them invaluable information in predicting the behavior of their opponents. They will be able to anticipate their next move.

For example, why do you think Wayne Gretzky, formerly of the National Hockey League, is one of the most prolific goal scorers of all time? Because, as the "Great One" himself has explained, he learned from studying countless hours of film that certain "shots on goal" ricocheted to specific locations on the ice rink. As a result, Gretzky knew exactly where to position himself on the ice to get the puck. And if you've ever watched him play he seemed to be in the right place, at the right time, all the time! Scoring goals became a science for him. Throughout his long career the lessons learned and implemented from watching game film have paid off handsomely in terms of goals made and games won.

Wilt Chamberlin, Bill Russell, Elgin Baylor, Larry Bird, and Earvin "Magic" Johnson (of National Basketball Association Hall of Fame status) have all studied game films of their respective eras. Game films taught them the fundamentals and subtleties of the art of basketball. Like Wayne Gretzky they learned how to position themselves to exploit their opponents' weaknesses.

In much the same way game film enables all great athletes to anticipate and predict behavior, studying charts will enable you to the same with individual stocks. (It's important to note that it really doesn't matter how old the charts are. Any chart will help you develop the ability to correctly identify and profit from repetitive price patterns. That's why I encourage members to frequently review archived editions of *Play of the Day* and *Chart of the Week* at www.mytradingdiary.com.)

Studying Charts Will Help You Know When to Buy and Sell

How could this be possible? Because after studying hundreds of charts you will begin to recognize various patterns that normally you wouldn't have noticed before. And because of such patterns and formations, charts won't appear to be merely composed of chaotic and random prices anymore. It will take the mystery out of knowing when to buy and sell!

It would seem logical that before making an investment in a particular stock you would consult a chart first. (Let's face it, how else would you know if it was a good time to buy?) Surprisingly, in working with thousands of investors over the years, I have found the opposite to be true.

Most investors never look at a chart before pulling the trigger. Some buy on a recommendation of a broker, friend, neighbor, or because of something they read in a magazine or newspaper. Consequently, they get hurt financially because their timing stinks (which should come as no surprise); they buy when they should sell, and sell when they should buy!

> Much like a detective gathers evidence to solve a case, you must gather evidence to support or disprove your notion of a stock's future direction.

While a chart offers no guarantees it will help you tilt the odds in your favor. How? By providing you with visual clues as to who's winning between the bulls and bears. Much like a detective gathers evidence to solve a case, you must gather evidence to support or disprove your notion of a stock's future direction.

Take a look at the chart of Hotel Reservations Network (ROOM).

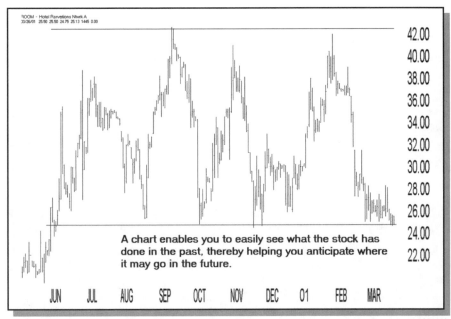

ROOM - Hotel Rsrvetions Ntwrk A
33/26/01 25.90 25.50 24.75 25.13 1445 0.00

42.00
40.00
38.00
36.00
34.00
32.00
30.00
28.00
26.00
24.00
22.00

A chart enables you to easily see what the stock has done in the past, thereby helping you anticipate where it may go in the future.

JUN   JUL   AUG   SEP   OCT   NOV   DEC   01   FEB   MAR

Courtesy of TC2000®.

At this point, would you be a buyer or a seller? Clearly, you would be a buyer. How long did that take you to reach that conclusion? Instantly! Yet I haven't told you anything about the company – their management team, earnings per share, gross revenues, book value, and so forth (boring stuff, to say the least!). Nevertheless you knew you wanted to buy. How? By looking at the chart. You can see exactly where you want to buy (and sell)!

Well, let's see if you made any money...

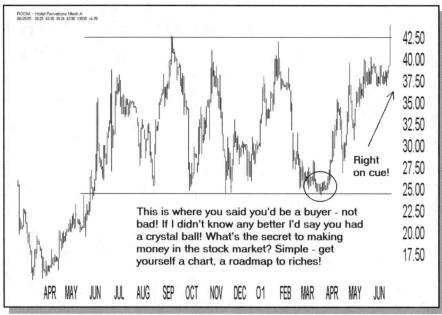

Courtesy of TC2000®.

Holy cow! You're brilliant. Your timing was perfect! Do you see how much easier investing becomes when you have a chart to look at? Pictures don't lie. Everyone understands pictures, particularly when you know what you're looking for. As a result, you can dramatically improve your timing.

Technical and Fundamental Analysis

As mentioned in a previous chapter, there are two schools of thought when it comes to analyzing stocks and/or the market: fundamental analysis and technical analysis.

Fundamental analysis deals with earnings, revenues, management, debt ratios, valuations, and the like.

Technical analysis deals with charts, price patterns, support and resistance, open interest, volume, and moving averages – to name a few. If the word "technical" turns you off think in terms of visual or chart analysis. You're simply looking at pictures.

Technical analysis revolves around the study of price patterns that help you forecast future price action. It teaches you that prices move in identifiable and predictable patterns – exactly what you experienced in the previous example.

The chart represents the battle between bulls and bears as price bars come together to form discernible and predictable patterns. Your task is to determine what those patterns mean and profit from it. Therein lies your key to riches!

The biggest challenge in using charts is remaining objective. Sometimes there's a tendency to see what you want to see. If you are

> The biggest challenge in using charts is remaining objective.

bullish, then you find ways for the chart to support your line of reasoning. Before long, the chart embodies your hopes and fears.

Therefore, always strive to remain objective and independent. Someone once suggested taking the following test to determine whether you're biased. Simply take the chart and turn it upside down. If it still looks bullish, you're biased!

While I'll primarily focus on daily and weekly charts in this chapter, you'll find that these same patterns work across all time frames. Due to their predictable nature, it is clearly in your best interest to learn how to identify and exploit them.

When you hear someone talk about charts, they usually speak of two types of patterns: Continuation and reversal patterns. Just like the names imply, prices will either continue in the prevailing direction or reverse. Once you learn to recognize these chart patterns, you'll trade with more confidence and better results.

Archimedes and The Most Reliable, Profitable, and Geometric Trading Pattern

Archimedes is considered the greatest mathematician of ancient times. Though he was born in about 300 B.C., his contributions to math and science are still in use today. Archimedes' greatest achievements may have been made in the area of geometry.

One of his greatest achievements involved the discovery of geometric patterns within straight lines. From this discovery he developed a series of theorems that could predict where the future movement of a line would go. Although Archimedes was not an investor, some of his most significant accomplishments, with respect to moving lines, are employed by thousands of technicians. Today, it's reassuring to know that such an exact geometric science can be used to reap huge profits in the stock market.

Let's take a look at one of Archimedes' discoveries and see how it evolved into a popular trading tool.

The Most Reliable Geometric Trading Formation: The Rectangle or "Cash-in-the-Box"

One of the easiest geometric chart patterns for you to recognize is a rectangle. It is a continuation pattern, meaning whatever trend was in place prior to a rectangle forming will likely continue once prices break out.

Rectangles form when a stock becomes stuck in a trading range, channeling between support and resistance. Such trading ranges often occur when stocks encounter heavy resistance and bedrock support. It is the easiest formation to spot and when a breakout occurs, it presents you with an explosive and highly profitable trading opportunity. That's why I call them "cash-in-the-boxes"!

Rambus (RMBS) provides a perfect example of a cash-in-the-box. Do you see how the rectangle immediately jumps off the page at you when you know what you're looking for?

Archimedes determined that when a line is forced to move in a specific direction, it will continue to move in that direction until the parameters or boundaries are changed. That is, a stock's price action is impeded by the boundaries of support and resistance.

Thus, if you take Archimedes' theorem into consideration, once a stock leaves or breaks out of a trading range, it's free to move in a new direction. Hence, the momentum tends to drive the stock in the direction of the breakout.

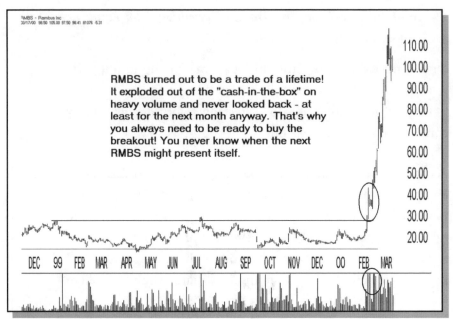

RMBS - Rambus Inc
3/17/00 98.50 105.00 97.50 98.41 81076 -5.31

RMBS turned out to be a trade of a lifetime!
It exploded out of the "cash-in-the-box" on
heavy volume and never looked back - at
least for the next month anyway. That's why
you always need to be ready to buy the
breakout! You never know when the next
RMBS might present itself.

Courtesy of TC2000®.

Do you see the direction the price goes once it breaks out of the trading range? Typically, when a stock breaks out from a cash-in-the-box, it tends to move in the direction of the breakout.

Just look at the obscene amounts of money you could have made, even though you didn't know a single thing about Rambus (RMBS). Charts are a veritable gold mine!

There will be times when your patience will be sorely tested. Sometimes prices snake along for months before breaking out. As a result, you must be prepared to take advantage of the opportunity when it presents itself.

Did you notice that RMBS moved along in a narrow channel for approximately one year? Granted, a year is a long time to wait for a trading opportunity, but look what happened once the stock broke out of the cash-in-the-box. The stock soared from around $30 on February 14 to a high of $117.75 on March 14, soaring 87 points in one month - not a bad reward for a little patience!

If you think one year is a long time take a look at the chart of Autozone (AZO). It was stuck in a trading range for eight years! When stocks break out from prolonged trading ranges, the more significant it becomes, that is, the larger the move. AZO went on to double in price in less than five months!

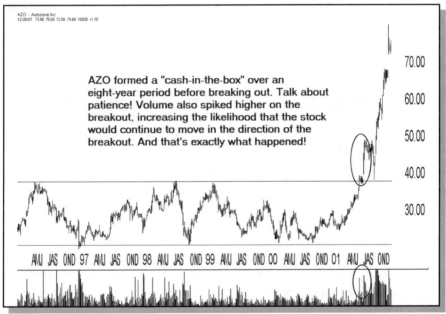

Courtesy of TC2000®.

USA Education (SLM) also found itself mired in a trading range for an extended period of time – over four years! But once it broke out, it almost doubled in price in less than a year.

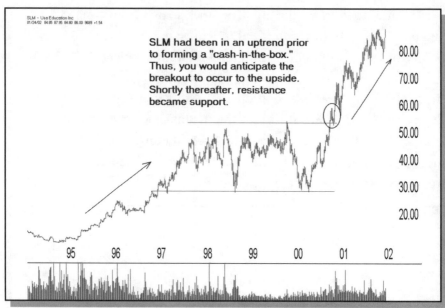

SLM had been in an uptrend prior to forming a "cash-in-the-box." Thus, you would anticipate the breakout to occur to the upside. Shortly thereafter, resistance became support.

Courtesy of TC2000®.

There are plenty of "parades" that will offer opportunities whose shape will resemble the most reliable geometric trading patterns. Invest in the opportunities when they present themselves and you will be greatly rewarded!

For example, stocks will break out of cash-in-the-boxes to the downside as well. Once again, you can anticipate the direction of the breakout by paying attention to the existing trend before the cash-in-the-box formed.

In this example, notice how Cable & Wireless (CWP) had been in a downtrend before forming a cash-in-the-box. Thus, you can expect the breakout to occur to the downside, which is exactly what happened.

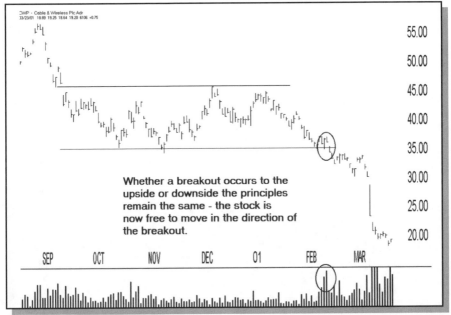

CWP - Cable & Wireless Plc Adr
3/23/01 18.89 19.25 18.64 19.20 6106 +0.75

55.00

50.00

45.00

40.00

35.00

Whether a breakout occurs to the upside or downside the principles remain the same - the stock is now free to move in the direction of the breakout.

30.00

25.00

20.00

SEP   OCT   NOV   DEC   01   FEB   MAR

Courtesy of TC2000®.

Volume should also be used to confirm the breakout. In fact, it is one of the most important indicators I use. What you are trying to determine is whether anyone cares about the change in price and/or direction. If prices are rising or falling on lighter volume, then it's clear no one is all that interested. As a result, the move is prone to failure, since it lacks the support of the "herd." There's no one to sustain it.

However, sometimes stocks can still pull it off without heavy volume, as was the case with Affiliated Computer Services (ACS).

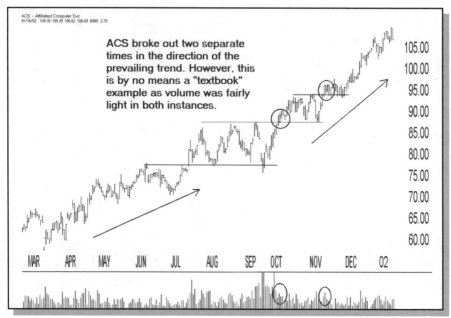

Courtesy of TC2000®.

It is bullish if prices are rising on heavier volume or if they are pulling back on lighter volume. It is bearish if prices are falling on heavy volume or rising on lighter volume. Volume confirms trend. Use it!

Most charting programs place volume in the lower part of the chart's window. This makes it easy to see if volume is rising or falling by noticing the height of the vertical bar. If the bars are getting taller, volume is increasing. If the bars are getting smaller, volume is decreasing. It's that simple!

How can you use this in conjunction with the pattern already discussed? If volume starts to increase as price approaches either support or resistance, a breakout is likely.

Take a look at the chart of InVision Technologies (INVN). Volume clearly confirmed the breakout.

> If volume starts to increase as price approaches either support or resistance, a breakout is likely.

Remember, a breakout is confirmed if prices continue higher or lower with an increase in volume.

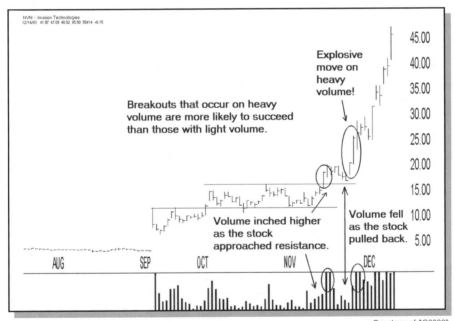

NVN - Invision Technologies
12/14/01 41.97 47.09 40.52 45.50 55414 +6.15

Explosive move on heavy volume!

Breakouts that occur on heavy volume are more likely to succeed than those with light volume.

Volume inched higher as the stock approached resistance.

Volume fell as the stock pulled back.

45.00
40.00
35.00
30.00
25.00
20.00
15.00
10.00
5.00

AUG   SEP   OCT   NOV   DEC

Courtesy of TC2000®.

Another thing to remember is if prices pull back or climb on lighter volume, it may indicate that the new roles of support and resistance will hold. Check out the chart of Dreyers (DRYR), as this is precisely what took place.

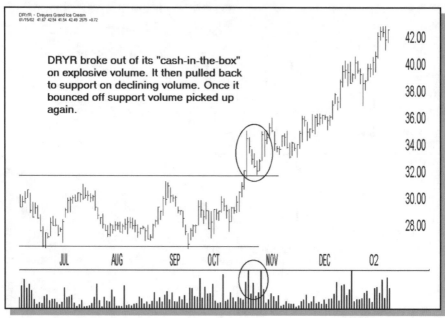

DRYR - Dreyers Grand Ice Cream
01/15/02 41.67 42.54 41.54 42.49 2575 +0.72

DRYR broke out of its "cash-in-the-box" on explosive volume. It then pulled back to support on declining volume. Once it bounced off support volume picked up again.

Courtesy of TC2000®.

If, on the other hand, prices pull back on heavy volume, it may be a false breakout. The breakout is not confirmed unless prices can hold at what was once resistance, and vice versa. If they don't, exit the trade immediately!

> The longer and/or taller a rectangle is, the greater the breakout will be.

The distance covered by a stock once it breaks out is determined by the length and height of the rectangle. The longer and/or taller a rectangle is, the greater the breakout will be.

There is a simple, two-step formula you can use to determine the projected price target for a stock once it breaks out. First, measure the height of the cash-in-the-box. Second, add this amount to the area of resistance for an upside breakout or subtract it from the area of support for a downside breakout. This will provide you with a rough estimate of the stock's potential target. This is an easy way for you to predetermine what your exit point should be and do it with razor-sharp precision.

Let's use Dreyers (DRYR) as an example of how this would work.

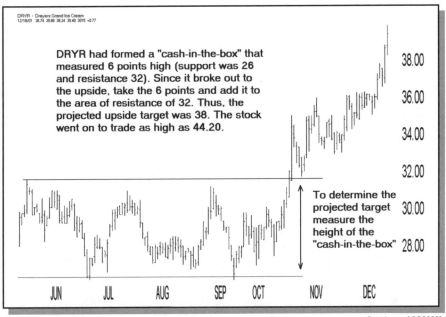

DRYR - Dreyers Grand Ice Cream
12/18/01 38.74 39.89 38.24 39.49 3015 +0.77

DRYR had formed a "cash-in-the-box" that measured 6 points high (support was 26 and resistance 32). Since it broke out to the upside, take the 6 points and add it to the area of resistance of 32. Thus, the projected upside target was 38. The stock went on to trade as high as 44.20.

To determine the projected target measure the height of the "cash-in-the-box"

38.00
36.00
34.00
32.00
30.00
28.00

JUN   JUL   AUG   SEP   OCT   NOV   DEC

Courtesy of TC2000®.

As you learned earlier, these levels of support and resistance are emotional strongholds for both bulls and bears. Once broken, they tend to reverse roles – support becomes resistance and vice versa. Use that to your advantage.

For instance, consider the chart of Loews Corp. (LTR). Even if you missed the initial breakout, there were still additional opportunities to enter the trade. Simply wait for the stock to pullback to support. Often, you'll get a second chance.

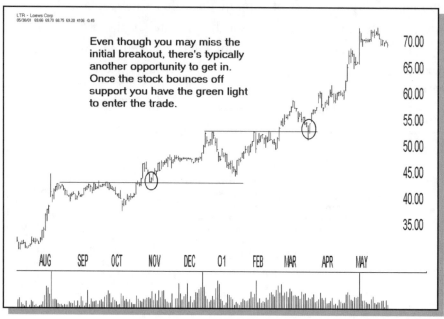

LTR - Loews Corp
05/30/01 69.66 69.70 68.75 69.20 4106 -0.45

Even though you may miss the initial breakout, there's typically another opportunity to get in. Once the stock bounces off support you have the green light to enter the trade.

Courtesy of TC2000®.

The wonderful thing about the stock market is that it offers you plenty of money-making opportunities in different shapes and sizes. You see, downside breakouts work just as well as their counterparts and what's more, the same principles apply.

In the chart below, Telecom Brazil (TBH) broke out to the downside and then quickly rallied back to the previous area of support. Unfortunately for the bulls, this was now an area of resistance and the stock continued its decline.

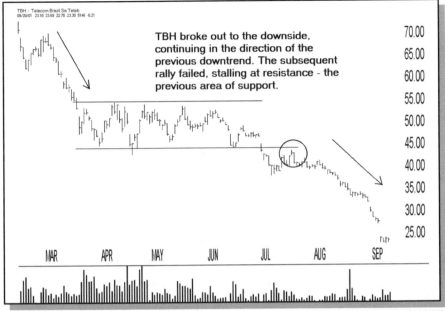

TBH broke out to the downside, continuing in the direction of the previous downtrend. The subsequent rally failed, stalling at resistance - the previous area of support.

Courtesy of TC2000®.

Manage your risk and money wisely by quickly exiting trades that give false signals. A simple exit strategy to use is placing your protective stop right above or below the new levels of support and resistance. That way, you won't be hurt by a false breakout. Once again, key in on volume. Retests on light volume should leave the breakout intact.

> A simple exit strategy to use is placing your protective stop right above or below the new levels of support and resistance.

Tails

Tails are those vertical bars that stick out like a sore thumb after an extended up or downtrend. They are powerful reversal patterns. They represent a fierce battle between buyers and sellers and as a result, they can provide you with some of the most profitable opportunities available to you.

As a quick review, remember that the top of the vertical bar on a daily chart represents the high of the day and the bottom of the vertical bar represents the low of the day. The longer the bar and higher the volume, the more extreme the battle was between the bulls and bears. Stocks tend to recoil from such extremes and move in the opposite direction.

The key is where the price closes at the end of the day. If the stock's price closes near the top of a long vertical bar on heavy volume after a prolonged decline, that means the market violently rejected the lower price. It usually leads to higher prices, sending the stock in the opposite direction of the tail. Often it is a powerful move, so be ready to implement a bullish strategy. You can see this very clearly on the chart of Pfizer (PFE).

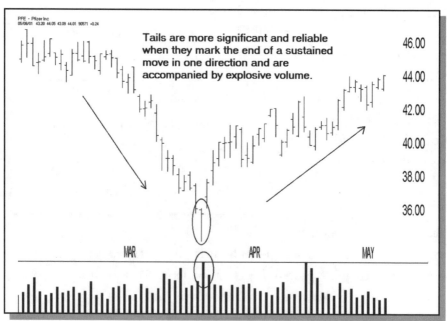

Courtesy of TC2000®.

Likewise, if prices close near the bottom of a long vertical bar on heavy volume after a sustained uptrend or sharp move higher, it means that the market rejected the higher price. If price sclose near the bottom of the vertical bar, you want to implement a bearish strategy.

This is exactly what happened to Broadcom (BRCM) on two different occasions:

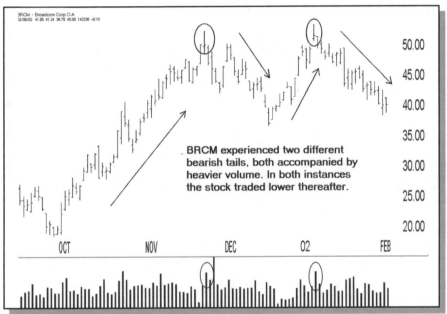

BRCM experienced two different bearish tails, both accompanied by heavier volume. In both instances the stock traded lower thereafter.

Courtesy of TC2000®.

Take a look at the chart of Ariba (ARBA). The bearish tail at the end of its sustained move higher had ominous implications.

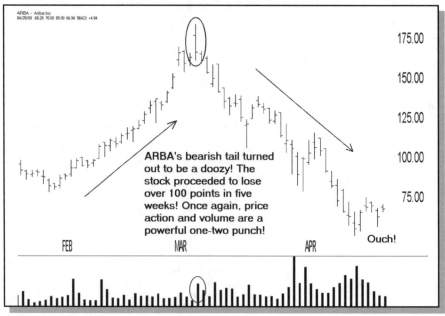

ARBA - Ariba Inc
04/25/00 68.25 70.00 65.00 66.94 56423 +4.94

175.00

150.00

125.00

ARBA's bearish tail turned
out to be a doozy! The
stock proceeded to lose
over 100 points in five
weeks! Once again, price
action and volume are a
powerful one-two punch!

100.00

75.00

Ouch!

FEB   MAR   APR

Of all the chart patterns you'll be exposed to, tails and cash-in-the-boxes are my two favorite patterns. It tells you there's a reversal brewing. And since you're looking for those accompanied by heavy volume it also tells you that people are heading for the exits! As a result, exploit it for all it is worth.

> A false signal would be given if the stock doesn't trade in the opposite direction of the tail within a day or two.

A false signal would be given if the stock doesn't trade in the opposite direction of the tail within a day or two. That is a sign to exit the trade. If you enter a trade based upon a bullish or bearish tail there should be immediate follow-through. If there isn't, it's most likely a dud. Get out!

You'll notice in the previous examples that prices followed through immediately – and in a big way! That's exactly what the doctor ordered!

Gaps

Gaps refers to a chart pattern where, just like the name implies, there is a gap or break in the chart pattern. It shows that no trades took place at a certain price, either higher or lower. This is due to an imbalance in either buy or sell orders, causing prices to gap higher or lower. This often occurs when news is released after the market closes or before the market opens. It represents the next price at which bulls were willing to buy or bears were willing to sell. Gaps can be either continuation or reversal pattern.

When you know that either the bulls or bears are hurting, you can determine which way the trend will go. Once a gap has occurred, if there is no follow-through

> Once a gap has occurred, if there is no follow-through to the upside or to the downside, it may be a false signal.

to the upside or to the downside, it may be a false signal. Don't wait around to find out. Like tails, either it's going to happen right away (a few days) or it won't happen at all. Since there are different types of gaps, let's take a look at each one and show you how you can profit from them.

A *breakaway gap* is the one you're after. This is where a stock breaks out of a trading area on heavy volume and establishes a new trend, indicating a dramatic shift in market psychology. A true breakaway is followed by a series of new highs or new lows, exactly what the chart of Northrop Grumman (NOC) illustrates.

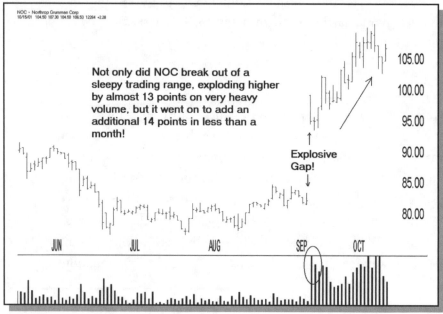

Not only did NOC break out of a sleepy trading range, exploding higher by almost 13 points on very heavy volume, but it went on to add an additional 14 points in less than a month!

Explosive Gap!

Courtesy of TC2000®.

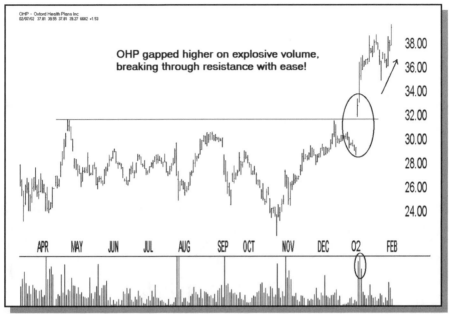

OHP - Oxford Health Plans Inc
02/07/02 37.81 39.55 37.81 39.27 6682 +1.53

OHP gapped higher on explosive volume,
breaking through resistance with ease!

Courtesy of TC2000®.

Below, Oxford Health Plans (OHP) demonstrates another valid breakaway gap.

A *continuation gap* describes a gap in the midst of an existing trend. If prices don't establish new highs or lows shortly thereafter, you may have an exhaustion gap (see below) on your hands.

This was not the case with InVision Technologies (INVN). Both continuation gaps were followed by higher prices.

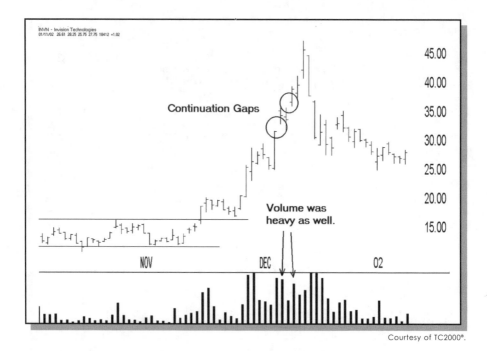

INVN - Invision Technologies
01/11/02 26.61 28.25 25.75 27.75 18412 +1.02

Continuation Gaps

Volume was
heavy as well.

Courtesy of TC2000®.

Exhaustion gaps do not establish new highs or lows in the direction of the gap, but tend to tread water, eventually filling in the gap. These occur at the end of a trend. The stock literally runs out of steam and can't continue. Exit the trade and wait for validation of the new trend.

More often than not, exhaustion gaps are followed by a reversal in direction. If one occurs at the end of an uptrend, buy puts or short the stock. If it occurs at the end of a downtrend, buy calls or buy the stock.

You'll notice that Research In Motion (RIMM) experienced all three types of gaps. In fact, you'll also see that the exhaustion gap coincided with a bearish tail – two good reasons to exit the trade!

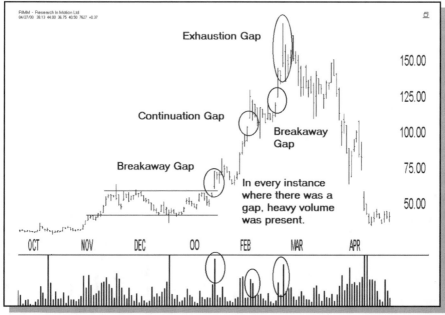

Courtesy of TC2000®.

Knowing what to look for will not only make you money but it will save from a lot of financial headache and heartache as well. Consider the plight of those who owned RIMM; it went on to lose over 100 points in the next two months!

The final gap worth considering, albeit rare, is known as an *island reversal*. This is where you have two gaps, in opposite directions, within a short period of time. This is a powerful reversal pattern!

What you're left with are one or more bars sitting by themselves – an "island" in no-man's land. Expedia (EXPE) provides a good illustration of a bearish island reversal. Once again, look for volume to confirm the reversal.

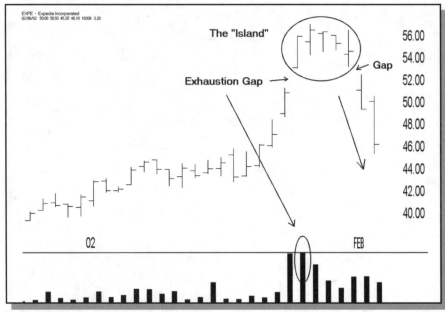

Courtesy of TC2000®.

This can be a very profitable and explosive reversal pattern, so always be looking for it. Praxair (PX) provides an excellent example of a bullish island reversal.

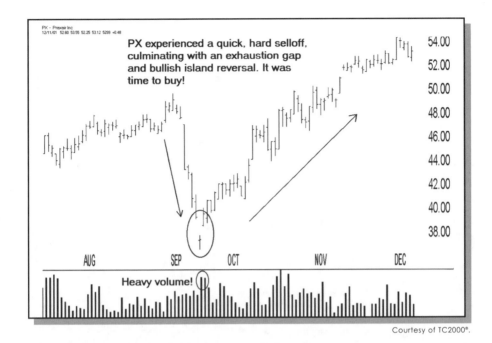

PX - Praxair Inc
12/11/01 52.60 53.55 52.25 53.12 5298 +0.48

PX experienced a quick, hard selloff, culminating with an exhaustion gap and bullish island reversal. It was time to buy!

Heavy volume!

Courtesy of TC2000®.

Finally, Shell (SC) ties everything together by providing you with an example of every single gap – all in one chart, to boot!

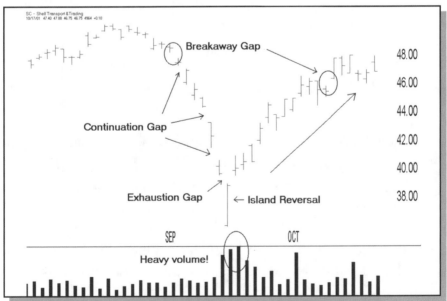

SC - Shell Transport & Trading
10/17/01 47.40 47.98 46.75 46.75 4964 +0.10

Breakaway Gap

Continuation Gap

Exhaustion Gap ← Island Reversal

Heavy volume!

Courtesy of TC2000®.

Double Top

A double top is a reversal pattern that looks like the letter "M." It is a bearish pattern that occurs in an uptrend. As you know, when a stock is trending higher, buyers are very much in control. However, there comes a point where new buyers are few and far between, enabling sellers to gain the upper hand. This is how a top is born. Consider the chart of Tyco (TYC).

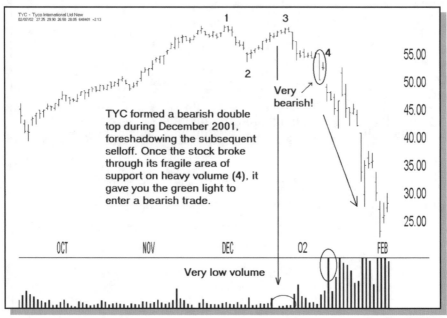

TYC formed a bearish double top during December 2001, foreshadowing the subsequent selloff. Once the stock broke through its fragile area of support on heavy volume (4), it gave you the green light to enter a bearish trade.

Courtesy of TC2000®.

The first peak (1) is established by the bulls' inability to push the stock any higher. This induces the bulls to take profits and the stock pulls back. However, it's not too long before buyers reemerge, helping the stock resume its uptrend (2).

As the stock rallies back to its previous high (1), the bulls grow tired and volume drops off. In fact, one of the characteristics of a double top is declining volume as the stock rallies back to its previous high (1). Lacking conviction and firepower, the bulls can't push the stock to new highs and it begins to roll over, forming a second peak (3). Vulnerable, the stock continues to fall and the bears begin licking their chops!

If the bears can gain the upper hand and drive prices below the minor area of support between points (2) and (4) then it signals that the double top is complete. It's time to enter a bearish position. If you want to trade this pattern more aggressively, you can enter a bearish position once the stock forms the second peak (3), validating it as an area of resistance. Your stop would be placed right above resistance. Once TYC broke through support, the bears had a field day as it proceeded to lose almost 60% of its value in three weeks!

Keep in mind that all these formations, including double tops, apply to both stocks and indexes alike. For example, in 2000 the NASDAQ experienced two double tops on two different occasions, letting you know that tech stocks were in trouble both times.

> Keep in mind that all these formations, including double tops, apply to both stocks and indexes alike.

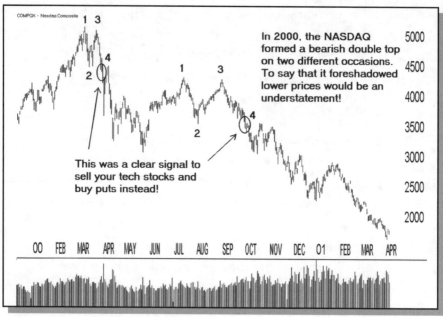

In 2000, the NASDAQ formed a bearish double top on two different occasions. To say that it foreshadowed lower prices would be an understatement!

This was a clear signal to sell your tech stocks and buy puts instead!

Courtesy of TC2000®.

Double Bottom

Downtrends end when bears run out of selling power and bulls reemerge to stem the tide. If you take a look at the chart of Idec Pharmaceuticals (IDPH), you'll see the stock had been declining since March on heavy volume. As it reached its lows (1), investors waved the white flag and dumped the stock. Keep in mind that heavy volume at the end of a downtrend typically indicates capitulation.

Now, prices have only one way to go-up, since everyone who wanted to sell has sold. Buyers reemerge and push prices higher. Since no one wants to get "burned" a second time, the stock rallies higher on lighter volume. Pretty soon it stalls (2).

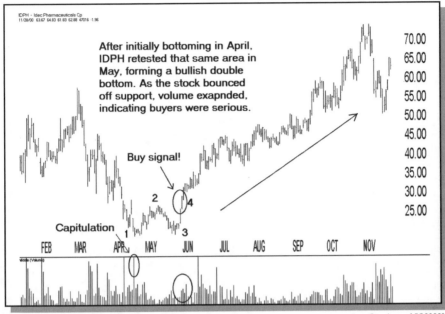

IDPH - Idec Pharmaceuticals Cp
11/28/00 63.67 64.83 61.83 62.88 47016 -1.96

After initially bottoming in April,
IDPH retested that same area in
May, forming a bullish double
bottom. As the stock bounced
off support, volume exapnded,
indicating buyers were serious.

Buy signal!

Capitulation

70.00
65.00
60.00
55.00
50.00
45.00
40.00
35.00
30.00
25.00

2   4
1   3

FEB   MAR   APR   MAY   JUN   JUL   AUG   SEP   OCT   NOV

Volume (Volume)

Courtesy of TC2000®.

This makes the bulls nervous and they take their money off
the table. Renewed selling drives the stock back to its
previous lows (1) and it retests support (3). Ideally, any retest
of the lows should be accompanied by lighter volume. This
lets you know the bears have truly finished selling the stock.
Moreover, the bulls see it is another opportunity to buy the
stock for peanuts.

Renewed buying forces the stock higher on expanding volume
(4), pushing it through resistance (2) and signifying the
completion of the double bottom. A new uptrend is underway.

Claires Stores (CLE) provides another example of a double bottom, with the same result – higher prices!

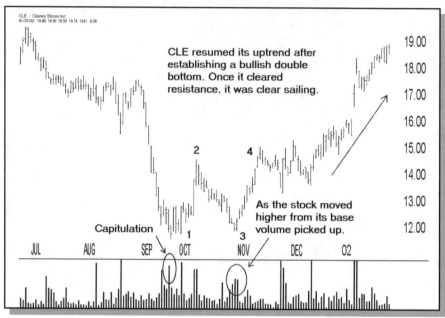

CLE - Claires Stores Inc
01/31/02 18.80 18.90 18.50 18.74 1241 -0.06

CLE resumed its uptrend after establishing a bullish double bottom. Once it cleared resistance, it was clear sailing.

As the stock moved higher from its base volume picked up.

Capitulation

Courtesy of TC2000®.

Triangles

Triangles are chart patterns that allow a stock or index to consolidate after a trend, either up or down. This allows the market to digest the recent advance before the trend resumes. It should be noted that a triangle may also represent the final stage of a trend, setting the stage for a reversal. Thus, triangles serve as both continuation and reversal patterns. All three types of triangles discussed below can fill both roles. I sometimes like to refer to these as "loaded springs." Prices wind up tighter and tighter, compressing energy so when prices do move, they tend to be explosive in nature. Let's explore them in greater detail.

An *ascending triangle* has a flat top (resistance) and a rising bottom. An ascending triangle, more often than not, is a bullish chart pattern resulting in a breakout to the upside. Just like any breakout, heavy volume is desirable to confirm its legitimacy.

Public Storage (PSA) formed a textbook ascending triangle, eventually resolving itself to the upside. The breakout occurred on heavy volume, which foreshadowed higher prices thereafter.

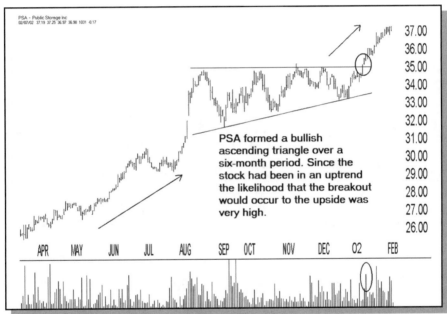

PSA formed a bullish ascending triangle over a six-month period. Since the stock had been in an uptrend the likelihood that the breakout would occur to the upside was very high.

Courtesy of TC2000®.

In exactly the same way you projected the price target for stocks once they broke out of cash-in-the-boxes, you can do the same for both ascending and descending triangles. Simply take the height of the triangle at its base and add it to the area of resistance for an ascending triangle and subtract it from the area of support for a descending triangle.

Since PSA broke out to the upside you calculate the projected price target by measuring its base (4 points) and adding it to the area of resistance, which is $35. Accordingly, your upside target would be $39.

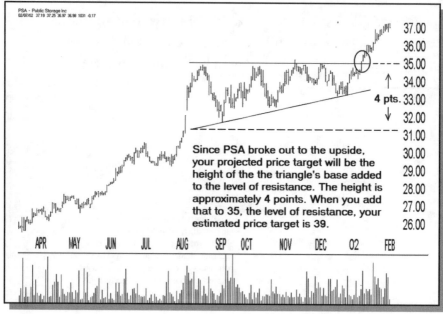

Courtesy of TC2000®.

A *descending triangle* has a flat bottom (support) and a downward sloping top. A descending triangle is typically a bearish pattern, resulting in a breakout to the downside. Once again, explosive volume should accompany the breakout.

Rambus (RMBS) formed two separate descending triangles. Both times the stock broke out to the downside on heavy volume. To say the least, it was not a good time to own the stock!

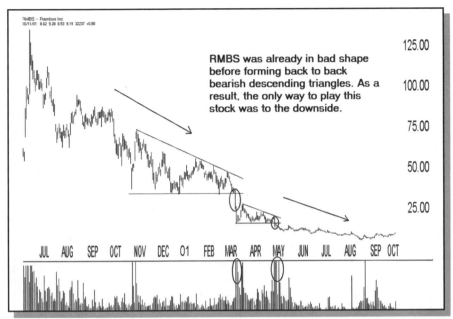

RMBS was already in bad shape before forming back to back bearish descending triangles. As a result, the only way to play this stock was to the downside.

Courtesy of TC2000®.

Once the stock breaks out, you can follow the same formula previously described to reach an estimated price target. However, in the case of a descending triangle you are going to subtract the height of the base from the area of support.

When Rambus (RMBS) broke out of its first descending triangle support was at 35. When you subtract the height of the base, you're left with a negative number – hardly a good sign for the stock! Suffice to say, the stock was headed lower.

Support for its second descending triangle was $16. By subtracting the height of the base (11) you're projected price target is $5. Accordingly, it should come as no surprise that RMBS closed at $4.86 on August 23, 2001.

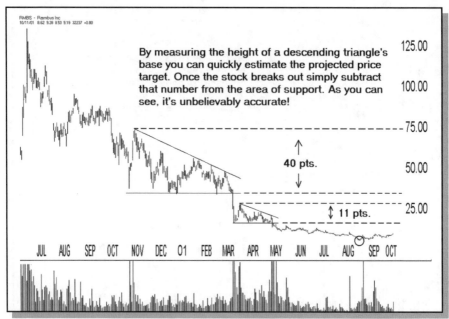

RMBS - Rambus Inc
10/11/01 8.62 9.20 8.53 9.19 32237 +0.00

By measuring the height of a descending triangle's base you can quickly estimate the projected price target. Once the stock breaks out simply subtract that number from the area of support. As you can see, it's unbelievably accurate!

40 pts.

11 pts.

125.00

100.00

75.00

50.00

25.00

JUL   AUG   SEP   OCT   NOV   DEC   01   FEB   MAR   APR   MAY   JUN   JUL   AUG   SEP   OCT

Courtesy of TC2000®.

Once the stock breaks out, support and resistance tend to reverse roles on subsequent pullbacks or rallies. As a result, be on the lookout for another opportunity to enter the trade if you miss the initial breakout.

The final type of triangle is known as a *symmetrical triangle.* This is where the upper and lower boundaries converge at the same angle. The bulls and bears are slowly losing ground to one another but no one is ready to give in just yet. Eventually, someone will!

Since this tends to be continuation pattern, you can anticipate the stock breaking out in the direction of the prevailing trend. In the following example, GTK was already in an uptrend before forming a symmetrical triangle. As such, you would expect the breakout to occur to the upside – exactly what happened!

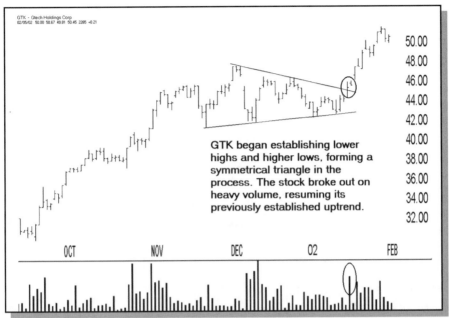

GTK - Gtech Holdings Corp
02/05/02 50.00 50.67 49.81 50.45 2285 +0.21

GTK began establishing lower
highs and higher lows, forming a
symmetrical triangle in the
process. The stock broke out on
heavy volume, resuming its
previously established uptrend.

Courtesy of TC2000®.

In similar fashion, you can project the up- or downside price target by using the same formula learned earlier. In the case of symmetrical triangles, you're going to add or subtract the height of the base from the point of breakout.

As usual, the formula worked like a charm. When you take GTK and add the height of its base to the point from which it broke out you get a projected price target of $51. GTK closed at $51.22 on February 1, 2002 – just nine trading days after breaking out!

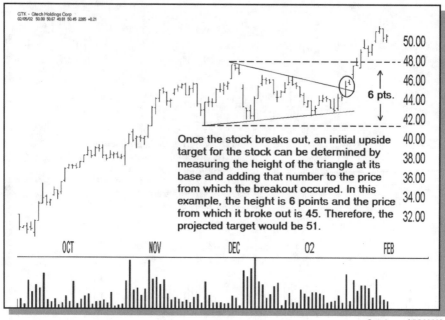

GTK - Gtech Holdings Corp
02/05/02 50.00 50.67 49.81 50.45 2285 +0.21

Once the stock breaks out, an initial upside target for the stock can be determined by measuring the height of the triangle at its base and adding that number to the price from which the breakout occured. In this example, the height is 6 points and the price from which it broke out is 45. Therefore, the projected target would be 51.

Courtesy of TC2000®.

For ascending, descending, and symmetrical triangles, breakouts will generally occur between half and three quarters of the way down the triangle. The closer it comes to the end of the triangle before breaking out, the weaker the breakout will be. In general, you want to avoid playing breakouts if they occur in the last third of the triangle. The stock is growing tired and the breakout becomes unreliable.

> In general, you want to avoid playing breakouts if they occur in the last third of the triangle.

However, this was not the case with W.R. Berkley (BER). Even though the stock finally broke out in the last third of the triangle, it still realized some explosive gains. The projected priced target was $59 – pretty intimidating, considering the breakout occurred at $41. Nevertheless, on November 6, 2001 the stock closed at $58.20!

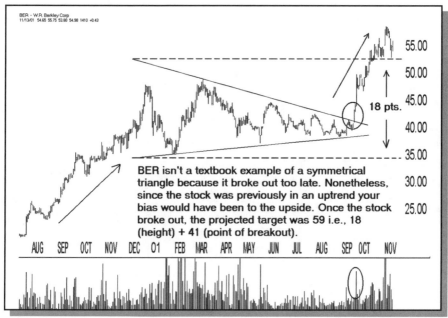

BER - W.R. Berkley Corp
11/13/01 54.65 55.75 53.90 54.98 1410 +0.43

18 pts.

BER isn't a textbook example of a symmetrical triangle because it broke out too late. Nonetheless, since the stock was previously in an uptrend your bias would have been to the upside. Once the stock broke out, the projected target was 59 i.e., 18 (height) + 41 (point of breakout).

Courtesy of TC2000®.

In conclusion, as you've just learned a picture is truly worth thousands of dollars! Harnessing the predictability of charts will be a snap, now that you know what to look for.

Make sure you take the time to study your "game film," by studying your charts. Learning how to identify cash-in-the-boxes, tails, gaps, double tops, double bottoms, and triangles will not only help you trade with more confidence, but it will take the mystery out of knowing when to buy and sell. Is it any wonder that charts are your roadmap to riches?!

Even though you have a map to point you in the right direction, realize that there will invariably be a few surprises along the way – the stock does the exact opposite of what you expected! That's why it's critical to cut your losses quickly, something you'll learn in Chapter 16 in greater detail.

Key Points to Remember

➤ Before you buy or sell a stock and/or option, take a look at the chart first.

➤ Trading without charts is like driving blindfolded – dangerous at best!

➤ Continuation patterns project that prices will move in the direction of the existing trend.

➤ Cash-in-the-boxes, ascending, descending, and symmetrical triangles are typically continuation patterns.

➤ Reversal patterns let you know the trend is going to reverse in the opposite direction.

➤ Tails, double tops, and double bottoms are reversal patterns.

➤ You can follow a simple, two-step formula to determine an estimated price target for the stock once it breaks out. First, measure the height of the cash-in-the-box or base of the triangle. Second, add that to the area of resistance for an upside breakout or subtract it from the area of support for a downside breakout. The resulting number is your projected price target.

➤ Charts aren't infallible; thus, it's always important to cut your losses if the stock does the opposite of what you expected.

CHAPTER 15

The Greatest Money Making Secret In the World!

Now that you've learned how to identify and capture explosive trading opportunities, I want to share with you the greatest money-making secret in the world. This secret has been mastered by every successful options trader! Yet, it is one of the most overlooked and misunderstood aspects of options trading by nonprofessionals. What is this secret? Determining the fair value of an option. Knowing whether an option is cheap, fairly priced, or expensive is paramount to your success. Over the next few pages you will be given an overview of how options are priced and you'll discover how to use the most important variable of all - volatility.

Approach the pricing of options the way you approach the pricing of a used car. When you shop for a new or used car, you probably have a "blue book" in hand to measure what the true value of the car should be. It would be very foolish for you to walk onto a dealer's lot and write out a check for the car you're interested in without first determining exactly what it's worth. Knowing that information gives you an edge in getting the best price possible.

In the options market, the same principle applies. When you decide to "shop" for an option, you need to know its true or theoretical value before you buy or sell it. Otherwise, you may pay too much or sell it too cheaply. But how many times have you bought an option without knowing exactly what you're getting yourself into? Does this ring a bell? "Hey Jim, buy me ten contracts of the XYZ $50 calls at market." I'm sure it sounds familiar. Isn't that the same thing as walking onto a dealer's lot and blindly writing out a check for the first car that catches your eye? It sure is. You really have no idea what the option is worth.

> When you decide to "shop" for an option, you need to know its true or theoretical value before you buy or sell it.

When you trade options, you need to know the actual value of the calls or puts that you're interested in buying or selling. The key to racking up huge gains is buying undervalued or cheap options and selling overvalued or expensive options. You want to buy low and sell high. So how do you know whether an option is cheap, expensive, or fairly priced? To answer that question you must first understand what variables determine the price of an option.

> The key to racking up huge gains is buying undervalued or cheap options and selling overvalued or expensive options

For example, suppose you call up your broker and get a quote on a particular Microsoft option. With Microsoft trading at $65 you inquire about the April $65.00 calls. Your broker quotes you a price of $7. How and why is it priced at $7? Well, there are six variables that determine the price of an option. The variables are:

1. The stock price
2. The strike price
3. Time until expiration
4. Volatility
5. Interest rates
6. Dividends

In looking at this list, which variables do you think have the greatest impact on the price of an option? Clearly, the first four do. Interest rates and dividends play a role, albeit smaller ones. Thus, for the purposes of this chapter we'll focus on the main four variables to help you better understand their respective roles in determining the price of an option.

Stock Price

The price of the stock is the single most important factor that determines an option's value. As the price of the stock rises, the value of calls increase while the value of puts decrease. As the price of the stock falls, the value of puts increase while the value of calls decrease.

Strike Price

As presented in a previous chapter, the relationship between the strike price and stock price determines an option's "time" and "intrinsic value." It also lets you know whether an option is in-the-money, at-the-money, or out-of-the-money. Intrinsic value is the "in-the-money" portion of an option. Time value represents everything else.

For example, if a stock is trading at $85 and the $80 call is trading for $7, the stock is $5 in the money. The $5 represents intrinsic value.

But if the intrinsic value is $5 and the option is trading at $7, what is the other $2? Time value. Time value is a "wasting asset," similar to an "ice cube." As time passes, the ice cube melts. If there's no time remaining your option becomes worthless. Intrinsic value, on the other hand, has tangible worth. At expiration, you can sell the option for its intrinsic value.

Thus, the stock price in relationship to the strike price has a great impact on the price of an option. Deeper in-the-money options cost more than those that are at or out-of-the-money because they have more intrinsic value. The further you go out-of-the-money, the less the option will cost, since it only consists of time value.

> Deeper in-the-money options cost more than those that are at or out-of-the-money because they have more intrinsic value.

Keep in mind that with puts the principle remains the same, although in-, at-, or out-of-the-money is just the opposite. With the stock trading at $85, the $80 put would be out-of-the-money, the $85 put would be at-the-money and the $90 put would be in-the-money.

Time

As discussed in the previous paragraph, an option can consist of both intrinsic and time value. Time value is what succumbs to the passage of time. It is referred to as "time decay." As expiration approaches, time decay accelerates. This reflected in this graph.

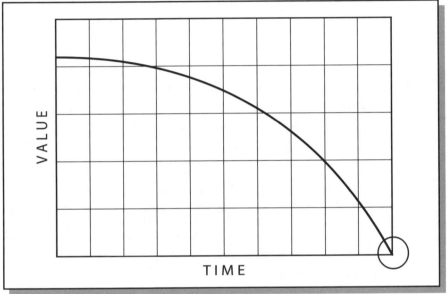

If you increase the amount of time until expiration, the value of both calls and puts will increase as well. Where there's more time, there is more value because the stock has more time to move in-the-money before expiration.

By way of review, when buying options always give yourself more time. As you learned in an earlier chapter, one of the biggest mistakes beginning option traders make is not buying enough time. As a result, often they pick the right stocks but run out of time.

Volatility

Having a sound understanding of volatility and its impact on the price of an option is critical to your success trading options. However, it is one of the most misunderstood aspects of option trading. This may be due to the fact that volatility tends to be rooted in mathematics (enough to make your head spin!) – a turnoff for many. Fortunately, you don't need to get caught up in the complexities of formulas and calculations to be successful trading options. Leave that to the professional trader. However, you do need to have a broad understanding of what it means and the role it plays. As you'll soon see, volatility has a huge impact on the price of options and your ability to trade them profitably.

You've probably realized that current volatility readings are not printed in *The Wall Street Journal* or *Investor's Business Daily* for you to read. Although you can quickly determine the other variables listed above, such as, stock price, strike price, the month of expiration, dividends, and short-term interest rates you can't determine, at first glance, the volatility of a particular stock. But since you do know the other variables, it becomes very easy to calculate what volatility is.

First of all, what is volatility? Volatility refers to the movement of a stock. It measures the amount a stock fluctuates, up or down, over a given period of time. The higher the volatility, the more likely the stock will experience greater movement.

Volatility is expressed in percentage terms on an annualized basis. For example, if Microsoft has a volatility of 30%, it tells you that Microsoft is on pace to be either up or down 30% over the next 12 months. If Microsoft is trading at $100, then its projected range would be between $130 and $70 over the next 12 months (30% x 100 = 30; add and subtract that from 100 and you get 130 and 70, respectively).

So how does volatility affect the price of the options? Consider for a moment two different stocks – Companies A and B. Company A is an up-and-coming star in a hot, fast-moving technology sector. Company B is in a slow, boring consumer products sector. Let's also assume both stocks currently trade at $50. Which stock's options do you think will cost more and why? Clearly Company A. Why? Because it can cover more ground quicker – it is more volatile. Company A is like a Ferrari and Company B is like an old clunker.

As a result, the higher the volatility, the higher the probability the stock will finish in-the-money at expiration. This is why the options are more expensive.

> Also keep in mind that as volatility increases, the price of both calls and puts increases as well.

Also keep in mind that as volatility increases, the price of both calls and puts increases as well. As volatility decreases, the price of the options decreases accordingly.

Let's say Company A $50 calls cost $13 and Company B $50 calls cost $5. Does this make Company A's options expensive and Company B's options cheap? Not necessarily. It's relative to what they're really worth. Consider the following example.

If I were to offer to sell you a car for $50,000, would that be a good deal? Well, it really depends on what kind of car it is. If it's a one-of-a-kind Porsche worth $200,000, then yes, $50,000 would be a steal of a deal! Why? The asking price of $50,000 is "cheap" relative to what the car is worth.

Conversely, if the car is a beaten-up clunker sitting out in a field then $50,000 is much more than the car is worth. In this case, $50,000 would be outrageously expensive. You see, a $50,000 car can be cheap or expensive depending on what its true value is.

So answering the question of whether a $13 option was expensive or a $5 option cheap ultimately depends on what the options are theoretically worth. If the $13 option is worth $17, then it would be considered cheap. If the $5 call is worth $3, then it would be considered expensive. As you can see, it is absolutely critical you know whether an option is cheap, expensive, or fairly priced. The key is knowing volatility.

Two Types of Volatility

If you assumed the role of market maker for a day, in what way would you use the stock price to determine the price of the options? Would you base the price of the options on how the stock traded in the past, or would you base them on how you think the stock will trade in the future? The future, you say. Why? The past doesn't necessarily predict the future. In other words, a stock may not move in the future like it did in the past. As a result, you need to be aware of two different types of volatility that exist: historical and implied.

Historical Volatility

As the name implies, historical volatility refers to the actual movement of the stock. Typically, you track it over a specific number of days. For example, at

www.planetcash.com/volatility.asp we track the 20-, 50-, and 100-day historical volatility.

But this brings us back to the same question – does the past always predict the future? No. It's one thing

> It is this predicted or estimated volatility that is referred to as implied volatility.

to know how a stock moved in the past (historical volatility), but it's much more difficult predicting how a stock will move in the future. It is this predicted or estimated volatility that is referred to as implied volatility.

Implied Volatility

Implied volatility represents the market's estimate or prediction of how volatile a stock will be until expiration. It's their "best guess" of how the stock will trade until expiration. Implied volatility is derived from the price of the option, something we'll cover shortly.

The lower the implied volatility, the cheaper the options. The higher it is, the more expensive the options are. So what would change or alter the market's estimation or prediction of where a stock may trade in the future? News!

> The lower the implied volatility, the cheaper the options. The higher it is, the more expensive the options are.

News creates uncertainty, and uncertainty equals risk in the market's eyes. Thus, the price of options rises (implied volatility increases) as things become more uncertain or volatile. It is a way for the market makers to reduce their risk much like an insurance company charges higher premiums to hedge against insuring a risky driver.

Can both good and bad news have an enormous impact on a stock's price? Yes! Consider the following examples. A good earnings report could cause the stock to skyrocket, whereas a bad report may send the stock into a free-fall. Hence, the anticipation of an earnings report before its release can cause implied volatility to rise dramatically. Anticipating an FDA ruling will inflate the price of options, despite little or no movement in the underlying stock.

Case in point: CV Therapeutics (CVTX) was awaiting results of the phase III trials for one of its products and the uncertainty regarding the outcome spiked implied volatility to 450%! Do you think those options were a bit pricey? You'd better believe it! Remember, implied volatility is the market's estimate or best guess of what they think may happen and not the actual movement of the stock. The bottom line? When the market or stocks face uncertainty, implied volatility typically soars!

Supply and Demand

In addition, don't forget that an option's price is also driven by supply and demand. If there is a lot of demand, prices will rise. If there is little or no demand, prices fall. Thus, implied volatility rises or falls as demand does.

You see this a lot with stock split announcements or the anticipation thereof. Have you ever bought an option on a stock split company, only to find by the end of the day that it's worth less than what you paid for it? Adding insult to injury, the stock may have even gone up in price! What's going on?

Most likely implied volatility bit you right in the wallet! Let's see what happens to the options when a company announces a stock split.

First of all, let's take a trip behind the scenes to see what happens in the pit where the options trade on a company that announces a stock split. Once on the floor, you notice a beehive of activity in the various pits located throughout the exchange. In some pits the traders are packed in like sardines, shouting "Buy" or "Sold." However, in the pit where the stock split company's options trade, there doesn't seem like much is going on. Heck, there's someone even playing a crossword puzzle. A few others are watching a NCAA playoff game on a TV perched between the bank of monitors displaying quotes.

All of a sudden the stock split announcement hits the newswire. Remember, order flow has been slow thus far but now things start picking up, and fast! Watch what happens to the options.

At my live seminars I like to demonstrate what happens next by using a balloon. The balloon represents the price of the option. The air inside the balloon represents implied volatility. I want you to visualize yourself holding a balloon that is partially filled with air.

Now let's pick up the story where we left off. You call your broker. "What are the $80 calls going for?" you ask. Your broker quotes $3.50 to buy. "Give me ten at the market," you respond. At the time you called, the option was selling for $3.50. Unbeknownst to you, as you're placing your order, hundreds of other orders to "buy" come streaming into the pit. What do you think happens to the price of the options? They begin to climb. But the stock isn't moving all that much, so what's driving the price higher? Implied volatility.

I demonstrate this by blowing up the balloon. The balloon, which once traded for $3, is now worth 4…4.50…4.75…and so on. In fact, it happens much quicker than I can blow air into the balloon. The price of the option inflates just like the balloon. Remember, implied volatility is the air inside of the balloon. As implied volatility expands, the options become more and more expensive.

Within minutes the $80 calls are trading at $6.50 and your *market order* is filled. You are the proud owner of an option at $6.50 that was just trading at $3.50 a few minutes ago. Once you get your fill back, you're absolutely flabbergasted. "This is highway robbery," you shout. "Those market makers are worst than thieves," you cry in disbelief.

By the end of the day, the stock closes up a few points and you decide to see how much money you've made. Even though you got a poor fill, at least the stock is moving in your favor. You call the broker and ask, "Hey Jim, what did the $80 calls close at?" They're currently 5.25 X 5.75 he reports. "Are you sure?" you say. Yep, he says. That's the closing quote. You hang up the phone in shock. Here, the stock moved in your favor with a stock split to boot, and you're *still* losing money? "I just don't get it," you say. "What in the world happened?" What *did* happen?

To begin with, when there are a lot of orders coming into a pit, the market makers do the best job they can filling them. Typically, the exchange implements what is referred to as "fast market rules." This gives market makers more time to fill incoming orders. To place a market order in such an environment is dangerous at best. You may be guaranteeing yourself the high of the day. Nevertheless, how did your option go down in value even though the stock closed higher?

Recall the analogy of the balloon. As demand increases, the market makers will continue to increase the price of the options until demand tapers off. This happens even if the stock isn't keeping pace. Implied volatility soars through the roof.

When demand drops off, volatility tends to return to lower levels, meaning air is let out of the balloon. That's how your option ended up finishing worth $5.75, even though the stock moved in your favor. This is often referred to as *volatility crush*.

You paid too much for the option. The market makers jacked up implied volatility and you bought the "balloon" when it was fully inflated. You see the option was really worth $3.50 but you paid $6.50 for it. As a result, in order to make money the stock has to make that much bigger of a move to compensate for the inflated premium. Hence, the odds were already against you before you hung up the telephone.

A recent illustration of this is the CV Therapeutics (CVTX) example I shared earlier. The news hit the wires that their product was approved by the FDA. Wonderful news, right? Well, the stock was up over 2 points during the day, but believe it or not, some options lost more than 50% of their value. Why? Implied volatility dropped back down to historical levels after hitting over three times their normal level going into the announcement. Talk about a volatility crush – all in a matter of seconds! Here's a perfect case where you can be right about market direction but still lose money. Knowing whether implied volatility is running high or low is mandatory to becoming a consistent and effective options trader!

> Trading off news, whether it comes from pagers or other portable devices, can be so dangerous.

This is why trading off news, whether it comes from pagers or other portable devices, can be so dangerous. Unless you are on the phone with your broker when such an announcement occurs, or you can route your order directly to the floor, it's very difficult to get a good fill trading off the news. It's like trading by the seat of your pants.

Market makers and other floor traders get the information as it hits the newswires just like everyone else, but they're always going to be quicker in those first ten seconds. By the time you call your broker, place the order and it hits the floor (even 30 seconds or a minute later), the options have most likely moved and implied volatility is already ramping. Plus, if fast market rules kick in, the odds of getting a poor fill increase dramatically. So how do you deal with demand-driven events such as stock splits, FDA rulings, or mergers? You have a couple of choices.

> Recognize that if you trade news announcements, you're always in danger of paying way too much for the options!

First of all, stand aside. Patience typically enables you to get a better price. Yeah, you may miss out on a couple of points, but I'd rather be "late" instead of paying too much due to all the hype and hoopla. Recognize that if you trade news announcements, you're always in danger of paying way too much for the options!

Second, implied volatility affects time value and not intrinsic value. In order to negate implied volatility's role a simple solution would be to buy deeper in-the-money options. Will it cost more money? Yes. Plus, committing more capital increases your risk in that trade. Additionally, it could price you out of doing the trade altogether. Nonetheless, it is one way you can avoid getting hammered by a collapse in implied volatility. Buy as much intrinsic value as you can afford, staying within your risk guidelines. If you avoid time value, you avoid the consequences of implied volatility.

Finally, on news-type events, Do Not Use Market Orders! Always use a limit order. If the option is

> On news-type events, Do Not Use Market Orders!

going at $4 by $4.50 and it's a stock split announcement, place a limit order at $5. It gives the floor broker more wiggle room to the upside to fill your order. If you enter a limit order at $4.50, you're going to be left in the dust. If you get filled, great. If you don't, no big deal, you can always get in later.

If volatility is so important, how do you figure it out? How do you determine what an option is really worth? You need an option-pricing model, just like professionals use. One such model is the *Black-Scholes* model. It is your blue book when you're "shopping" for options. It will tell you exactly what you need to know!

The Black-Scholes Model

Since an option's price is determined by the stock price, strike price, volatility, time until expiration, interest rates, and dividends, it would seem logical that a formula could be used to calculate the theoretical value of an option. That's exactly what the Black-Scholes model does. This was one of the first models, introduced in 1973, shortly after listed options started trading. Its purpose is to calculate the theoretical value of an option. In fact, in 1997 its creators won the Nobel Prize for its effectiveness and usefulness in the pricing of derivatives – options. As far as the formula itself, you don't want to do this by hand. Use a software program to do the work for you. I use a program I've created called the *Option Explorer*.

The Option Explorer is an easy-to-use software program that harnesses the power of the Black-Scholes model. All you need to do is input the variables and it does the rest! Once you input the variables, you can quickly and easily determine the theoretical price of an option. This tells you whether an option is cheap, fairly priced, or expensive. This frees up your time to make trading decisions instead of crunching numbers. It also gives you the ability to determine implied volatility! By making use of this program you have the rare ability to measure the true value of your investment (options) through scientific means.

One way to do so is by plugging in the known variables into the formula – stock price, strike price, time until expiration, short-term interest rates, and historical volatility.

As I mentioned previously, you can get the historical volatility (courtesy of options guru Larry McMillan) for optionable stocks and indexes by visiting **www.planetcash.com/volatility.asp**.

Once there, you'll notice that the stocks are arranged alphabetically by ticker symbol. The next three columns (left to right) provide the stocks' 20- (20hv), 50- (50hv), and 100-day (100hv) historical volatility. This helps you see the trend of volatility over time. It tells you whether the stock is becoming more or less volatile. When choosing which historical volatility to use, I like the 50-day historical volatility.

Option Explorer will then determine the value of the option – in milliseconds! By comparing this value against the quote you get from your broker, you can determine whether or not you're buying a fairly priced option. For example, if Option Explorer told you the option was theoretically worth $2 but the current price is $3.50, you know immediately that the option is expensive based upon the assumptions you've made with the option-pricing model. The theoretical value of the option is less than the current market value of the option.

Now the question becomes: Is using the 50-day historical volatility a fair representation of future volatility? Or could recent volatility in the stock justify a higher premium? Or perhaps it's too high. As discussed previously, the dilemma facing every option trader is trying to predict the future movement of the stock. What you can do is analyze the current price of the options and determine what kind of future movement the market is "implying" in their price. You want to find out what the implied volatility is. You want to know the market's current estimate of where the stock may trade until expiration. This is the second way that Option Explorer proves invaluable.

If you run the Black-Scholes model as demonstrated, you can calculate the value of an option given the current stock price, strike price, time, volatility, and short-term interest rates. You can likewise run the Black-Scholes model "backward," this time solving for volatility. (Sorry, but a quick trip to math class is in order.) You do this by leaving volatility blank and putting in the current price of the option. In a nutshell, Option Explorer is going to solve for volatility.

Once this is done, Option Explorer will provide you with implied volatility, as reflected by the current price of the option. Now you can determine whether an option is cheap, fairly priced, or expensive. How? By comparing implied volatility against historical volatility.

Is the Option Cheap or Expensive?

By comparing the historical and implied volatility, you can determine whether an option is cheap, fairly priced, or expensive.

When implied volatility is greater than historical volatility, the option is said to be "expensive."

When implied volatility is less than historical volatility, the option is "cheap."

When volatility is similar to historical volatility, the option is fairly priced.

A Shortcut

Another way to determine whether an option is cheap, fairly priced, or expensive is to use the percentile rankings found at **www.planetcash.com/volatility.asp**.

You probably already noticed the additional four columns to the right of the historical volatility readings. They are:

"Date" refers to the last date upon which the data was calculated.

"Curiv" refer to the composite or average implied volatility reading for all options that trade on the underlying security.

"Days" refers to the number of days for which implied volatility has been calculated.

"Percentile" is the rank of the "curiv" as compared to the past number of daily implied volatility readings.

For example, if the current implied volatility ranks in the tenth percentile, what this means is that the current implied volatility ranks higher than 10% of all past daily readings. Another way of looking at it is that 90% of all past readings have been higher. It's in the lower end of its range when compared to the past daily readings. This means the options are cheap.

If the implied volatility ranked in the 98th percentile then the options would be very expensive since it's in the higher part of its range when compared to its past daily readings. You see, only 2% of all past daily readings have been higher.

So the rules of thumb are as follows:

When the options on the underlying security you're interested in rank in the 90th percentile or higher, the options are considered expensive.

If the options rank in the 10th percentile or less, they're considered cheap.

As I'm sure you've already figured out, if they rank in the 50th percentile, they're fairly priced.

As the rankings fall above or below these "extremes," recognize that the options are becoming more expensive or cheaper. You're able to gain an edge by exploiting opportunities that arise when their rankings are above or below the extremes.

> By knowing whether options are cheap, expensive, or fairly priced you'll always know which strategy or strategies to implement.

Remember, pillar two of your trading plan is choosing the appropriate strategy. By knowing whether options are cheap, expensive, or fairly priced you'll always know which strategy or strategies to implement.

How can options can become mispriced if everyone can easily calculate its theoretical value? It boils down to emotion. It is the one thing you can't "bottle" when it comes to trading stocks and/or options market. Options, being highly leveraged instruments, exaggerate the emotional optimism or pessimism of the market, causing option prices to vary widely from their true worth.

Moreover, when you use words like "estimated," "predicted" or "best guess," is there room for error? Sure. You see, no one knows whether the market makers will be proven right in their assumptions until time passes or the news event occurs. It is this disparity between perception (implied volatility) and reality (historical volatility) that you can exploit as an option trader. If you're anchored in a well-crafted game and you know what to look for, you can take advantage of the anomalies that repeatedly pop up in the marketplace.

> It is this disparity between perception (implied volatility) and reality (historical volatility) that you can exploit as an option trader.

Choosing the Appropriate Strategy – Exploiting Volatility for Maximum Gains!!

There are times when stocks experience high volatility and periods of low volatility. This could be due to an earnings release or other news-driven events. The important lesson to be learned, however, is that regardless of how high or low volatility becomes, it tends to return back to normal, historical levels.

To better understand how this affects options is to view volatility like a rubber band. Take a rubber band and place it in your hand. This starting point represents historical volatility. This is how it normally behaves. Now, if you stretch the rubber band one way or the other it's similar to increasing or decreasing implied volatility.

> Regardless of how high or low volatility becomes, it tends to return back to normal, historical levels.

Thus, as it's stretched to the right an option is becoming more and more expensive (implied volatility is greater than historical volatility). As you stretch it to the left, it is becoming cheaper (implied volatility is less than historical volatility).

However, regardless of how far you stretch the rubber band (without breaking it, of course), it will ultimately return back to where it began – historical levels.

So how do you profit from this recurring phenomenon? Let's think it through. If options are expensive (90th percentile or above), what would you rather be, a buyer or seller? A seller. You want to receive that juicy premium! But if options are cheap, what would you rather be, a buyer or seller? A buyer. In short, you want to buy low volatility and sell high volatility. That gives you an edge. So what strategies should you implement?

This topic is discussed at length in my sequel to this book, *High Octane Options*, but let me whet your appetite with a few ideas.

Choosing the Appropriate Strategy When the Options Are Expensive

If options are expensive, the preferred approach includes strategies that involve selling premium. By the way, before you engage in any strategy, make sure you understand the risks inherent to it.

If the trend is bullish, then you could choose from these bullish strategies: writing covered calls, selling naked puts, bull put spreads, bull call spreads, and call ratio backspreads.

If the trend is bearish, you can choose from: selling naked calls, bear call spreads, bear put spreads, and put ratio backspreads.

If the stock is stuck in a trading range, you can implement neutral strategies such as selling naked combinations or straddles.

Don't forget that pillar number one is still paramount – the trend is your friend! It does you no good to buy cheap puts on a stock in a strong uptrend, and in the same way, putting on a bull put spread on a stock in a strong downtrend would be foolish.

The key is to correctly identify the trend and then choose the appropriate strategy based upon how the options are priced.

Each one of these strategies has both positives and negatives to consider – something we'll tackle in *High Octane Options*. Nonetheless, the general benefits of selling premium are twofold.

1. You benefit from time decay. As a buyer, the melting "ice cube" costs you money. As a seller you make the money!
2. Volatility, over time, reverts back to historical levels. By selling inflated premium, you have the ability to pocket "extra" premium and benefit from a collapse in volatility.

Furthermore, once you correctly understand how to take advantage of volatility, you don't necessarily have to predict the direction of the move, but the magnitude of the move. Thus, you can construct trades with very little risk, be totally wrong about market direction, and still make a killing! How do you like the sound of *that*?

> you can construct trades with very little risk, be totally wrong about market direction, and still make a killing

Important note: If you are selling overvalued options, you want to be aware of the risks inherent with such strategies. The options may be overvalued for a reason. If there is a merger or acquisition on the horizon, or if there is a FDA approval in the works, the value of the underlying security could skyrocket or plummet. Avoid such situations. However, there are plenty of times when options become undervalued or overvalued for no apparent reason. It's these situations that you want to capitalize on.

For example, let's say 3M (MMM) is trading at $95. An at-the-money call option with 43 days remaining until expiration is worth $4.81 at a 35% volatility level, but worth an amazing $6.75 at a 50% volatility level. Out of-the-money comparisons are even more dramatic. A fifteen-point out-of-the-money call option (110 strike price) with 43 days remaining until expiration is worth only $0.75 at a 35% volatility level. That same option is worth 2.06 at a 50% volatility level. This means that you can sell an option at $2.50 that is normally worth $0.75 based upon the stock's historical movement. Can you see how knowing the theoretical value of an option can unlock lucrative trading opportunities?

Strategies When Options Are Cheap

When options become cheap (10th percentile or less), your "edge" comes from implementing buying strategies. You can buy a call or buy a put, or you can buy both. This is a neutral strategy called a straddle. A straddle involves buying both a call and a put on the same stock, at the same strike price, for the same month. You're playing both sides of the fence! This is an awesome strategy as well.

> One of the great benefits of a straddle is that you don't have to pick market direction.

One of the great benefits of a straddle is that you don't have to pick market direction. You don't care whether the stock goes up or down; you just want it to go somewhere! That's why I refer to it as my "be in a good mood all the time" strategy! The last thing you want, though, is for the stock to do nothing.

Another awesome benefit of buying options when they're cheap is that you'll benefit as implied volatility returns back to historical levels. As it does, both your calls and puts increase in price, increasing the overall value of the straddle. In this case, you could theoretically make money without the stock moving anywhere! How's *that* for a change?

So what do you do if you just want to buy calls and puts or you are unfamiliar with these other strategies? Can you still trade? Of course. But as I mentioned before, if you identify options that are expensive, you need to take measures to neutralize implied volatility's role. How? The key is choosing the correct strike price.

Strike Price is Critical

Once you identify the trend, should you buy at-the-money, in-the-money, or out-of-the-money options? The answer depends on how the options are priced and what type of move you expect the stock to make. Once you know the answers to these two questions you will be better suited to pick the appropriate strike price.

First of all, let's tackle the issue of how the options are priced. If the option is cheap or fairly priced, you have the "green light" to buy the option. Then the strike price you choose is based upon the expected move in the underlying stock. But what if the option is expensive?

As mentioned before, buying expensive options can be quite a frustrating experience, particularly if you're right about the direction of the stock but your option still loses money. The solution is to buy deeper in-the-money options. By buying more intrinsic value and less time value, you not only avoid time decay but you also negate the affects of implied volatility. How?

> By buying more intrinsic value and less time value, you not only avoid time decay but you also negate the affects of implied volatility.

In the balloon example, implied volatility represented the air inside the balloon. This can also be considered the "time value" portion of the option. The less you have, the less a collapse in crush can affect your position. So if you determine the options you're interested in are expensive then buy in-the-money calls or puts, depending on the trend of the stock.

Now let's address the second part of our question. What kind of move do you expect the stock to make? A small one, perhaps a three- to five-point move? Or do you think the stock's going to move eight to ten points? Do you feel it's going to explode and run 20 to 30 points, maybe more? In order to select the correct strike price you have to make some kind of assumption as to the expected move in the underlying stock. This will enable you to choose an option that will adequately leverage the resulting move. How do you know how closely the option will mirror the stock? The delta will.

What's delta? It tells you how sensitive your option is to the underlying movement of the stock. It answers the question,

"For every one dollar the stock moves, how much will your option go up or down?" Each strike price has a corresponding delta. It is typically expressed as a decimal, for example, 0.42 or 0.95. You can also view it as a percentage: 0.42 = 42% and 0.95 = 95%. Option Explorer will calculate the delta for any strike price you choose.

> What's delta? It tells you how sensitive your option is to the underlying movement of the stock. It answers the question, "For every one dollar the stock moves, how much will your option go up or down?"

So if you buy the $65 calls with a delta of 0.42, then if the stock moves $1.00, your calls would increase by 42% of that one-dollar move, or 42 cents. A 0.95 delta would yield a 95-cent increase in the calls.

Would you prefer a higher or lower delta as an option trader? Higher! If you have 100% delta, your option will move "tick for tick," meaning that if the stock goes up one dollar, your call option will go up one dollar. Also keep in mind that delta is a two-edged sword – it works both directions. If the delta is 0.95 then if the stock falls $1.00, your call option would lose ninety five cents.

> The deeper you go in-the-money, the higher the delta will be.

So the $64,000 question is, where do you find the higher deltas? In-the-money. The deeper you go in-the-money, the higher the delta will be. If the stock is at $85, the $80 calls will have a higher delta than the $85 calls, and the $75 calls will have a greater delta than the $80 calls. The farther out of-the-money you go, the smaller the delta will be.

How does this affect the strike price you choose? It ties back into what you're looking for. The smaller the move you expect, the higher the delta you'll need to be profitable. You want your option to mirror as closely as possible the movement of the stock. Thus, you'll need to buy deeper in-the-money options. If you believe the stock is going to make a bigger move, then buy at- or out-of-the-money options. Initially, you have a smaller delta, but as the stock moves in your favor your delta increases in your favor. Plus, buying at or out of-the-money options takes advantage of leverage, since you're putting up less money.

> The smaller the move you expect, the higher the delta you'll need to be profitable. If you believe the stock is going to make a bigger move, then buy at- or out-of-the-money options.

With puts it works the same way. If you think the stock's going to drop tremendously, go out of-the-money. If you think it's going to drop a fair amount, buy at-the-money. If you think it's just going to drop a little bit, maybe three or four points, buy in-the-money.

If the market is trending strongly or stocks are breaking out, you would typically buy at- or out-of-the-money options. You expect a big move; thus, you want to harness the power of leverage. If the market is choppy or more volatile, you want to buy in-the-money options, looking to capture smaller moves. At such times, my preferred style of trading is *swing trading*.

Since I'm getting in and out quicker, I need the option to mirror the movement of the stock more closely. As a result, I buy options with a higher delta.

In conclusion, knowing whether an option is cheap, expensive, or fairly priced is crucial to your success as an options trader. It dictates the appropriate strategy to choose. It will also help you determine the correct strike price. When you identify options that are cheap, you want to implement buying strategies. When options are expensive, you want to implement selling strategies. Clearly, there is no magic formula that guarantees profitable results. However, by using this invaluable information in your trading decisions, you can increase the odds of success dramatically. It is truly the greatest money-making secret in the world!

That's why it's critical you minimize your losses and maximize your gains! In short, you need to know when to hold'em and know when to fold'em.

Key Points to Remember

➤ *In-the-money* options consist of intrinsic and time value. They are the only options with any value at expiration.

➤ *At-the-money* and *out-of-the-money* options have no intrinsic value and consist of time value only.

➤ *Time decay* refers to the wasting portion of an option. It pertains to time value only.

➤ Having more time until expiration will increase the value of both calls and puts. A decrease in time will decrease the value of both calls and puts.

➤ *Volatility* refers to the speed with which a stock may move either up or down over a given period in time.

➤ The higher the volatility, the higher the price for both calls and puts. This is due to the fact that the probability of the stock finishing in the money is greater.

➤ There are two types of volatility: *historical* and *implied*. Historical volatility represents that actual movement of the stock. Implied volatility is the market's estimation of how the stock will move until expiration.

➤ You can determine the theoretical value of an option using an option-pricing model such as the Black-Scholes. By inputting the stock price, strike price, time until expiration, volatility, and short-term interest rates, you can determine the value of an option.

➤ You can use the same model to compute the current implied volatility. By merely leaving volatility unknown and plugging in the current value of the option, the model will tell you exactly what implied volatility is.

➤ By comparing implied volatility against historical volatility, you can determine whether an option is cheap, fairly priced, or expensive. When implied volatility is less than historical volatility, the option is said to be cheap. If implied volatility is greater than historical volatility, the option is expensive.

➤ Generally speaking, you want to be a buyer when options are fairly priced or cheap. You want to be a seller when they are expensive. When trading options, you want to buy implied volatility when it's low and sell it when it's high.

➤ An option may be compared to an insurance policy: the higher the risk, the greater your premium. Likewise, the more volatile a stock is, the higher the option premium. Therefore, it behooves option traders to track volatility closely. In fact, it is mandatory.

➤ By knowing the true value of an option, you can implement strategies that exploit cheap or expensive options. When options are cheap, you can buy calls or puts, or both as in a straddle. When options are expensive, you can implement sell naked calls or puts, buy or sell spreads, and sell naked strangles or straddles.

➤ By knowing both the historical and implied volatility you can put on a trade, be totally wrong about market direction, but still make money. The edge exists in knowing the range of the move, not necessarily the direction of the move.

➤ Delta tells you how much your option will go up or down for every one dollar the stock moves. You can find higher deltas as you go deeper in-the-money. The further you go out of-the-money, the lower the delta will be.

➤ If you expect the stock to make a smaller move, buy in-the-money options. If you expect a larger move, buy at- or out-of-the-money options.

CHAPTER 16

Know When to Hold'Em, Know When To Fold'Em

"Who are those guys? They never know when to hold'em or fold'em. They just can't make up their minds."
– Butch Cassidy

Your success as a trader is dependent upon your ability to manage your risk and money wisely. Remember, the third of the three pillars that form the foundation of a successful trading program is risk and money management. While everyone begins trading with the hope of making bushels of money, the sobering reality is that you will lose money along the way! The difference between lasting success and certain failure is how you handle your profits and losses. Therefore, your primary focus should be protecting the equity in your trading account.

With that in mind, in this chapter you will be introduced to some conservative and simple money management tools that are easy to implement. They will provide a reliable anchor so you can weather the tumultuous emotional storms found on Wall Street. By the time you're done, you'll have the necessary tools so you can know exactly "when to hold'em and when to fold'em!"

Do you nip a loss in the bud or do you let it get out of hand? Do you make the most of your winning positions? Do you execute your stop-loss according to your game plan, or do fear and greed prevent you from taking the appropriate action? How you answer these questions will either put you on the path to wealth and happiness or poverty and despair.

The key to succeeding in this or any business is paying attention to your bottom line – are you making or losing money. When your money is at risk, it has a strong impact upon you and your emotions. Unfortunately, emotional traders are almost guaranteed to lose in the stock market. The most effective strategies in the world will not help you if you allow your emotions to affect your buying and selling decisions.

Frankly, before you can become skillful at making money, you need to become even more adept at losing money first! Wow! Did that grab your attention? Well, it's true. Your success is rooted in your ability to avoid large losses and taking small ones! It's that simple. You must learn and master the art of losing money. You must be constantly "pruning" your portfolio in much the same way you would prune a bonsai tree.

Bonsai is the ancient art of growing miniature trees in pots or containers. For thousands of years, bonsai (pronounced BAHN-sy) has been considered a very specialized, delicate, and unique art form. Although the practice of developing

Lilliputian trees originated in China around 200 A.D., the Japanese popularized and named the practice. "Bonsai" is a Japanese word, which literally means "potted tree."

There are many ways to start a bonsai, but maintaining and nurturing a tree through many stages of maturity requires an understanding of proper pruning techniques. Knowing how to prune the limbs and roots will enable a tree to live for years. In fact, there are many trees that have lived for hundreds and, in some cases, thousands of years!

Why is cutting so important? Because it helps a bonsai maintain its shape. And more importantly, "cutting it back" creates longevity. You see, bonsai trees are trained to live within their boundaries so no limb or root is allowed to create a loss of growth space. By constantly trimming and clipping the tree, it fosters long-term growth and development.

And so it is with trading. It's critical to constantly cut your losses. Bad trades are like overgrown limbs and roots that will eventually inhibit financial growth. By frequently "pruning" losing trades, your account will enjoy longer and lasting growth. Thus, becoming a profitable trader has very little to do with your entry points and everything to do with your exit points! Mastering this aspect of trading will also help you avoid wild fluctuations in the size of your trading account.

A timeless trading adage states, "Cut your losses short and let your profits run." Consequently, your highest priority should not be achieving a high winning percentage (although that's admirable), but rather making a lot of money when you are right. Regrettably, most traders let their losses run and take their profits early. They may even have a high winning percentage, yet they are still broke! They have it all backward.

For example, one investor could win 80% of the time but still lose his shirt, while another may lose 80% of the time and strike it rich! The difference revolves around each trader's ability to maximize gains and minimize losses. The reality is that your emotions, fear and greed, tend to prohibit you from executing such a trading plan. As a result, you make irrational decisions – risking too much money on any one trade or exiting a profitable trade too early – the Achilles heel of every investor!

Thus, you will find safety and refuge in staying committed and focused on your game plan. Speaking of focus, it reminds me of the following story.

A young boy traveled across Japan to the school of a famous martial artist. When he arrived at the dojo, he was given an audience by the sensei.

"What do you want from me?" the master asked.
"I wish to be your student and become the finest karateka in the land," the boy replied. "How long must I study?"
"Ten years at least," the mastered answered.
"What if I studied twice as hard as all your other students?"
"Twenty years," replied the master.
"Twenty years! What if I practice day and night with all my effort?"
"Thirty years," was the master's reply.
"How is it that each time I say I will work harder, you tell me that it will take longer?" the boy asked.

"The answer is clear. When one eye is fixed upon your destination, there is only one eye left with which to find the way."

This enlightening story clearly underscores the importance of focusing on your journey (execution) and not on your destination (profits). Don't allow yourself to get sidetracked by the amount of money you hope to make. Avoid thinking that each trade will be a big winner. Don't mentally "spend" the money you haven't realized yet. Doing so only leads to sloppy execution, putting you on the fast track to frustration and failure.

By staying focused on your game plan you will be pleasantly surprised with the results. There will be some months where the total of your profits will shock you. Some of my biggest months have absolutely amazed me. I had no idea I was doing as well as I was. You see, my sole focus was on making good trades and executing my game plan in maximizing my gains and cutting my losses. By focusing on protecting my trading capital, the profits took care of themselves.

As you know, the stock market is full of surprises. No matter how well you do your research, trades go bad. Quickly recognizing when you are wrong is key to maintaining a positive attitude while trading. When you take a loss, simply view it as an opportunity to "upgrade" your money to a better position! Always view the glass as being half full. Develop a proactive mindset and get in the habit of taking losses quickly. Playing the game of "Oh, I'm sure it's going to turn around" will get you into trouble. In fact, it's often a one-way ticket to huge losses.

Another thing to consider, which is often overlooked, is the emotional toll a losing position has on you. It becomes a proverbial ball and chain, dragging it around with you wherever you go. By cutting it loose you can move on to bigger and better trades.

One of the great joys of teaching people how to trade is hearing about their successes. But with the good comes the bad, so I also hear of the losses as well. While losses inevitably occur, many could have been dramatically reduced. People let losses get way out of hand. I'm sure you have a few "war stories" of your own. Unfortunately, everyone will go through the same learning curve unless they, like you, take the time to master the principles in this chapter.

For some, however, it is a longer and more painful process than with others. It's the "school of hard knocks." We've all been there at one time or another. As I reflect on the many lessons I've learned (and still learn!), many of them could have been avoided if I had known then what I'm sharing with you now.

When I first started trading, I made some great money, but then I found myself giving it back due to poor decisions. It was like I was taking two steps forward and one step back. Sound familiar? To say the least, that got old, fast! So why do most traders suffer this same fate? Simple: fear and greed! It is human emotion rather than logic that puts traders between a rock and a hard place.

Fear

Purchasing a stock or option involves risking the loss of your entire investment. This is why risking too much capital on any one trade only magnifies the problem. You see, when the trade moves against you, you fear taking a loss because your potential loss is that much bigger now. You hang on, hoping the trade will turn in your favor. Too often, you watch hopelessly as your money goes right down the drain! I can tell you right now, with a high degree of confidence, that "hoping" is not a very successful trading strategy!

Greed

This is the flip side of the "emotional coin." Greed comes in two seductive and dangerous forms. First of all, although you may be disciplined enough to cut your losses short, you may find that you are never satisfied with your profits. You'll reason that, "If I can double my money, why not triple it?" Frankly, this was one of my biggest weaknesses when I started trading. Unfortunately, this comes back to haunt you as sizable paper gains evaporate into thin air, or worse, turn into losses.

For example, shortly after placing a trade, I found myself with almost a 200% gain! I thought I had struck the mother lode! Did I sell? No. "Since I have so much time remaining before expiration I'm going to make a fortune," I whispered to myself. Sadly, the story didn't have a happy ending. My option proceeded to fall back to breakeven and then I watched in despair as it eventually expired worthless. I couldn't believe it. I was in a state of shock. How in the world did I let this happen? I left so much money on the table it made my stomach turn. It was my first, but not my last, run-in with the ruthless taskmaster known as greed.

In retrospect, one of the worst things that happened to me as a rookie was having some impressive wins right out of the gate. Success actually became a major stumbling block. Why? I was lulled into thinking that I was invincible! (Just like trees grow to the sky.) I got too big for my britches. This led me to violate another important money management rule.

The second trap you can fall into is thinking, "More is better." When I first started trading, if I made money I always wished I would have bought more. If I had bought ten contracts I told myself I should have bought 20. Thus, on my next trade I ended up doing just that, committing way too much capital to that one position in the process. As soon as that trade moved against me, what do you think I wished I had done? Exactly! I wished I had bought less – a lot less! Talk about an emotional rollercoaster!

However, little did I know that my time at the school of hard knocks was far from over. Now, I found myself holding losing positions. I watched the trades move against me, but I didn't take action. I didn't realize it at the time, but I was paralyzed by the fear of taking a loss.

"There's no way I'm going to lose $5,000," I said to myself. Like many investors, I felt it would turn around. "Plus, if I sell now I'll miss the next move higher." So a $5,000 loss turned into a $15,000 loss.

Next, I grappled with my own fallibility. "Me, wrong? No way. I know I'm right. How can the stock be going down? Don't they know the company announced better-than-expected earnings?" I was frustrated with the market's "ignorance." I couldn't accept the fact that I was wrong. I was more concerned with being right than making money. I didn't realize that the market is always right!

The bottom line is that I squandered a lot of my hard-earned money because I didn't have a predefined exit strategy. As a beginning trader, I let fear and greed rule my buying and selling decisions. Don't let the same thing happen to you. (Forewarned is forearmed!) So how do you guard against committing these same mistakes? You need a game plan. (Ring a bell?)

You need a plan, system, or way to help you know exactly when to buy and sell. You need a simple way of knowing when to cut your losses or take your gains. By having objective, preset exit points, both on the upside as well as the downside, you can conquer your emotions.

Scared Money

Before we move on to more specific money management principles to help meet these challenges, let me touch upon an important investment principle. You should never invest in the stock market, let alone options, unless you can afford to lose the money to begin with. While you can implement certain strategies to substantially reduce your risk, the possibility of loss is real. It is very hard to make money with "scared money" – money that is needed for another purpose, such as bills, food, or rent. Your emotions will be easily affected, thus making the trading process all the more difficult. Can you make a fortune starting on a shoestring? Yes! That's what the American Dream is all about. I meet people all the time who have enjoyed tremendous success after getting started with very little money. Nonetheless, you must understand and control your risk at all times.

Risk

The first rule of money management is predefining the amount of money you're willing to lose on each and every trade. Risk is simply the difference between your entry and exit. Thus, before you enter a trade you must know exactly when (time) and where (price) you will exit. This applies to not only cutting your losses, but with taking profits as well. Here are a few ideas to consider.

Time

A significant aspect of money management that is often overlooked, particularly when trading options, is the element of time. As you know, an option is a wasting asset so you need to close out your positions before the acceleration of time decay kicks in. You need an exit strategy based on time.

Here's a basic rule of thumb you can use: If you own calls or puts, exit them with four to five weeks remaining before expiration, regardless of price. A good time to exit your positions is the week of expiration of the month before your option expires. If you hold a May option, you should liquidate it the week of expiration for April. Even if the option has not hit your target, exit the position

What should you do if your position is profitable and the "trend is still your friend"? You should still close out the position but then roll up (choose a higher strike price that is at- or slightly in-the-money) and out to a further month (two months minimum). That way, you give the stock more time to hit your target.

Let's say in August you decide to buy a November 50 call for $5. The stock is trading at $49. Now, two months later, the stock has rallied to $60. Your option is worth $11. The stock is in a nice uptrend and there are no red flags: the stock isn't climbing too sharp, too fast. However, it's the week of expiration for October, so you're supposed to exit the trade. What should you do?

Since the trend is still your friend, sell your November 50 call and use part of the proceeds to reestablish another position. So you decide to roll up and out. You buy the January 60 call for $6. The benefits are twofold:

First of all, time is back on your side. This slows down the effects of time decay. How often have you picked the right stock, but ran out of time? Second, you "ring the register"! By taking some money off the table, you reduce your exposure, thereby placing yourself back in a leveraged position – you have $6 at risk and not $12. And, above all, the trend is still your friend! Then again, what happens if the trend is not your friend? At what point should you cut your losses? Moving averages are part of the answer.

Moving Averages as an Exit Strategy

Not only will moving averages help you identify and position yourself in the direction of the trend, they will also become an integral part of your risk management program. If used correctly, they will tell you exactly when to cut your losses, something you don't want to take lightly.

As you learned in a previous chapter, moving averages are a lagging indicator. That's why you can't afford to wait for the moving averages to cross to generate a sell signal. You'll be too late and your losses will be substantial. As you realize by now, entering a trade late shouldn't bother you, but exiting a losing trade should. You must cut your losses sooner rather than later! What's the solution? Pay attention to where the stock closes in relationship to its key moving average. This will enable you to exit your trades quicker and keep the losses smaller.

Which moving average should you use? That depends upon your tolerance of "financial pain." If you use a longer moving average you will stick with a trade longer and potentially suffer larger losses! If you take a look at the chart of Deluxe (DLX) below, you can see the stock in a beautiful uptrend. If you decide to use the 200-day moving average as your stop, the stock could make a sizable move against you before you exited the trade – something I don't recommend!

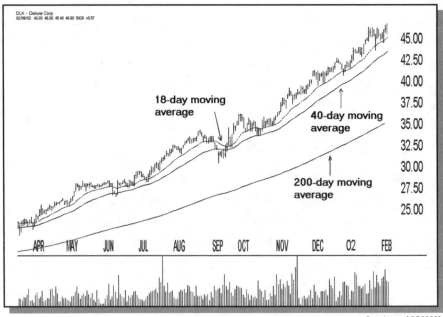

Courtesy of TC2000®.

If you use a shorter moving average you will get out quicker since it mirrors the price of the stock more closely. Note how the eighteen-day moving average is much closer to the current price of the stock. I tend to give the stock the benefit of the doubt if it's in a strong uptrend. As a result, I typically don't exit a losing position until the stock closes below the 40- or 50-day moving average. If it does, it goes on "sell alert" status.

The reverse would be true for exiting bearish positions. Once the stock closes back above your chosen moving average, then you would exit the trade. Similarly, the shorter the moving average you use, the quicker the sell signal. By using a longer moving average, you give the stock license to rally too far before stopping yourself out, potentially wiping out most, if not all your profits. You can readily see how this would be the case with Ariba (ARBA). Note how far away the 200-day moving average is from the stock.

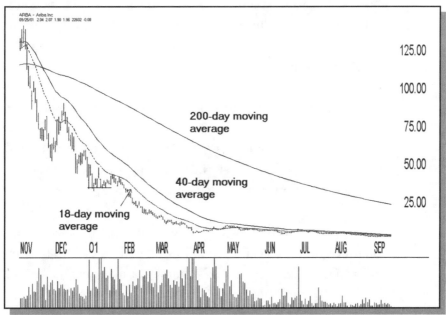

Courtesy of TC2000®.

Avoid using too tight of a moving average because it will nickel-and-dime you to a death of a thousand cuts. Yes, you keep the losses small but you don't allow the stock any "wiggle" room. Thus, the slightest gyrations will repeatedly stop you out of the position. Having said that, remember to always choose something that fits your personality and trading plan.

It's important to realize that by following this trend-based approach, you aren't confined to watching real-time quotes during the day. Granted, prices could breach your chosen moving average during the day, but you will only take action once they close above or below the moving average. This helps you avoid the "noise" of the market.

Too often, traders react to prices on an intraday basis; in so doing they stop themselves out of a position due to fear. But by the time the market closes, prices may have rallied back above the moving average. In other words, they sold too early and they end up missing out on the resumption of the uptrend! There are two blatant and common mistakes made in this situation:

1. Emotion took control of the decision-making process.

2. They cut their losses based on a short-term signal (intraday chart) yet their strategy was based upon a long-term trend (40-day moving average).

Since you will be looking at charts after the market closes, you'll need to take action the following trading day. That's why I refer to it as "sell alert" status. You may or may not take action.

In effect, you have until the end of the next trading day to see if prices follow through or reverse. It's what I call my "one day rule." If prices don't look like they'll close back above the moving average before market close, exit your bullish trade. The reverse would be true for your bearish positions. This gets you out of potentially big losses early.

For example, if you review your charts in the evening and you find XYZ stock has closed below its 50-day moving average, the stock is then on sell alert status. The following day you periodically check the price of the stock to see how it's faring. With 30 minutes to go before market closes, the stock is trading down $1. You realize it's not going to close back above the 50-day moving average. You exit the trade.

Take some time, go back, and review some of your losing trades. Apply this simple exit strategy. What do you think you'll find? Invariably, you'll recognize that you would have exited the position much earlier than you did. When prices start closing above or below the moving average, it's a warning shot across the bow of your "financial ship." The trend is changing! Your position is in jeopardy! Get out!

As you can see, it's a very simple technique to implement. Granted, there are times when a stock gaps up or down, making the position instantly worthless, but those are few and far between. More often than not, you have plenty of time to sell your option at much higher prices. Isn't it wonderful to know exactly when to sell a losing position?

Take a look at the chart of Expedia (EXPE).

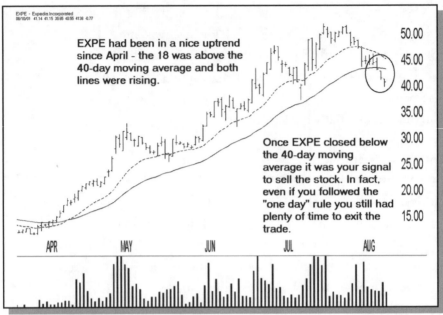

EXPE - Expedia Incorporated
08/10/01 41.14 41.15 39.95 40.95 41.39 -0.77

EXPE had been in a nice uptrend since April - the 18 was above the 40-day moving average and both lines were rising.

Once EXPE closed below the 40-day moving average it was your signal to sell the stock. In fact, even if you followed the "one day" rule you still had plenty of time to exit the trade.

APR   MAY   JUN   JUL   AUG

Courtesy of TC2000®.

Note that since the beginning of April, the stock traded below the eighteen-day moving average (on an intraday basis) a few different times, but it only closed once below its eighteen-day moving average. It quickly resumed its uptrend shortly thereafter.

However, in August prices closed five days in a row below the eighteen-day moving average – definitely a red flag! When stocks start closing below their key moving averages it's a sign momentum is waning and the trend may be poised to reverse.

Even if you didn't use the eighteen-day moving average as an exit strategy, when prices began closing below the 40-day average, it was a clear signal to exit the trade. Remember, before a stock ends up on its "shoe tops," it will cross its eighteen- and 40-day moving averages first.

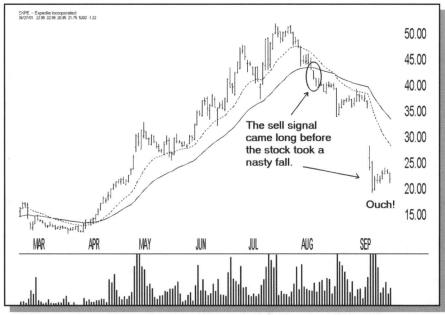

EXPE - Expedia Incorporated
39/27/01 22.99 22.99 20.95 21.75 5202 -1.22

The sell signal
came long before
the stock took a
nasty fall.

Ouch!

50.00
45.00
40.00
35.00
30.00
25.00
20.00
15.00

MAR   APR   MAY   JUN   JUL   AUG   SEP

Courtesy of TC2000®.

By using this simple exit strategy you wouldn't have suffered all that hardship and heartache watching the stock freefall, wiping out your hard-earned money in the process. Even if you missed it the first day, you would have had a few more days to exit when the stock was still trading around $40.

By the way, if you trade options instead of the stock, you would use the same sell signal to exit your positions. Additionally, you might be wondering, "Steve, I have a call option with three months remaining. Since I have so much time left do I need to adhere to this exit strategy?" Yes!

I can rattle off a myriad of positions where I had three or four months remaining before expiration, but prices never recovered. I watched my money go right down the drain. I would rather get out too early than get out too late! You can always get back in if the trend reverses. Remember, protecting your capital is more important than focusing on the money you want to make. It will help you cut your losses faster and preserve more of your gains.

Risk/Reward

As previously mentioned, before you put on a trade you need to determine what you're willing to lose if the position moves against you. Hence, risk is the difference between when you enter a trade and stop yourself out at a loss.

Understanding the relationship between risk and reward can help you better position yourself to minimize risk while at the same time maximizing reward. Once again, your objective is not winning every time but making the largest amount of money when you do!

When you buy a stock or option, how much of your money is at risk? 100%. Obviously you don't want to lose 100%, but it is a distinct possibility. Just consider the plight of Enron, Kmart, and Global Crossing shareholders! By approaching each and every trade from the worst-case scenario it will keep you alert and on your toes.

Therefore, you always want to make sure your reward is equal to, if not greater than, your risk. For example, if you decide to stop yourself out of a stock once it has fallen 8%, then your targeted reward must be 8% or greater.

If you decide to trade options, risking 100% of the capital in a position, then at a minimum your reward should be 100%! If you buy an option for $4, your upside target should be $8. If you buy an option at $16, your target is $32, and so on.

Obviously, there will be times when you won't achieve such results, but always strive to make sure your reward is equal to or greater than your risk. Why is this so important?

The numbers tell the story. A 5% loss requires a 5.3% gain to breakeven, not including commissions. For example, let's assume you start with $100,000 and proceed to lose 5% or $5,000. Your account is now worth $95,000. In order to get back to breakeven, you'll need to make back your $5,000. Thus, 5.3% of $95,000 is $5,035, bringing your account back to where you started.

And it only gets worse from there. A 10% loss requires an 11.1% gain to breakeven. A 33% loss requires a 50% gain to breakeven. A 50% loss requires a 100% gain to breakeven!

If you let your losses get too large it becomes almost impossible to dig yourself out of the hole. Plus, if you take smaller gains you're putting way too much pressure on yourself to have a big winner. Keep your losses smaller and let your winners run. That's the recipe for success.

If you buy stocks, don't risk more than 10% before stopping yourself out. With options, instead of risking 100% of the premium, stop yourself out once you've lost half, no matter how much time you have until expiration.

If you buy an option for $6, then your "stop" or exit should be $3. This is on a closing basis. By targeting a 100% gain and limiting your losses to 50%, you create an ideal "reward to risk ratio" of 2 to 1. You're making $2 for every $1 you lose. Realistically, target a ratio of $1.50 to $2 made for every $1 you lose. Apply this same methodology to stocks as well. If your stop is 8%, then your upside target should be 16%.

In fact, a good exercise for you to do (right now if possible) is to calculate what your reward to risk ratio is for a sample of your most recent trades.

What you're computing is the amount of money you make on average when you win divided by the amount of money you lose on average when you suffer a loss. Once again, this ratio should fall somewhere between $1.50 to $2.

Below, I've chosen a random sample of some of my actual option trades to demonstrate the exercise. The calculations are based upon one contract, and commissions have been excluded.

Symbol	Mo./Strike	Entry	Exit	Gross	Per 1 Contract
ABI	Mar 80p	9.900	14.100	4.200	$420.000
NBL	Mar 40c	5.900	7.500	1.600	$160.000
ARTG	Mar 35c	8.500	5.750	-2.750	-$275.000
QQQ	Feb 55c	2.450	4.400	1.950	$195.000
JNPR	Feb 85c	5.215	10.750	5.535	$553.500
VRTS	Feb 75c	4.000	8.625	4.625	$462.500
MERQ	Feb 70c	7.375	12.250	4.875	$487.500
CHKP	Feb 86.625c	5.000	10.000	5.000	$500.000
CMVT	Jan 130c	10.250	8.125	4.200	-$212.500
EXDS	Jan 85c	11.375	9.500	1.600	-$187.500
SUNW	Jan 75c	6.750	5.625	0.000	-$112.500
ADIC	Jan 50c	5.250	3.375	-2.750	-$187.500
BMY	Jan 65c	7.125	4.625	-2.500	-$250.000

ORBK	Jan 65c	8.500	13.250	5.535	$475.000
CPTL	Jan 35c	5.625	5.375	4.625	-$25.000
SHPGY	Jan 45p	4.500	8.000	3.500	$350.000
BRCM	Jan100c	15.625	19.625	4.000	$400.000
WM	Jan 45c	2.938	6.125	3.187	$318.700
BA	Jan 65c	7.625	3.875	-3.750	-$375.000
ABK	Jan 75c	6.500	7.000	0.500	$50.000
VRTS	Jan 95c	15.125	23.250	8.125	$812.500
EMC	Jan 75c	8.125	10.500	2.375	$237.500

From this sample of trades you learn the following:

>   22 total trades
>   14 winners for a combined gain of: $5,422.20
>   Average per win: $387.30 ($5,422.20/14)
>   8 losers for a combined loss of: $1,625.00
>   Average per loss: $203.13 ($1,625.00/8)
>   Reward/risk ratio: $1.91 ($387.30/$203.13)
>   63% winning percentage (14/22)

This is exactly the process you should use every single month to analyze your trades. Once you take the opportunity to "look" inside the numbers, it will open your eyes to how you manage your gains and losses.

Granted, I randomly selected the sample I used, but if you could model these numbers it would be exactly what you're looking to accomplish. Notice the reward to risk ratio is an impressive 1.91! What that means is that I made $1.91 for every $1 I lost. In simpler terms, I'm taking almost two steps forward and only one step back.

The winning percentage is also very respectable. If you have a higher reward to risk ratio you can post a lower winning percentage but still be very profitable. If you have a lower reward to risk ratio then you'll need to have a higher winning percentage to remain profitable. This basic exercise underscores the importance of keeping your losses small while maximizing your gains. So the $64,000 question is: How?

Maximizing Your Gains

If you have correctly identified the trend and it isn't showing signs of stalling, then you should milk it for all it's worth. That's not greed, but sound trading technique. Don't misunderstand me. If news comes out that changes your opinion or the profitability of the trade, use common sense and sell if need be. At the same time, don't let fear of losing a profit spook you into selling early. Stick with your game plan.

To win at this game, your gains must exceed your losses. If you take smaller profits how many large losses will it take to wipe out your tiny gains? Just a few! Once again, you could win on eight out of ten trades yet still lose money because your profits are too small and your losses are too large. Your winning percentage plays a secondary role. Focus on quality rather than quantity. You want bigger wins and smaller losses.

Nevertheless, you don't want greed to remain unchecked. So how do you maximize your gains without capping your upside? And at the same time, how do you avoid letting sizable "paper gains" fall by the wayside by holding onto a position too long?

The solution is to use a trailing stop in the form of a shorter moving average. This is also referred to as a *mental* or *visual stop*. It's not an order you give to your broker or enter into your online trading account. It's something you keep an eye on via the chart.

I recommend you use something between a five- and ten-day moving average. If you place a GTC ("good-till cancelled") order to sell at a predefined price (although you can) it limits your upside, preventing you from maximizing your gains. Since a shorter moving average mirrors the price of the stock closely, it will act as a "safety net." Therefore, at the first sign of weakness (the stock closes below the moving average), you exit the trade. This accomplishes two things. First, it removes any limit to the amount of money you can make on the trade. Second, it defines exactly where you'll get out if the stock begins to falter.

My very first trading "home run" came when I bought calls on a company called Zitel. I bought some March $25 calls for $9.25. At the time the stock was trading at $30. Over the next ten days the stock ran up to $72. I was tickled as can be! Obviously, I had some outrageous paper gains, but I didn't want to cash in too early. I also didn't want to watch my paper profits disappear into thin air! So what did I do?

I kept moving my mental exit point right up behind the price of the stock. If the stock began to pull back, I'd exit the trade. The stock hit $72 and began to fall. I sold my option when the stock was at $66 for $40.125. Wow! I realized over a 400% gain in just ten days. What's sobering is that the stock proceeded to fall as low as $35, eventually closing at $41. By then my option was only worth $16. A lot of money would have been left on the table had I not used a trailing stop.

Diversification

The great thing about options is that they give you total flexibility to make money, regardless of market direction. You can also trade options with many different companies in different sectors. Clearly, not all stocks go up, and so puts provide you with a great opportunity to make money from stocks in downtrends. By using the trend analysis techniques discussed earlier, you can identify stocks in downtrends or those in uptrends.

A simple way to reduce your exposure to any one stock is by spreading your money across different companies in different sectors. That way, you give yourself a better chance to win. However, make sure those companies don't reside all in the same sector. This avoids falling victim to the "domino effect." Let me give you an example. I wanted to diversify by buying options on different stocks, but I didn't understand the importance of diversifying in different sectors as well.

I bought options on companies like Intel, Micron, Applied Materials (AMAT), Cypress Semiconductor (CY), not realizing they were all in the same sector. In my mind I was diversified. But what happens if Intel sneezes? They all catch a cold. Bad news for one stock may mean lower prices for every other stock in that same sector. They tend to fall like dominoes. I soon found myself with losing positions across the board (an expensive lesson!) because I was not diversified across different sectors and industries.

Capital Allocation

Besides minimizing your risk by using calls and puts on stocks in different sectors, another very important aspect to risk management is deciding on the amount of capital to spend on any given trade. It answers the question, "How much should you buy?" I realize that for those of you who have less capital to start with, this becomes even more challenging. If you do fall into that category, you still must use strict capital allocation.

First of all, if you decide to trade options, then no more than 25% of your trading capital should be set aside for that purpose. If you have a $100,000 account, then no more than $25,000 should be spent buying options. You see, if you really drop the ball and lose the entire $25,000 you still have $75,000.

This rule also applies if you're trading with a smaller account. If you have a $10,000 account, then you shouldn't exceed $2,500. Why so stingy? If you lose $2,500, then you have $7,500 left to trade with. Your primary objective is survival – longevity your priority! You give yourself more opportunities to win by staying in the game longer.

Next, how much money should you invest in any one position? Don't commit more than 2% to 5% of your trading account per trade. If a trade goes against you, the losses are minimal compared to the overall size of trading account.

Let's say you have a $20,000 account. You decide to risk 5% per trade. That would allow you to risk $1,000 per position. If the trade turns sour and you stop yourself out, you still have $19,000 left in your account. If you have a $50,000 account and decide to risk 3%, you would be risking $1,500 per trade. If you end up losing on the trade, you're still left with $48,500. Yes, it hurts, but since it's a fraction of your overall equity it doesn't cripple your ability to trade.

Deciding to stop yourself out of any stocks you own once they lose 10% (or less) or 50% (or less) with options will provide your account with another safety net. With options, you could also assume the worst-case scenario, basing your initial capital allocation upon a 100% loss – even though you're still shooting for 50% stop.

If you define 50% of the value of an option as your risk, then it would allow you to commit more capital to any particular position. Once you define your risk (how much you're willing to lose) beforehand, you can determine how many contracts or shares you can buy. Let's take a look at three different investors and see how these principles would be implemented.

Case Study 1

Malorie has a $100,000 trading account.

She's decided to allocate 3% of her trading capital per trade.

She's interested in buying the October 50 call, quoted at 8 x 8.50. So one contract would cost her $850.

How many contracts is she allowed to buy?

Before you can answer that, you need to compute exactly how much money she can allocate per trade, plus you must define her risk.

3% of $100,000 = $3,000. This is her "budget," or the amount of money she's allocated per trade.

Malorie decides to play it close to the vest and assumes she'll lose the entire investment. Thus, her risk is $850. One contract (100 shares) x $8.50 = $850.

You can determine the number of contracts she's able to buy by dividing her "budget" per trade, which is $3,000 by her risk per trade, which is $850.

As a result, she's able to buy 3.52 contracts ($3000 / $850 = 3.52).

Malorie decides to buy three contracts and spends $2,550, excluding commissions.

If you assume the worst-case scenario, then Malorie would lose the entire $2,550, amounting to 2.5% of her trading account. While not pleasant, it's definitely within the risk parameters we've discussed. Better yet, she still has 97.5% of her account to fall back on!

Case Study 2

Brittany has a $12,000 trading account.

She decides to allocate 5% per trade.

She's interested in buying the September 25 puts, quoted at 3 x 3.25. Thus, one contract would cost $325.

How many contracts should she buy?

First, you need to determine her budget. If you take 5% of her $12,000 trading account, she's able to risk $600 per trade (5% x 12,000 = $600).

Now you need to define her risk. Brittany determines beforehand that she will sell the option if it closes at $2 or $200 per one contract. This equates to a loss of $1.25 or $125 per contract ($325-$200 = $125).

To determine the number of contracts she can purchase, divide her budget, which is $600, by the risk, which is $125, leaving her the ability to buy 4.8 contracts ($600/$125 = 4.8).

Brittany decides to buy five contracts for $1,625 (5 x $325).

If the stock begins to rally, forcing Brittany to sell her puts at the predefined loss outline above ($125 per contract), she would end up losing $625 (5 x $125) or 5.2% of her account. Once again, not exactly what she's hoping for, but the loss isn't devastating either.

Case Study 3

Zack has a $300,000 trading account.

He decides to allocate 2% per trade.

He wants to buy Home Depot, quoted at 49.90 x 50.00.

How many shares can he buy?

First, you determine his budget, which is $6,000 (2% x $300,000)

Second, you quantify his risk. Zack uses a 10% stop on all stock purchases. To compute his risk, take 10% of $50 (the price he'll buy it at), which is $5. Thus, he'll sell the stock if it closes at $45 (50-5 = 45).

Third, you determine the number of shares he can buy. Divide his budget, which is $6,000, by his risk, which is $5. The result is 1,200 ($6,000/$5 = 1,200). This means Zack can buy 1,200 shares of Home Depot.

Zack buys 1,200 shares, spending $60,000 (50 x 1,200).

Even though Josh has 20% of his trading account tied up in Home Depot, his risk is still only 2%. If his stop is triggered and he has to sell his Home Depot shares for a $5 loss, the loss amounts to $6,000 or 2% of his trading account.

As you can see, a string of bad trades wouldn't damage Zack's account too severely, giving him time to adjust his trading plan. In fact, a string of bad trades for anyone following this approach wouldn't be fatal. Painful – yes; fatal – no.

Using this percentage-based approach to capital allocation enables you to gain more exposure when you're winning and reduces it when you're losing. The reason why is that the amount of capital you spend per trade is a set percentage. Thus, the more money you have in the account, the larger the amount you can commit per trade. The smaller the account, the lower the amount.

Your success is predicated upon avoiding large losses. Besides, cutting your losses when it represents such a small percentage of your overall trading account is so much easier to do.

Most traders get wiped out by throwing too much money at too few deals. A couple of winning trades lures them into betting too much money and a string of losses causes irreparable harm.

They may even increase their trading size during a losing streak so they can make back their losses quicker. Exactly what you shouldn't do! They dig themselves into a deeper hole by trying to get it all back on the next trade. It's a loser's game at this point. Good money management will keep you out of the hole to begin with. By clearly defining your risk and then allocating the proper amount of capital per trade, you will greatly enhance your ability to withstand the losses that inevitably occur.

In conclusion, to be a successful trader you must implement a disciplined and rigorous risk management program. This final pillar to your game plan will ensure your longevity in the market, whether trading stocks or options. With this in mind, your focus should always be on protecting what you have (your trading account), instead of focusing on what you want to make. While it is tempting to "swing for the fences," avoid that type of trading at all costs! Above all, "Cut your losses short and let your profits run!"

Key Points to Remember

➤ Use a percentage-based approach when allocating money for a specific trade. Restricting it to 2% to 5% of your trading account will help you avoid putting too much money into too few deals.

➤ Always predefine your *risk*. Risk is the difference between where you buy and sell. Know exactly where you'll get out if the trade moves against you.

➤ Divide your budget by the risk to determine the number of shares or contracts you can buy.

➤ Know your profit target at all times. Trail your stops to maximize your gain.

➤ The key to your success is making as much money as you can when you're right and *minimizing* your losses when you're wrong.

➤ You should be more concerned with your *reward* to *risk ratio* than your winning percentage.

➤ Don't risk more than 10% of the purchase price when buying stock.

➤ When buying options, *avoid* risking more than half the premium, regardless of the time remaining before expiration.

➤ Since options are a wasting asset, it's important you implement a "time stop" as well.

CHAPTER 17

25 Ways to Improve Your Trading NOW!

Napolean Hill once said, "You're paid not merely for what you know, but more particularly for what you do with what you know." He also said, "Knowledge is not power – it is potential power. It becomes power when it organized into definite plans of action and directed to a definite end."

With that in mind, I've summarized everything that I believe will help you become a more productive and effective investor into 25 specific guidelines.

Post these in a conspicuous place and review them often. It will help you stay on track. It will also provide you with definite plans of action which, if adhered to, will enable you to trade with more confidence, less stress, and better results.

1) *If you fail to plan, you plan to fail.*

Trading without a game plan is like skydiving without a parachute-deadly! What type of stocks do you play? Do you base your decision on chart patterns, fundamentals, or news? When do you cut your losses? How much money do you commit to options and each individual trade? If you can't answer these questions quickly, you need to sit down and revise your game plan. Go back and review Chapter 10. Moreover, even if you have a plan it is worthless unless you write it down.

2) *Fear and greed cloud the mind – avoid them at all costs.*

Letting emotion get the best of you will result in impulsive trades and irrational decisions. If you trade according to your emotions, you will develop a herd mentality. You will lose your independence and trade according to what someone else thinks – your broker, analyst, guru, whoever. A rational individual trades with intellect. An emotional trader trades impulsively. By executing your game plan, you will remain on a planned course that will keep emotions at bay. Discipline and objectivity are the keys to success.

3) *The trend is your friend.*

Trade with the trend, not against it. Use moving averages and/or trendlines to help you better identify trends. Trying to pick market tops and market bottoms is a one-way ticket to the poorhouse. If the trend changes, cut your losses and run.

4) During a losing streak, cut back your trading and/or take a break.

A surefire way to create more trouble is to double up on a position to win back your losses all at once. Do not add to a losing position, trying to average down your loss – you're only digging a deeper hole for yourself. Like most things in life, trading successfully is directly correlated to your level of confidence. If you hit a losing streak, take a timeout!

5) Only trade with risk capital.

Never trade with money you can't afford to lose. Never trade with money earmarked for bills and living expenses. Allocate only 25% of your trading capital to option trading. Adhere to the 2% to 5% rule, which states, that only 2% to 5% of your trading capital should be committed to any one trade. Smaller accounts (less than $10,000) should risk no more than 10% per individual trade.

6) Know exactly where your buy and sell signals are.

Determine where and when you'll exit before entering a new trade. This will help you avoid second-guessing yourself later on. A very simple tool to help you know when to sell is moving averages. Once a stock closes below (for calls; above for puts) your chosen moving average, exit the trade.

Second, keep your risk/reward ratio in proper alignment. Target a 1.5 - 2 to 1. If you buy an option for $4 then your upside target would be $8 and your stop loss would be $2. That's a 2:1 reward to risk ratio. Thus, if the option falls to $2, exit the trade. If you hold onto a losing position, you will create an emotional ball and chain.

Finally, with options you also need an exit strategy based on time. With four to five weeks remaining before expiration, exit your position. Time decay starts to accelerate in those final few weeks. If your target has not been met, and you have run out of time, exit the trade. If the trend is still intact, roll out to a further month. This will give you more time to secure profits.

7) Trade according to your personality.

Stay within your comfort level for both strategy and risk. If you are looking to buy and sell in a matter of a few days or weeks, then buying LEAPS® is not the strategy for you. If you take a more conservative approach, then don't buy short-term options. Align your trading style with your lifestyle.

8) Cut your losses short; let your profits run.

If the trade goes against you, get out. Don't fear taking a loss-it will happen. Move quickly and don't hesitate. Cut your losses short. Don't take your profits off the table before your predetermined objective has been hit. Fear of losing a profit is real. Avoid it by sticking with your game plan. Use common sense. If the trend has changed or if news affects the viability of the trade, get out.

9) Only trade when you have an edge.

Make sure the odds are in your favor: sentiment, trend, volume, and news.

Don't trade just to trade. If there isn't a clear reason for putting on the trade, pass on it.

10) Admit when you're wrong.

Don't blame external forces or events for your losses. It's only one trade out of hundreds you'll make. Denial won't turn a bad trade into a winner but it will destroy your trading account!

11) Don't be a "Jack of All Trades and Master of None."

Focus and become the "master of one." As you increase your expertise, you can add other strategies to your trading repertoire. Remember: Keep it simple!

12) When in doubt, stay out. When in doubt, get out.

Too often, traders seek the opinions of others. Opinions are a dime a dozen. It demonstrates a lack of conviction on your part. If you need to ask anyone's opinion whether you should put on or liquidate a trade, you've lost your edge. Get out or stay out. Develop confidence in your own decision-making process. No one will look out for your money the way you will.

13) Remain flexible (markets move up and down).

Look for both bullish and bearish opportunities. Stocks go down in strong markets and stocks go up in weak markets. Maintain an open mind and consider all possibilities.

14) Diversify (don't put all your eggs in one basket).

Spread your risk across different companies from different sectors.

15) Quality is better than quantity.

Maximize your gains rather than the number of wins. By focusing on quality, you will keep your losses to a minimum.

16) Pull the trigger.

Buying and selling is where the money is made. Standing on the sidelines does no good. Get in the game. Your game plan should foster the confidence to enter and exit trades quicker and with razor-like precision.

17) Get in a zone.

Trading should be effortless. If there is strain, stress, force, or struggle, it's wrong. Focus on becoming a good trader and execute your game plan.

18) You can't go broke taking a profit!

That's exactly why traders do go broke. They absorb large losses and take small profits. By practicing good money management and making the trend your friend, you will position yourself for bigger gains and smaller losses.

19) Don't try to catch a falling knife (you'll get hurt sooner or later).

Stocks get slammed for various reasons. If you buy a stock in freefall, make sure your reasons for doing so are well founded. Sometimes "dead cats" don't bounce.

20) Never trust a naked tailor.

Surround yourself with people who do what you are trying or wanting to do. Make sure they "talk the talk" and "walk the walk."

21) Buy high, sell higher.

Avoid weak stocks. They are weak for a reason. Buy strength and sell more strength. Buy stocks in strong uptrends. Avoid the "dogs," soar with the "eagles."

22) Don't buy calls on stocks pulling back or puts when they're rallying.

Another key to success is letting the stock and/or index prove itself before you enter the trade. Instead of trying to pick bottoms and tops, let the stock hit your "trigger" before entering a trade. Thus, before initiating a bullish position, make sure the stock has "bounced" higher and taken out at least the previous day's high. Before initiating a bearish position, wait for the stock to roll over and trade below the previous day's low.

23) Keep a trading diary.

Write down your thoughts and impressions of the market on a daily basis. Make note of seasonal tendencies, patterns, and market-moving news. If you put on any trades, jot down the reason why. Review your performance regularly. Learn from your mistakes and duplicate your successes. By keeping a diary you'll begin to recognize the rhythm of the market. By the way, make sure you stop by **www.mytradingdiary.com** and you can see exactly how I do it!

24) Don't trade to be right – trade to make money!

Often, people want to be right and look smart and it ends up costing them money. How many traders went broke betting against YHOO, AMZN, EBAY, CMGI, and LCOS due to poor fundamentals? Ultimately, they were vindicated but it was too late. Instead of admitting they were wrong and cutting their losses, they let their ego get the best of them. Remember, Wall Street is based on perception, not reality.

25) Avoid watching the market all day long.

Another common mistake that traders make is trading too much. Avoid watching real-time quotes all day long. It's too easy to get caught up in the noise of the market and trading when you should be doing nothing. The best time to make your buying and selling decisions is when the market is closed. It's okay to watch CNBC, CNNfn, and Bloomberg – just make sure the volume is off!

Whether you're a seasoned pro or a complete beginner... this trading system will give you the financial boost you've always dreamed of...

"Discover A Proven Formula That Will Help You Rack Up Outrageous Profits, Without Ever Buying A Single Stock, Bond, Or Mutual Fund... Whether the Market Soars or Crashes... And With Limited Risk!"

"Now, at last, you can get your hands on a *simple trading formula* that can help accelerate your profits... in good times or bad... right from the comfort of your own home. It will enable you to trade with *more fun and less stress*; plus you can put it on "autopilot" so you can spend more time doing what you love to do (e.g., golf, fish, hang out with family or friends... or... whatever else you feel like doing!)."

"If you qualify and decide to pursue this can't-miss opportunity, you'll be richly rewarded for your effort. It will help you achieve greater results - both profits and success - than you ever imagined possible. More importantly, this rare and risk-free opportunity offers you disarmingly simple and powerful techniques to take your trading to a whole new level!"

To find out what the fuss is all about go to this web site right now...

www.highoctaneinvesting.com

All the best,

Steve Wirrick

P.S. Plus, if you *qualify* you'll receive 3 sizzling bonuses (a $1,697 Value)... absolutely *FREE*... while supplies last! Go! Go! Go!

What Others Have to Say About Steve...

"WOW! This site is incredible! MyTradingDiary.com is truly a **blueprint for success.** So many traders desperately need what Steve has to share. The **High Octane Options** homestudy course is by far my favorite trading-related homestudy course of all time! Trading without the proven strategies, tips and ideas that Steve reveals is like driving blindfolded - hazardous at best! *MyTradingDiary.com is a bargain at ten times the price."*

Tracy C., Programmer, Memphis, TN

"Finally, a simple and practical approach for anyone who wants to learn how to trade more effectively. **Frankly, MyTradingDiary.com is absolutely ingenious! It could not be easier.** Anyone who dreams of making a lot of money from the stock market would be well advised to sign up for MyTradingDiary.com immediately! In fact, **you can't afford not to become a member!** This is the real deal!"

Scott L., Author/Real Estate Investor, Boise, ID

"Steve is **the best trainer I have heard yet.** He clearly knows his material and tell us in an entertaining manner. He is great!"

Matt B., Austin, TX

"...This time, **my $2,737.50 investment yielded a $4537.50 profit in two weeks time.** Again, thanks goes to Steve for his outstanding teaching ability, and the clarity that the 18 and 40 day moving averages provide regarding the timing of trades."

Elliott C., Salt Lake City, UT

"I'm excited about the impact these strategies will make on my trading. Steve really understands how the market works and **makes it easy to understand how to use that knowledge to make money, but more important to me, how to keep it.** Concrete exit strategies... Nobody I've ever seen has such a grasp on how to make money in options. It's obvious he's been there and has a double-simple approach that anybody should be able to do. I look forward to his two day workshop."

Eric G., Washington

"Right after taking the HOOPS class, I used Steve's strategy analyzing TC2000 charts...I got out when the stock price indicated and using Steve's taught exit strategy. I ended up making *$1600 profit after deducting fees etc. in less than two months.*"

Bill C., Austin, TX

"I have gone to every seminar...*I would give up all the classes, even wealth, for High Octane Options.* I've learned so much..."

Ray K., Redondo Beach, CA

"Steve, I purchased your High Octane Options...Following your advice to the letter, I took my IRA account from *$35,000 to $87,500 in less than 4 weeks.* My regular trading account from *$27,000 to $61,000 in the same amount of time...*"

Brian, D.

"Your tape course is excellent. Since listening to High Octane Options I have made a *$8,000 profit on a $4,000 investment....*"

Ralph G.

"One hour into this seminar I had figured out why my options strategies weren't working as well as I wished. I could have gotten back on the plane, gone home, and my $695 would have been well spent (Plus airline fare)."

Jack K., Devine, TX

"Thank you!!! I am finally free from the fear that caused me to lose money in the market. *I see the light now and it is brighter than the sun at noonday.*"

David D., Taylorsville, UT

"This seminar should be mandatory for anyone wanting to deal in options. Steve's knowledge and attitude are a great assets to this seminar."

Duane D.

"This seminar helped me to pinpoint the things that I have done wrong in the past and reminded me what I need to do in the future with my options. ***This seminar is definitely explosive and high return.*** Steve Wirrick is so exciting to watch, his eyes are just full of explosion, you can tell his mind is working just as fast as a computer, his is so much fun to watch."

Casey W., Renton, WA

I had to get this off my chest before I explode…

151% in 16 days… 100% in 5 days… 139% in 8 days… 103% in 13 days…191% in 2 days… 194% in 4 days…

Attention Stock and Option Traders! Learn How To Gain An Unfair Advantage In The Stock Market With The Fastest Wealth-Building Trading Secrets Known To Man!

This is an exclusive opportunity to learn how to build your cash flow, grow your profits, and minimize your risk… regardless of market conditions!

Announcing...

Swing Trading – A No Holds Barred, In Your Face, And Turbo-Charged Trading System!

These simple and easy-to-use wealth-building strategies are now available to a select group of traders - and you can be among them if you act quickly. Learn the "secrets" that can help you generate eye-popping profits in today's wild and crazy stock market!

So, if you're serious about making money please visit…

www.getrichswingtrading.com

It may be the most important thing you do today!

About the Author

Steve Wirrick is the founder and president of *Planetcash.com* and *MyTradingDiary.com*, two popular web sites dedicated to teaching people how to trade stocks and options more effectively.

Steve graduated cum laude from Brigham Young University and shortly thereafter began his speaking career. His simple and easy-to-understand approach to trading have made him a popular radio and TV guest, along with being a dynamic trainer, author, and public speaker.

Over the past ten years, Steve has taught tens of thousands of people from all over the country his unique blend of money-making strategies. He has shared the speaking platform with world-acclaimed Zig Ziglar, Dr. Denis Waitley, Tom Hopkins, Paul Harvey, Robert Allen, and former U.S. President, Gerald Ford.

Tony Robbins, international best-selling author and honored by Accenture as one of the "Top 50 Business Intellectuals in the World," had this to say about Steve,

> *"I thoroughly enjoyed your teaching...You did an outstanding job of taking a complex subject and making it simple, entertaining and fun, not to mention profitable."*

He is also the creator of various home study courses and live seminars, including the wildly popular: *High Octane Options, High Impact Trading, Winning on Wall Street,* and *Swing Trading.*

Steve is currently working on his latest book, *High Octane Investing.* You can get more information at *www.highoctaneinvesting.com.*